Computing Projects
in
Visual Basic

Derek Christopher

Published by
Payne-Gallway Publishers Ltd
an imprint of Harcourt Educational Ltd
Halley Court, Jordan Hill, Oxford, OX2 8EJ

Web site www.payne-gallway.co.uk

Acknowledgements

I would like to thank my wife, Bozena, for her great support while I worked on this book. Thanks are due also to my Advanced GNVQ students who struggled through a version of the sample project as part of their assessment. Their feedback was very useful in writing up this part of the book.

Cover picture © 'The Descending Orange' by Hsiao-Mei Lin
Cover photography © Mike Kwasniak, 160 Sidegate Lane, Ipswich
Cover design by Tony Burton

First edition 2000. Reprinted 2001, 2002, 2003, 2005

10 9 8 7 6 5

A catalogue entry for this book is available from the British Library.

10-digit ISBN: 1 903112 33 8
13-digit ISBN: 978 1 903112 33 5

Copyright © Derek Christopher 2000

Printed in Great Britain by
W M Print Ltd, Walsall, West Midlands

Preface

Aim

This book has been written mainly for students of AS/A level Computing, 'A' level ICT and Advanced VCE ICT. This book assumes no knowledge of programming and covers everything needed to write a large program. Students on other courses of a similar standard, such as BTEC National, and first year HND and degree courses, should also find the material useful.

AS/A level Computing

Depending on the Examining Board computing students may need to produce a small project or write a number of programs for the 'AS' part of the course. For 'A' level a substantial piece of programming may be needed. The theory part of the course covers a number of important programming concepts, which are far better learned through practical programming than only through the pages of a textbook. Visual Basic is an excellent, modern language through which to learn these concepts.

Advanced VCE students

An optional unit on programming using an event-driven language such as Visual Basic is offered by all the Boards. One of the Boards offers two units. Although the amount of programming is not expected to be as much as an A level student of Computing would do, it is still substantial.

How the book is structured

The book is divided into three Parts.

Part One goes through all the main programming concepts carefully. These need to be understood by all students.

Part Two covers a variety of topics which for some students will prove useful in their project work. These cover items such as designing menus, printing reports and interfacing with the Internet.

Part Three goes through the main stages of producing a project to 'A' level standard by using a sample project based on a snooker club. All the programming concepts used in the sample project are covered earlier in the book.

The approach throughout is a very practical one. Running throughout Parts One and Two are 47 programs, with step-by-step instructions explaining how to build them and explanations about how they work. In Part Three you are taken through each stage in the design and coding of the full project, again using a step-by-step approach for the coding.

Table of Contents

Introduction

Visual Basic

In recent years Visual Basic has become one of the world's most popular event-driven programming languages. An event-driven language is one that responds to events – clicking a button, selecting an item from a list, tabbing out of a control and so on. The most popular non-event-driven languages in schools and colleges in the last decade or two have been BASIC and Pascal, but the new 'A' level and Advanced VCE specifications for 2000 and onwards have shifted the emphasis away from these traditional languages. Visual Basic is likely to be the main teaching language for the foreseeable future.

Editions of Visual Basic

Visual Basic has gone through several versions. Recent versions have offered three editions – the **Learning** or **Standard**, **Professional** and **Enterprise** editions. The Learning edition contains all that is required by a student to learn the language and to be able to produce a project of 'A' level standard, and a great deal more. The other two editions are really only for professional Visual Basic programmers. Everything in this book can be done using the Learning Edition.

How to use this book

The book is divided into three sections. Part One covers the key topics you are likely to need to produce a project to 'A' level standard. Part Two covers several topics which you may find useful in your project work and one topic, debugging (in Chapter 11), which you are encouraged to look at after you've done some of the work in Part One. In this chapter program 11.1 can be done after Chapter 5 and program 11.2 after Chapter 7. Chapter 12 is necessary if you want to send reports from your project to the printer. The sample program in this chapter requires an understanding of text files, which are covered in Chapter 10.

Part Three covers a sample 'A' level Computing project. It takes you step-by-step through analysing, designing and building a Visual Basic application for a snooker club. All the coding concepts used in this project are covered in Part One and in Chapter 12 of Part Two. Appendix A lists the things in Parts One and Two that are essential in understanding the sample project. Part Three also covers a number of methods you might use for documenting the design and implementation of your own project.

The structure of each chapter in Parts One and Two is the same. There are one or more sections explaining the main concepts and up to four complete programs to illustrate them. Each program consists of step-by-step instructions telling you how to build it, interspersed with any essential explanation. These programs should be done as practical exercises – you don't learn much programming by only reading about it! There are 47 of these programs and they are summarised in Appendix B.

Take it from here…

All the chapters in Part One and most of those in Part Two have a *Take it from here…* section. This contains several suggestions for follow-up work related to the topics covered in the chapter. Visual Basic Help is likely to be a useful source for many of the answers. You are encouraged to do these if you have the time and interest. There is nothing in this section which *must* be understood to do the exercises at the end of the chapter or to understand the sample project.

Questions on the programs

Most of the sample programs have suggestions for more practical work to develop a concept further or extend what the program does. It would be sensible to do these as soon as possible after completing the program in the main part of the chapter. These questions are graded using from one to three stars.

End of chapter exercises

The exercises at the end of most of the chapters ask you to build your own programs. A few of these involve something new that has not been directly covered in the current or previous chapters. These exercises are also graded using from one to three stars.

Saving your work

In Chapter 1 you'll learn that a Visual Basic program consists of at least three files. Only the sample programs in this chapter tell you to save your work but it would be sensible to save everything you do. Sometimes a sample program or an end of chapter exercise may be needed again for another program or exercise, and so should definitely be saved. These are as follows:

Program/exercise	*Also required for*
Program 2.4	Program 7.1
Program 3.4	Program 7.2
Chapter 3, exercise 4	Chapter 8, exercise 3
Program 7.2	Program 11.2
Program 8.1	Program 8.2

Code

Code extracts are always presented in a shaded format as in the example below.

```
Password = "secret"                          'initialise variables
Attempt = 0
Do                                           'start of loop
   Attempt = Attempt + 1
   InputPassword = InputBox("Enter password. This is attempt " & _
               "number " & Attempt)
Loop Until (Attempt = 3) Or (InputPassword = Password) 'end of loop
```

This extract illustrates three important coding conventions:

- The 4th line of code has an underscore character (_) at the end. This means that the line has been broken into two lines because it is too long to fit into the page width of this book. When copying code into your program you *could* break it into two lines in the same way. Visual Basic accepts the underscore character as the connection between the split lines, but note that there must be at least one space before it. On the other hand you can type the two lines as one line into your program, but remember to leave out the underscore. You cannot break code in the middle of text that is in quotes.

- Three lines of code have an apostrophe (') followed by a short explanation of what the line means. Such explanations are called **comments** and must come after the apostrophe. In this book the code and the comments are formatted differently. Comments are in italics and are not bold. When you run your program Visual Basic skips over the comments – they are there for human use only. If you are doing an assessed project using Visual Basic you will be expected to write comments as appropriate. There are rather more comments provided in the code extracts in this book than you should write in your own programs, but they have the extra role here of teaching you how the code works. You do not have to copy these comments when you write the sample programs, but if you do you will certainly find them helpful when returning to your code later.

- The lines of code between the words **Do** and **Loop** are **indented**. Indenting code in a consistent way is an invaluable aid to understanding what you have written. Visual Basic doesn't insist on it; like commenting you do it for human use only. In this book indents are three characters in size.

Web site

The publisher's web site contains a variety of support material on www.payne-gallway.co.uk/vb that you can download.

- A few of the programs and end-of-chapter exercises use programs or files. These are:

Program/File	Type of file	Required for
Stack.exe	Executable	Exercise 8, chapter 8
GNVQStudents.txt	Text	Exercises 1 and 2, chapter 10
Sales.txt	Text	Program 12.1
GardenCentreProducts.dat	Random access	Exercise 2, chapter 12
GNVQStudents2.txt	Text	Exercise 3, chapter 12
Numbers.txt	Text	Program 14.3
SoftwareSales.txt	Text	Exercise 4, chapter 14
HolidayHomes.mdb	Access database	Programs 15.1 and 15.2
Alevels.mdb	Access database	Program 15.3
GNVQStudents.mdb	Access database	Exercises 1, 2, 3, 7, chapter 15
Repayments.mdb	Access database	Exercise 4, chapter 15
Wards.mdb	Access database	Exercises 5 and 6, chapter 15

- A Word file on object-oriented programming in Visual Basic. This is written in the same style as the chapters in this book.

- Teachers can download solutions to the end-of-chapter exercises. These are stored as Visual Basic forms, one for each exercise. To use the form open a new project and add it to the project. You will also need to tell Visual Basic to use this new form when the program runs (see steps 4 – 5 of program 8.2) because it is set up to run the default form, Form1, provided with a new project.

- Teachers can also download a Word file giving explanations and coded solutions to many of the exercises on the programs.

Part One – Basic Topics

Chapter 1 – Introducing Visual Basic

A Visual Basic Project

Event-driven languages like Visual Basic are built using one or more **forms**. On these you place a variety of **controls** and attach code to some or all of them to suit the purpose of your program. All except one of the programs you will do in Parts One and Two of this book have only one form; it's surprising how much you can pack into such a program. The sample 'A' level project in Part Three needs only four.

Figure 1.1 shows a form. In this program the user clicks the Start button and then types as fast as they can in the white area. The number of seconds that have elapsed ticks over on the right, and after 60 seconds they are told how many words they have typed in.

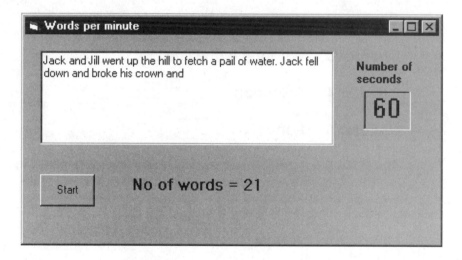

Figure 1.1: A program made up of one form

The example above is a **program**. It has one form with several controls and some code hidden from view which runs when the user clicks the Start button. It is also an example of a Visual Basic **project**. If we called this program WordsPerMinute Visual Basic would save it as a project file called **WordsPerMinute.vbp**. The **vbp** extension means **v**isual **b**asic **p**roject. It would also save the form as a separate file, with a name of your choice, and give it a **.frm** extension.

The Visual Basic programming environment

The programming environment of a language refers to the interface the programmer uses to build a program and then to run and test it. It is the screen in front of you, including all its menus, icons and buttons. Let's have a practical tour of the Visual Basic environment.

Starting a new project

1. Load Visual Basic and you'll get the New Project window shown in figure 1.2. This will contain two or more icons, depending on which edition of Visual Basic you are using. Select **Standard EXE** and click **Open**.

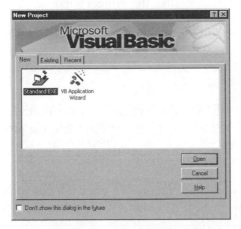

Figure 1.2: The New Project window

2. You're now in Visual Basic's programming environment. The screen has several windows, menus and toolbars. These are shown in figure 1.3.

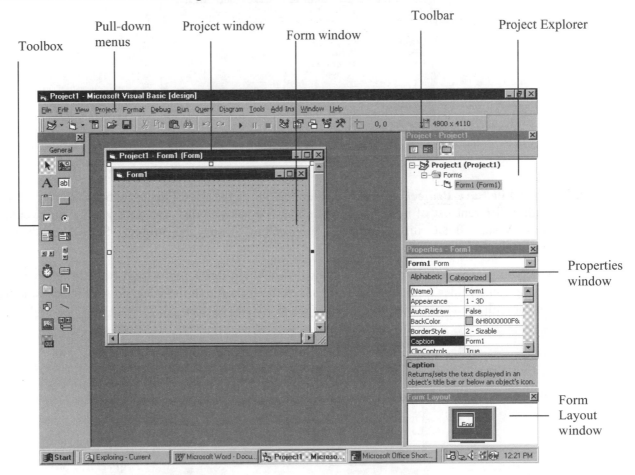

Figure 1.3 – The Visual Basic programming environment

The Project and Form windows

The idea that a form is part of a project can be demonstrated by these two windows.

3. Drag the base of the Project window down to reveal the base of the Form window. Resize the Form window and you'll find it cannot be larger than the Project window.

4. Maximise the Project window and you can then make the Form window fill much of the central part of the screen.

The Form Layout window

5. Resize the Form window again and look at the changes in the Form Layout window. This window shows you the position the form will occupy on the screen when the project runs.

The Project Explorer

The **Project Explorer** is the window at the top right of the screen. It contains details of all the forms your project contains. When you start a new project it contains just the one form, which has the name Form1 – twice!

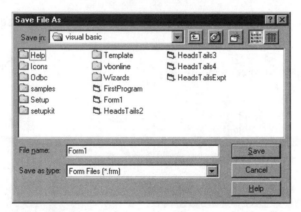

Figure 1.4: Saving a form

6. Select **File/Save Project As** from the menu. You get the Save File As window shown in figure 1.4 (with a different list of items) and the default file name Form1. Because you haven't yet saved the form, Visual Basic insists you do this before saving the project. Save it with the name **FirstProgram**.

7. Now you get the Save Project As window as shown in figure 1.5. Visual Basic assumes you wish to use the same folder as the one you just saved the form file in. It is a good idea to save the form and project with the same name. Save the project as **FirstProgram**.

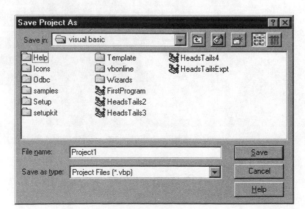

Figure 1.5: Saving a project

8. These names are now listed in the Project explorer, as shown in figure 1.6.

9. The Project Explorer has three small buttons at the top left. Two of these are named in figure 1.6. Make sure the form is selected and then click the **View Code** button. You are now in the Code Window for the form where you write the program's code. At the moment it's empty. Click the **View Object** button to take you back to the form.

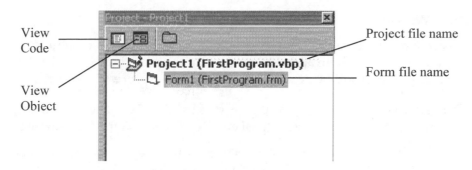

Figure 1.6: The Project Explorer

The Toolbox

The **toolbox** contains icons for each control you can put on your forms. Figure 1.7 shows the controls on the toolbox, but there are several others, known as custom controls, that you will use in this book with more specialised jobs. You add these to the standard toolbox as the need arises. In figure 1.7 most of the controls have two names. The name inside the brackets is the technical Visual Basic name and the other one is the 'ordinary' way of referring to a control. Thus we would talk in the ordinary way about a list box but the technical term is a ListBox.

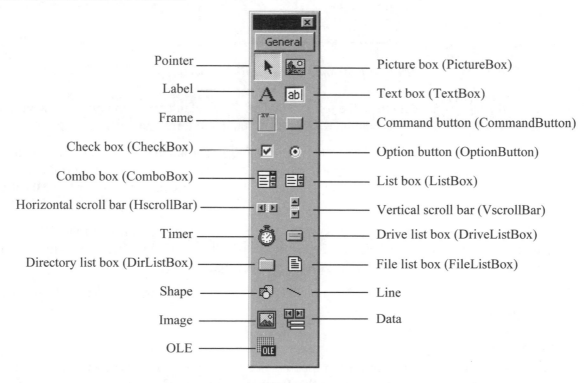

Figure 1.7 – The toolbox

10.   Click on the command button control in the toolbox and then draw a rectangle anywhere on the form with the left mouse button down. Release the mouse button to get a command button drawn on the form with the word Command1 in it.

11.   Practise placing a variety of controls on the form. Note how the name that appears with some of these controls reflects the type of control. Thus you get Label1, Frame1, Option1 and so on. Place the same control again on the form and the name will be Label2, Frame2 etc.

The Properties Window

When you place a control from the toolbox onto a form it is an example of an **object**. The form itself is also an object. All objects can have **properties**, and most of these can be seen in the Properties window, which is below the Project Explorer. **A property is a descriptive feature of an object.**

12.   With the form selected scroll through its 50 properties listed in the Properties window. Some of these are shown in figure 1.8. These are listed alphabetically but click on the **Categorized** tab and they are arranged by category.

Figure 1.8: Some of the form's properties

13.   The selected property by default is the form's Caption. The default value is Form1. Change this to **My First VB Program** and this caption will be displayed in the form's title bar.

14.   Find the Name property of the form. This is the most important property you will use in your programs. All controls have a Name property; it refers to the name by which the control is known in your Visual Basic project. Select the form and change its Name property from Form1 to **MainForm**. Names cannot have any spaces.

15.   In the Project Explorer the name you gave your form in step 14 appears in front of the file name you gave it in step 6. Note that the Name of the *project* is still the default Project1. You will never need to change the default name of any of the projects in this book.

16.   Close the project by selecting **File/Remove Project.** Save the changes if you wish, though the program doesn't do anything.

Menus and toolbar

Along the top of the screen are the pull-down **menus**. You will use many of these as you work through the programs in this book. Below the menus is the **Toolbar**. Nearly all the buttons on the toolbar have a corresponding menu item.

PROGRAM 1.1 *Display your name*

Specification   Display your name on a form in large letters

Designing the form

1. If you are loading Visual Basic select **Standard EXE** from the New Project window (see figure 1.2) and click **Open** to start a new project. Otherwise select **File/New Project** and then **Standard EXE**.

2. Make sure Form1 is selected in the Project Explorer, and then in the Properties window change its Caption property from Form1 to **Print my name**.

3. Find the form's Font property in the Properties window. Click on the button to the right with the three dots and in the Font window set the font to **30 bold**. When your name appears on the form let's have it in large letters!

Coding

Code may be executed when a particular event occurs. The event in this program is the displaying of the form. The event is called the Load event, and when it happens your name should appear.

4. Double-click anywhere on the form and you'll be given the code template shown below. You can tell the type of event from the phrase **Form_Load**. The meaning of the other parts of this template will be explained in later chapters.

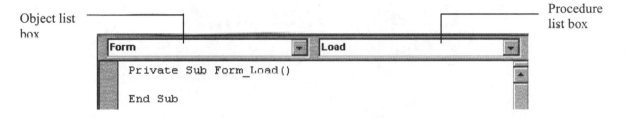

Figure 1.9: The code template for the form's Load event

When you double-click any control on a form, or the form itself, Visual Basic supplies the code template for the event which the makers of the language think is the most common one for that control. For a form they think the Load event should be the default one. Some controls have the Click event as their default one.

5. To see the events you can have for a form click the small button in the Procedure list box (see figure 1.9.) It will display a list of 16 possible events associated with a form, from **Activate** to **Unload**.

6. Between the two lines of the template type two lines of code to tell Visual Basic to print your name on the form. Put your own name between the quotation marks.

```
Private Sub Form_Load()
   Form1.Show
   Form1.Print "Derek Christopher"
End Sub
```

Note the following:

- The two lines of code are **indented**. Indenting code in a consistent way is a very important part of writing good code. It makes code easier to read, as you will appreciate when writing more complex code later. A three-character indent is used in this book.

- **Show** and **Print** are two of the form's **methods**. All objects have methods – **actions you can perform on an object**. Note the dot separator between the name of the object and its method.

Running the program

To run a program its code must be changed from the words you have written, commonly called **high-level** or **source code**, into something your computer can understand. Computers only understand 1's and 0's; this sort of code is called **binary** or **machine** code. The Visual Basic **compiler** changes the source code into binary code and stores this in the computer's memory so that the program can run.

If you select **Run** on the menu bar there are two available options at present. These are:

- **Start** – this will run your program but the program will stop when a line of source code contains an error that the compiler picks out. There are two alternative ways of doing this – press the F5 function key or click the Start button on the toolbar.

- **Start with Full Compile** – the compiler will first check all your code for errors, and only if it can't find any will the program begin to run. The alternative way is Ctrl + F5.

Figure 1.10: Program to display a name

7. Run the program using one of the methods above and your name should appear in 30 point bold font as shown in figure 1.10. If the program does not run properly check the code you wrote in step 6 above.

8. Close the program by closing its window in the way you would normally close a window – click the small button with an 'x' at the top right or click on the small icon to the left of your form's caption and then click close, or simply press Alt + F4.

9. Select **File/Save Project As** and then save first the form and then the project file using the same name.

end of Program 1.1

Naming objects

Many Visual Basic programmers use a naming convention that adds a lower case three-character prefix to the name they give a control. For example if the purpose of a text box is for the user to type in a person's salary then you might name it txtSalary. Whenever you come across this in your code you would know it was a text box from the txt prefix, and the 'Salary' part would give a strong clue as to its purpose. The point was made earlier that names of controls are not allowed to have any spaces.

Figure 1.11 lists the prefixes for all the controls on the standard toolbox that you will need to refer to in code in the programs in this book.

Control	Prefix
Check box	chk
Combo box	cbo
Command button	cmd
Common Dialog Control	dlg
Data	dat
Form	frm
Frame	fra
Horizontal scroll bar	hsb

Control	Prefix
Label	lbl
List box	lst
Menu	mnu
Option button	opt
Shape	shp
Text box	txt
Timer	tmr

Figure 1.11: Prefixes for naming controls

PROGRAM 1.2 *Change a message*

Specification When a command button is clicked the message "I LIKE Visual Basic" appears. When a second command button is clicked the message changes to "I HATE Visual Basic"

The finished program can be seen in figure 1.12.

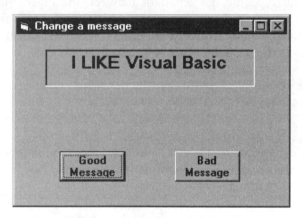

Figure 1.12: Program 1.2

Designing the form

1. If you are loading Visual Basic select **Standard EXE** from the New Project window (see figure 1.2) and click **Open** to start a new project. Otherwise select **File/New Project** and then **Standard EXE**.

2. Make sure Form1 is selected in the Project Explorer, and then in the Properties window change its Caption property from Form1 to **Change a message**.

3. Click on the Label control in the toolbox, and then with the mouse button down draw a rectangle in the upper part of the form.

4. Find the label's Name property in the Properties window and change it from Label1 to **lblMessage**, using the 'lbl' prefix as explained earlier.

5. Set the label's Caption property to blank by deleting the default value 'Label1'.

6. The default value for the label's BorderStyle property is 0 – None, meaning that no border will be shown when the program runs. To get a border change this to **1 – Fixed Single**.

7. Set the label's Font property to **14 Bold**.

8. Drag a command button from the toolbox and draw a rectangle at the bottom left of the form. Set its Caption property to **Good Message**. Change its Name property to **cmdGoodMessage**.

9. Place a second command button at the bottom right of the form. Set its Caption property to **Bad Message**. Change its Name property to **cmdBadMessage**.

Coding

10. Double-click on the Good Message command button and you'll get the code template for its Click event shown below. The Click event is the one Visual Basic associates most commonly with a command button.

```
Private Sub cmdGoodMessage_Click()

End Sub
```

11. Type the line of code below to set the Caption property of the label to the message you wish to output. As soon as you type the dot separator between the object (lblMessage) and its property (Caption), pause and look at the list of properties which pop up (see figure 1.13). This very useful feature of Visual Basic is called **Auto list members**. You can select a property from this list by double-clicking it or type the property name in yourself.

```
Private Sub cmdGoodMessage_Click()
   lblMessage.Caption = "I LIKE Visual Basic"
End Sub
```

The '=' sign means *store or assign the text inside the quotation marks into the Caption property of the label*. Technically it is known as an **assignment statement**.

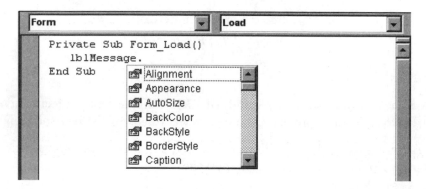

Figure 1.13: Auto list members for a label

12. Get the code template for the Bad Message command button. Do this by returning to the form (by clicking the View Object button in the Project explorer) and then double-click the command button. Alternatively, as you are in the Code window already, just select **cmdBadMessage** from the Object list box at the top left (see figure 1.9) and its default code template will be provided.

13. Type in a line of code similar to that in step 11 to output the appropriate message when the button is clicked:

```
Private Sub cmdBadMessage_Click()
    lblMessage.Caption = "I HATE Visual Basic"
End Sub
```

Running and saving the program

14. Run the program using one of the methods listed before step 7 in program 1.1. Click on each of the two command buttons to check that the message changes.

15. Save the project and the form using the same file name, e.g. Message.frm and Message.vbp.

end of Program 1.2

Summary of key concepts

- A Visual Basic **project** (program) is made up of one or more **forms**. The project and each form must be saved as a separate file.

- To build a program you place **controls** from the toolbox onto a form. Controls are examples of **objects**. Most controls have many **event procedures**. The code inside these procedures is fired off when the particular event occurs. A common event is the Click event.

- Objects have **properties** and **methods**. A property controls the appearance and behaviour of an object whereas a method is an action that can be done on the object.

- To **compile** a program is to change the **source code** you have written into **machine code** that the computer can understand.

- It is standard practice in this book to prefix the Name property of objects that will be referred to in code by three letters that indicate the type of control, e.g. txt for a text box, cmd for a command button.

- The '=' sign is often used as an **assignment statement**. It assigns the item on its right to the item on its left, e.g. lblMessage.Caption = "Hello"

Take it from here....

1 In Windows locate the two files you saved for Program 1.2 – the project file and the form file. There is a third file called a VBW file ('W' stands for Workspace) that Visual Basic created when you saved the project file. All three are text files which Visual Basic reads when you open the program. Open each of these files in Notepad or WordPad and see if you can identify some of the pieces of information stored in them.

2 Use Visual Basic's Help to find out how it presents information about controls' properties, methods and events. Select the first item in the **Help** menu, select the **Index** tab and then type in the type of control, e.g. **CommandButton**.

3. The few properties looked at in this chapter are all examples of those that can be set at **design** time. Most design-time properties can also be set by your code at **run** time. Choose some controls and compare the properties listed in the Properties window (design-time properties) with those listed in Help. Any extra ones in Help are likely to be run-time properties only.

4. The **Object Browser** is something else you can use to look through the properties, methods and events of controls. Explore this feature of Visual Basic by selecting **View/Object Browser**.

5. Visual Basic comes with a wide variety of sample projects to explore. Where they are stored depends on which version of Visual Basic you are using. The best large-scale project is **biblio.vbp** (a Books project which uses an Access database). If you don't know where they are found click the **Start** button in Windows and then **Find/Files or Folders**. Then enter ***.vbp** to search for all Visual Basic project files.

6. You can make an **exe**cutable file of a program from the **File** menu. You can run this file from Windows without Visual Basic on your computer. Make an exe file of one of your programs and try this out.

Questions on the Programs

Program 1.1

*1. Add code to display your address after your name on the form when the program runs.

End of chapter exercises

*1. Write a program that changes the title of the form to **Welcome to Visual Basic** when a command button is clicked.

*2. Put two command buttons on a form and set their captions to **Show** and **Hide**. Clicking the Show button should display a label with the message **Hello**. Clicking the Hide button should remove the label and its message. Use the label's Visible property to show and hide it.

**3. Write a program so that the words typed into a text box change to red or blue when an associated command button is clicked (see figure 1.14). You will need to

- set a property of the text box in the Properties window to allow word wrapping.

- assign **vbRed** or **vbBlue** in your code as appropriate to the property of the text box that determines the colour of its contents (see Color Constants in Visual Basic Help).

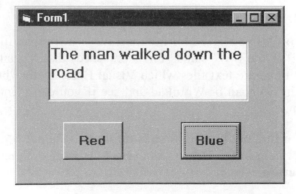

Figure 1.14: Exercise 3

Chapter 2 – Working with Controls

In Chapter 1 you used two controls from the toolbox – a label and a command button. In this chapter you will use another six controls which will allow you to design a wide range of interfaces in your programs. To get these controls to work for you requires an understanding of some of their properties, methods and events.

The Text Box

Text boxes are used for entering and displaying data. The property you will use most commonly is the **Text** property. The commonest method you will use is **SetFocus**, which positions the cursor inside the text box. If you had a text box named txtName, then the code below would print whatever has been typed into it on the form, clear its contents by setting its Text property to blank (**""**), and finally put the cursor in the text box ready for the next piece of data to be typed in.

```
Form1.Print txtName.Text
txtName.Text = ""
txtName.SetFocus
```

The List Box

Use a list box if you want to select one or more items from a list of items. Figure 2.1 shows an example of its use - the query wizard in the database package Access. The list box on the left lists the fields that can be selected. When selected they are moved to the other list box on the right.

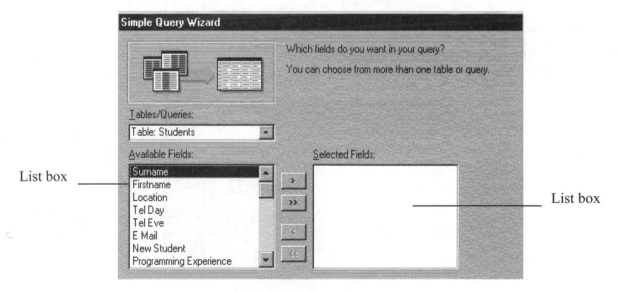

Figure 2.1

The following are the properties and methods of the list box that you will commonly use:

Properties

List   Contains all the items in the list box. The first item is indexed (numbered) by Visual Basic as 0, the next as 1 and so on.

ListCount   Contains the number of items in the list box.

ListIndex   Contains the index or number of the item currently selected. For example, if item number 6 is selected ListIndex contains 5 (since the first item is numbered as 0).

Sorted   Specifies whether the items in the list box are sorted or not.

Text   Contains the currently selected item from the list box

Methods

AddItem   Adds an item to the list box.

Clear   Removes all the items from the list box.

RemoveItem Removes an item from the list box.

PROGRAM 2.1   *A list box of countries*

Specification Allow the user to enter the names of countries in a text box. They should be able to click command buttons to display all the names alphabetically in a list box, to delete a selected country from the list box, or to delete all the countries from the list box.

Designing the form

1. If you have Visual Basic open already select **File/New Project** from the main menu, otherwise load Visual Basic from Windows. Select **Standard EXE** from the New Project window and then click **OK**.

2. Change the Caption property of the form to **Using a List Box**.

3. Drag a text box, three command buttons and a list box onto the form and position them as shown in figure 2.2.

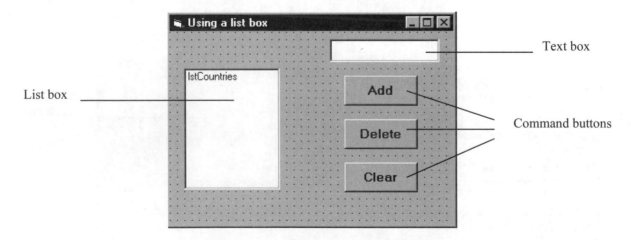

Figure 2.2: Design of program 2.1

4. Set the properties of these controls as shown in figure 2.3. The purpose of the List property at design time is to populate the list box with items before the program runs. To do this click the small button in the List property and type in the three countries listed in figure 2.3. Figure 2.4 shows what to do. You must press Ctrl + Enter to get to a new line.

Control	*Property*	*Property setting*
Text box	Name Text	txtCountry blank (i.e. delete *Text1*)
Command button	Name Caption	cmdAdd Add
Command button	Name Caption	cmdDelete Delete
Command button	Name Caption	cmdClear Clear
List box	Name Sorted List	lstCountries True Spain USA Austria

Figure 2.3: Design-time property settings for controls in program 2.1

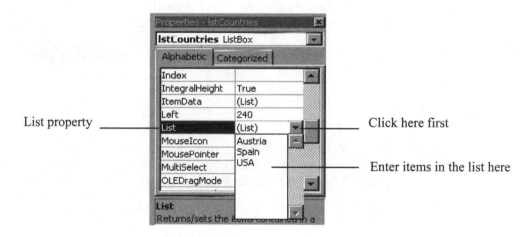

Figure 2.4: Entering items into the List property

Coding

5. Double-click the Add command button to bring up its Click event procedure code template. Complete the code as shown below.

```
Private Sub cmdAdd_Click()
    lstCountries.AddItem txtCountry.Text  'add contents of text box to list
                                          'box display

    txtCountry.Text = ""                  'clear the text box
    txtCountry.SetFocus      'put cursor in text box ready for next country
End Sub
```

6. Get the code template for the Click event of the Delete command button. As you are currently in the Code window you can click the Object list box (figure 1.9) and then click cmdDelete from the drop-down list of controls on your form. Alternatively you could return to the form by clicking the View Object button in the Project Explorer (figure 1.6) and double-clicking the Delete command button.

7. Enter the code below.

```
Private Sub cmdDelete_Click()
    lstCountries.RemoveItem lstCountries.ListIndex  'delete selected item
End Sub                                              'from list of displayed items
```

The RemoveItem method is told what to delete by giving it the value of the list box's ListIndex property. This contains the number of the current selected item. Items are numbered from 0.

8. Get the code template for the Click event of the Clear command button and enter the following:

```
Private Sub cmdClear_Click()
    lstCountries.Clear              'delete all items displayed in list box
End Sub
```

Running the program

9. Run the program by selecting **Run/Start** or clicking the **Start** button on the toolbar. Enter several country names into the text box and click the Add button after each one. The names will be displayed in alphabetical order in the list box because its Sorted property is set to True. If you fill the list box a scroll bar will automatically be added. Try out the Delete button.

end of Program 2.1

The Combo Box

The term 'combo box' is short for 'combination box' because this control combines the features of the text box and the list box. You use exactly the same properties and methods described earlier for the list box to make a combo box work. The two main differences between combo and list boxes are:

- With some types of combo box you can edit any of the displayed items or type in an item that is not listed.

- The standard combo box must be clicked to reveal its items. It therefore takes up less room on a form.

Examples of combo boxes can be found on Word's Formatting toolbar, and two of these are shown in figure 2.5. By clicking the small button the list of fonts is revealed. If the one you wish to use is not listed you can type it in the edit part of the combo box and Word might be able to switch to it. The list of font sizes does not include every number. Again you enter the number you want in the edit part.

The Option Button

Option buttons are used to allow the user to select one option from two or more options. A common example is Word's four options when you wish to print a document, as shown in figure 2.6. You can only select one of these four.

Edit part of the
combo box

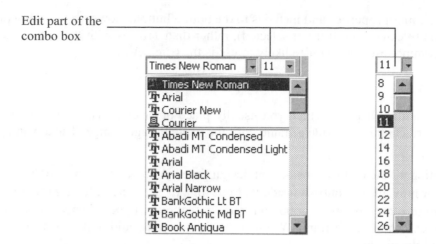

Figure 2.5: Combo boxes on Word's Formatting toolbar

Note the following about the option button:

Properties   Apart from the Name and Caption properties, the most useful property is **Value**. It holds True if the option button is selected or False if it is not selected. You need to understand about selection in Chapter 4 to use this property.

Methods   You are most unlikely to use these.

Events   The **Click** event is the only one you are likely to use.

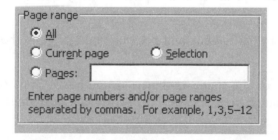

Figure 2.6: Option buttons when printing from Word

The Check Box

The check box is similar to the option button in that you can test its Value property to see if it is selected. Unlike the option button you can select more than one at a time. A common use of check boxes in Windows applications is setting general default values through the **Tools/Options** menu. Figure 2.7 shows an example from the spreadsheet Excel. All but two of the check boxes in this example have been selected.

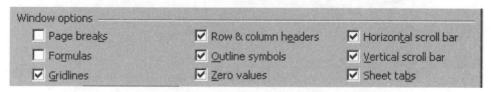

Figure 2.7: An example of the use of check boxes in Excel

The check box has similar properties and methods to the option button. However its **Value** property stores 1 if the check box is selected (and 0 if not selected), rather than True as with the option button. Like the option button, the commonest event you're likely to use is the Click event.

The Frame

The frame is a rectangular shape in which you usually place other controls. In figure 2.6, for example, four option buttons are contained inside a frame with the caption Page Range. The advantages of using a frame are:

- You can reposition all the controls inside it at design time by moving the frame only.
- You can show or hide all the controls inside it at run-time by showing or hiding the frame only.
- If you want two or more groups of option buttons, so that one can be selected from each group, then you *must* put each group into a frame. Without the frames you could only select one button from all the buttons in all the groups.

You are most unlikely ever to use the frame's methods and events. The **Visible** property can be a useful one. It can hold True or False. Set it to False to hide the frame and all its controls. The sample project in Part Three uses this technique a lot.

PROGRAM 2.2   *Option buttons, check boxes and frames*

Specification   Demonstrate the use of two groups of option buttons and a group of check boxes

1. Open a new project and change the form's Caption property from Form1 to **Option buttons, check boxes and frames**.

2. Drag a frame control from the toolbox and position and size it as shown in figure 2.8. Change its Caption to **Gender**.

3. Place two option buttons on the frame as shown in figure 2.8. Draw them as rectangles in order to reveal their captions. Change their Names to **optMale** and **optFemale** and their Captions to **Male** and **Female**.

Note: If you had first placed the option buttons outside the frame and then moved them onto the frame, they would not 'belong' to it. You must drag them straight from the toolbox to the frame.

4. Move the frame and both option buttons should move with it.

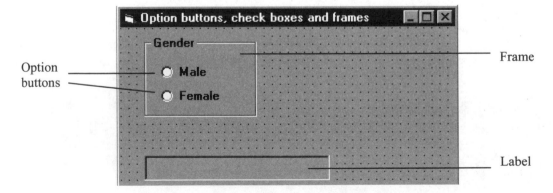

Figure 2.8: Design of program 2.2

5. Place a label below the frame. Set its Name to **lblSelection**, its Caption to blank and its BorderStyle to **1 - Fixed Single**.

6. Double-click the Male option button to bring up the code template for its default event procedure, the Click event. Type in the code below:

```
lblSelection.Caption = "You selected Male"
```

7. Get the Click code template for the Female option button and enter the code:

```
lblSelection.Caption = "You selected Female"
```

8. Run the program and try out the two option buttons.

9. Place another frame on the form and change its Caption to **Age** as shown in figure 2.9.

10. Place three option buttons in this frame. Keep the default Names but change their captions to those in figure 2.9.

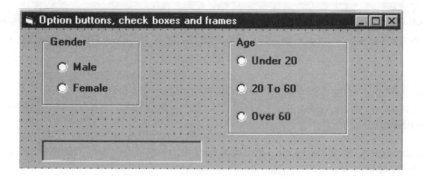

Figure 2.9

11. Run the program to demonstrate that you can select one option from each of the two groups.

12. Place a third frame on the form and change its Caption to **Replies** as shown in figure 2.10.

13. Place three check boxes on the frame and set their Captions as shown in figure 2.10.

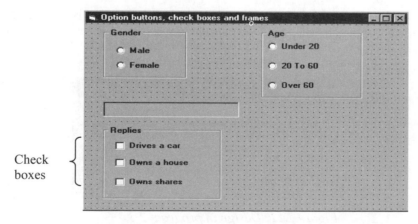

Figure 2.10

14. Run the program and select as few or as many check boxes as you wish.

end of Program 2.2

The Timer

The Timer is one of several toolbox controls that are not visible at run time, which means that you can place it anywhere on the form. It only does one thing: it checks the system clock. It has no methods but two important properties. These are:

Enabled   This holds True or False. An enabled timer is able to carry out what you have coded in its Timer event (see below), but a disabled timer cannot.

Interval   This is measured in milliseconds. A value of 1000 represents 1000 milliseconds or 1 second.

The Timer only has one event, called the **Timer** event. If the timer is enabled, when the time represented by its Interval property has elapsed, it generates its own Timer event. For example an Interval value of 500 would call the Timer event every half a second.

PROGRAM 2.3   *Displaying the time*

Specification   Display the time to the nearest second on a form

1. Open a new project. Place two labels on the form. Set the Caption of the left label to **The time is**. Delete the Caption of the right label, set its Name to **lblTime** (see figure 2.11) and its Style property to **1 – Fixed Single**.

2. Place a timer control anywhere on the form. Set its Name to **tmrTimer** and its Interval property to **1000** so that the Timer event is called every second.

3. Double-click the timer to bring up the code template for its Timer event. Add the line of code that follows:

```
Private Sub tmrTimer_Timer()
    lblTime.Caption = Time          'display current time in the label
End Sub
```

Time is the first example of a Visual Basic **function** you have met. A function is a piece of code built into Visual Basic that returns a value, in this case the current time. You will meet many more functions throughout this book.

Figure 2.11: Design of program 2.3

4. Run the program. You can't see the timer but the time should 'tick' away to the nearest second.

End of Program 2.3

The Scroll Bars

The toolbox has a **horizontal scroll bar** and a **vertical scroll bar**. They are identical except for their orientation on a form. They are used to increase or decrease a value. They have starting and finishing values, represented by the two ends of the scroll bar, and all the values in between. A scroll box is moved between the two ends to set the value.

Scroll bars have no important methods but the most useful properties and events are:

Properties

Max   The highest value, represented by the right side of a horizontal scroll bar or the bottom of a vertical scroll bar.

Min   The lowest value.

Value   The number represented by the current position of the scroll box – between Min and Max.

Events

Change   Occurs when the Value property changes at run time. This in turn results from the user moving the scroll box. The event is triggered *after* the user has moved the scroll box. This is the scroll bar's default event.

Scroll   Similar to the Change event but is triggered *as* the user moves the scroll box.

PROGRAM 2.4   *Changing a form's colour using scroll bars*

Specification	Use three horizontal scroll bars so that the form's colour changes as the user moves their scroll boxes.

To understand how this program works you need to understand the Visual Basic function **RGB** (which stands for **R**ed, **G**reen, **B**lue). The function provides a colour by mixing proportions of these three primary colours. Each of the three colours can have a value from 0 to 255. So the code

```
Form1.BackColor = RGB(255, 0, 0)
Form2.BackColor = RGB(0, 255, 0)
Form3.BackColor = RGB(125, 125, 125)
```

would set Form1's BackColor property to red and Form2's BackColor to green. Form3 gets equal amounts of the three colours to produce a grey. The three numbers given to the function are called **arguments** or **parameters**.

1. Open a new project and set the form's Caption to **Change the form's colour**.

2. Place three labels and three horizontal scroll bars from the toolbox onto the form as shown in figure 2.12.

3. Change the Captions of the labels to **Red**, **Green**, **Blue**.

4. Name the scroll bars **hsbRed**, **hsbGreen** and **hsbBlue** as appropriate.

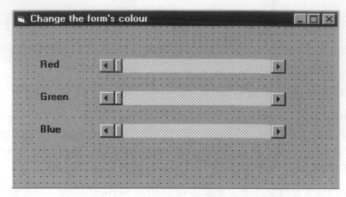

Figure 2.12: Design of program 2.4

5. As the default **Min** property of a scroll bar is 0 leave this alone. Set the **Max** property of the scroll bars to **255**. To set all three at once select one of them, and with the Shift key pressed down select the other two. When you have two or more controls selected the Properties window lists those properties that the controls have in common.

We will use the Scroll event rather than the Change event for each scroll bar to change the form's colour as this will give a more continuous change. Since the Change event is the default event, double-clicking the control on the form will bring up the wrong code template. There are two methods of getting the code template for an event that is not the default one. Steps 6 and 7 cover both methods.

6. Click the View Code button in the Project Explorer (see figure 1.6) to bring up the Code window. From the drop-down list at the top left select **hsbRed**. You're given its default Change event template. From the right hand drop-down list select **Scroll** and you'll get the code template you want. You can delete the code template for the unwanted Change event. Make sure the code is as follows:

```
Private Sub hsbRed_Scroll
   Form1.BackColor = RGB(hsbRed.Value, hsbGreen.Value, hsbBlue.Value)
End Sub
```

The three arguments passed to RGB are the numbers (from 0 to 255) stored in the Value property of each of the scroll bars.

7. As an alternative to getting a code template you can type it in yourself. Press Enter a couple of times and then type in the three lines below for the second scroll bar.

```
Private Sub hsbGreen_Scroll
   Form1.BackColor = RGB(hsbRed.Value, hsbGreen.Value, hsbBlue.Value)
End Sub
```

8. Repeat either step 6 or 7 for **hsbBlue**.

9. Run the program and as you move the scroll boxes the form's colour will change. You will use this program again in program 7.1 so make sure you save it.

End of Program 2.4

Summary of key concepts

- The **text box** is used for entering and displaying data.

- The **list box** and **combo box** are used for displaying a list of items from which the user can select an item. With a combo box you can edit the items at run-time.

- Two or more **option button**s allow the user to select an option. If the option buttons are not grouped on a frame only one button on the form can be selected at once. When option buttons are grouped on frames one button can be selected from each group. The **Value** property holds True if the button is selected and False otherwise.

- Any number of **check box**es can be selected at the same time. The **Value** property holds 1 if the box is selected and 0 otherwise.

- A **frame** is often used to hold groups of option buttons or check boxes. If a frame is moved or made invisible, then all its controls move or become invisible.

- A **timer** has a Timer event that is called after an elapse of time equivalent to its **Interval** property value. The **Enabled** property of the timer must be True for the Timer event to be called. An Interval value of 1000 represents 1000 milliseconds or 1 second.

- A Visual Basic **function** returns a value. Some functions do not require any **arguments** or **parameters** to work (e.g. the Time function). Others require one or more arguments (e.g. RGB).

Take it from here...

1. The **Style** property of a list box has two settings. The default one used in this chapter is **0 – Standard**. Experiment using the other style, **1 – Checkbox**.

2. The **Style** property of the combo box has three settings. Experiment using each of these.

3. Drop two option buttons on a form and set their **Style** property to **1- Graphical**. Run the program to find out how this style differs from the standard one.

4. The Value property of the list box and check box can be True or False. The check box also has a third setting. Investigate what this does.

5. Investigate the **SmallChange** and **LargeChange** properties of scroll bars.

6. Investigate the similarities and differences between the **Image** and **Picture** controls on the toolbox.

7. The RGB function has a simpler sister function called **QBColor**. Investigate this function.

8. Three controls that are non-standard and must be added to the toolbox are the **Slider**, **ProgressBar** and **TabStrip** controls. Select **Project/Component** from the menu and in the Components dialog box click the check box with **Microsoft Windows Common Controls** (plus the version of Visual Basic you are using). Note you should not select *Microsoft Windows Common Controls-2*. Click **OK** and several controls will be added to the toolbox, including the three mentioned above. Experiment using these controls using Help to find out about their important properties and methods.

Questions on the Programs

Program 2.1

*1. Run the program and do the following:

- Enter **turkey** (with a lower case 't'). Then click the Add button.
- Enter **austria** (with a lower case 'a'). Then click the Add button.
- With no data in the text box click the Add button.

What can you conclude about the Sorted property of a list box from these three examples?

*2. In Program 2.1 you could only select one item from the list box. The **MultiSelect** property allows you to select more than one. It has two types of multi-selection. Try out both types.

**3. Add labels below the list box to display the number of countries currently in the list box and the name of the country currently selected.

Program 2.2

*1. Add another label below the Age frame to indicate which of its option buttons is currently selected.

*2. Make the Age frame (and the label in question 1 above if you added this) invisible when the program runs. When the user first selects a gender option make this frame (and label) appear.

Program 2.4

*1. To the right of each scroll bar place a label to display the current position of the bar's scroll box (i.e. a value from 0 to 255).

*2. To see the difference between the Scroll and Change events change the first line of **hsbRed**'s Scroll event so that it is a Change event. Run the program and move the scroll box in this scroll bar.

End of chapter exercises

*1. Use a vertical scroll bar to simulate volume control on a radio. Use three option buttons which will position the scroll box at one-third, half and two-thirds the volume when they are clicked.

**2. Build a program using two list boxes as shown in figure 2.13. One of these, called lstEmployees, lists all the employees in a firm. The other, called lstExcursion, lists those employees taking part in the firm's annual outing. Populate lstEmployees at design time using its List property. When the program runs the user can click a button to copy the selected name from lstEmployees to lstExcursion. A second button should let them delete a name from lstExcursion in case they have made a mistake. Display the number of people on the firm's excursion.

**3. Build a program to implement the two list boxes shown in figure 2.1. Items can be moved between the two list boxes. You will only be able to move one item at a time rather than the two or more which this actual example allows because you have not done Chapter 4 yet. In figure 2.1 the lower two buttons, which move items from the right list box to the left one, are dimmed because there are no items to move in this direction. Find out which command button property allows this and disable the appropriate button on your form. As soon as an item is moved into the right list box allow the button to be used. (You won't be able to enable it when the right list box becomes empty again without knowing about selection, covered in Chapter 4.)

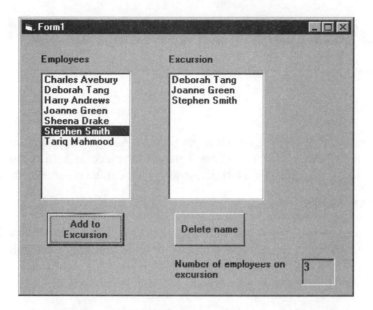

Figure 2.13: Exercise 2

***4**. Build a simple text editor as shown in figure 2.14. The user writes in the large text box and can change this to bold and/or italics by clicking the check boxes, and they can alter the font size by using a combo box. You need to use the **FontBold**, **FontItalic** and **FontSize** run-time properties of the text box to do this.

To get the command buttons working you need to find out about the **Clipboard** object. In a Windows application when you copy or cut something it is saved in an area of RAM known as the Clipboard. You will need to use three of the Clipboard's methods called **Clear**, **SetText** and **GetText**. You will also need the **SelTest** property of the text box.

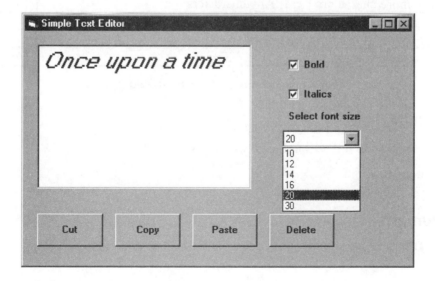

Figure 2.14: Exercise 4

Chapter 3 – Working with Data

Variables

When a program runs, any data that it uses must be stored in RAM. A variable is a name made up by the programmer to identify the address in RAM where a particular piece of data is stored. Our programs so far have managed to avoid using variables but this restricts what can be done. For example the code

```
Form1.Print txtNumber.Text
```

displays whatever the user has typed into the textbox txtNumber. But to *store* what is in the textbox and use what is stored after the user has typed something else into the text box, we would need a variable.

Data Types

Every variable must be of a given **data type**. The main data types you will use in your Visual Basic work are summarised in figure 3.1.

Data type	*Used for storing...*	*Possible stored values*	*Storage required (bytes)*
Integer	Whole numbers, e.g.8, 453	-32,768 to +32,767	2
Long	Whole numbers	-2,147,483,648 to +2,147,483,648 (approx. –2 billion to +2 billion)	4
Single	Numbers with decimal places, e.g. 4.76, 98.00	Very large range indeed, from very small to very large	4
Currency	Numbers with 4 decimal places, e.g. 34.8765. Monetary values	Very large range indeed, but not very small numbers	8
String	One or more characters	Any characters	1 per character
Date	Dates and time	Dates from 1 Jan. 100 to 31 Dec. 9999 Time from 0:00:00 to 23:59:59	8
Boolean	True or false values	True, False	2

Figure 3.1: Summary of the main data types

Declaring variables

To declare a variable means to tell Visual Basic two things about it:

- Its name or **identifier**.
- Its **data type**.

The Dim statement

Use the keywords **Dim** and **As** when you declare a variable. The code below declares three variables of different data types.

```
Dim Number As Integer
Dim Payment As Currency
Dim DateOfPayment As Date
```

Note:

- Always use meaningful identifiers. The three variables could have been declared as A, B and C but these would tell you nothing about what they are supposed to store.
- Identifiers cannot have spaces. When you use two or more words you could join each by an underscore, e.g. date_of_payment, or you could omit the underscores and make each start with an upper case letter, e.g. DateOfPayment. In this book underscores are not used and single-word variable identifiers will begin with an upper case letter (except when naming controls with their prefix).

Option Explicit

Using the declaration above, suppose you later assigned the following values to your variables:

```
Number = 24              'programmer assigns value to variable
Payment = txtPay.Text    'value assigned from user input
Name = txtCustomer.Text  'value assigned from user input
```

Whether Visual Basic will accept the third assignment given that you have not declared the variable *Name* will depend on whether or not you use **Option Explicit**:

- If you *do not* use Option Explicit you do not need to declare a variable before using it.
- If you *do* use Option Explicit you must declare a variable before using it.

A good rule is always declare a variable before using it. If you don't then your code is more likely to contain errors that are hard to spot. You can do this in two ways:

- Write Option Explicit before declaring your variables, e.g.

```
Option Explicit
Dim Number As Integer
'other variable declarations
```

- Select **Tools/Options** and click the check box **Require Variable Declaration**. Visual Basic will automatically put Option Explicit at the head of the Code window the next time you load it.

1. Select **Tools/Options** and tell Visual Basic that you want to be made to declare your variables.

PROGRAM 3.1   *Add two numbers*

Specification   Allow the user to enter two numbers and display their sum.

You could get input from the user using two text boxes, but this program will introduce you to another method of getting simple input, the **input box**.

1. Open a new project and get to its Code window by clicking the **View Code** button in the Project Explorer (see figure 1.6).

2. If you told Visual Basic above to make you declare your variables, the words **Option Explicit** should be there. If you did not then write them in yourself now (see code in step 3).

3. Note the word **General** in the Object list box at the top left. The General part of any form code is where you declare your variables (though see the later section on Scope of Variables). Declare the following:

```
Option Explicit
Dim FirstNumber As Integer          'stores the first number
Dim SecondNumber As Integer         'stores the second number
Dim Total As Integer                'stores sum of the 2 numbers
```

4. Get the form's Load event code template by clicking **Form** in the Object list box (figure 1.9) and type in:

```
Private Sub Form_Load()
    Form1.Show
    FirstNumber = InputBox("Enter your first number")
    SecondNumber = InputBox("Enter your second number")
    Total = FirstNumber + SecondNumber
    Print "The total is", Total
End Sub
```

Note:

- The words in brackets after InputBox will be displayed in the input box.
- You assign whatever the user types into an input box directly to a variable.
- FirstNumber + SecondNumber adds the contents of the two variables (and not their names!)
- The Print statement has two parts separated by a comma. The part inside quotation marks is output as it stands. The part not in quotation marks, Total, outputs the *contents* of this variable.

5. Run the program. The input box below will appear first (figure 3.2). Type in a small number and click **OK**. Another input box appears asking for the second number.

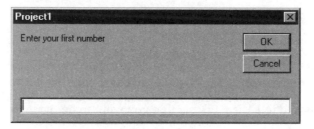

Figure 3.2: The first input box

6. Run the program again and this time enter a number that is too big for FirstNumber to hold, (figure 3.1 shows that Integer values can go up to 32767), a situation called **overflow**. You will get a run-time error message. Click **Debug** and you'll be taken back to the code, with the line that caused the error highlighted in yellow. Select **Run/End** to stop the program or **Run/Restart** to start it again.

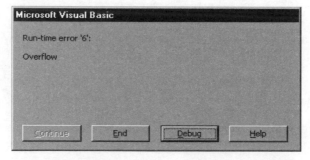

Figure 3.3: The run-time error message indicating overflow

To add numbers that are too large for Integers you must declare the variables as Long instead.

end of Program 3.1

Scope of variables

The **scope** of a variable refers to the part of the program that can use it. There are two main types of scope:

- **global**
- **local**

Global scope

A form variable with global scope can be used anywhere on the form, i.e. in any of its event procedures. In program 3.1 the variables were declared in the General part of the program and this gives them global scope throughout Form1. The code inside the form's Load event used them, and so could code in any other event procedure we might have on Form1.

Local scope

Local variables are declared inside a procedure and can be used only by code inside that procedure. In program 3.1 we could have declared the variables inside the form's Load event instead of in the General part of the code. A good rule is **always declare variables with as narrow a scope as possible**. It will lead to fewer errors.

It is possible to give a global variable and a local variable the same identifier. Program 3.2 shows what happens in this situation.

PROGRAM 3.2   *Illustrating global and local scope*

| Specification | Demonstrate the difference between a global variable and a local variable |

1. Open a new project. Place a command button on the form and name it **cmdOK**.

2. In the General section of the Code window declare a global variable:

```
Dim Surname As String
```

3. In the form's Load event procedure make sure the code is as follows:

```
Private Sub Form_Load()
   Form1.Show
   Surname = "Green"
   Form1.Print "The global variable stores "; Surname
End Sub
```

The semi-colon (;) in the Print command prints the contents of Surname directly after the part inside quotes (rather than leaving a few spaces which was the output in program 3.1).

4. In the Click event procedure of the command button declare a local variable using the same identifier as the global one and display its contents:

```
Private Sub cmdOK_Click()
  Dim Surname As String
  Surname = "Brown"
  Form1.Print "The local variable stores "; Surname
End Sub
```

5. Run the program. The name 'Green' is printed on the form, since the global variable is being accessed by the form's Load event. Click the button and 'Brown' is now printed since the local variable is now being used (figure 3.4).

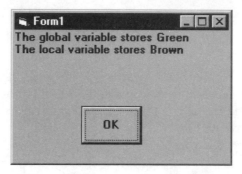

Figure 3.4: Program 3.2

end of Program 3.2

Static variables

Variables no longer exist when they go out of scope. A global variable ceases to exist when the form is closed and a local variable ceases when its event procedure has finished. Sometimes you need to keep the value stored in a local variable until the next time the event in which it is declared is called. You need to declare the local variable as **static** as the next program shows.

PROGRAM 3.3   *Using a static variable*

Specification   Demonstrate the use of a static variable

1. Open a new project. Place a command button on the form and name it **cmdOK**.

2. Make sure the button's Click event code is as follows:

```
Private Sub cmdOK_Click()
  Dim Number As Integer
  Number = Number + 1                      'add 1 to Number
  Form1.Print "Number of clicks = "; Number 'display number of clicks
End Sub
```

3. Run the program and click the button a few times. The printed message will keep saying you have only clicked the button once (figure 3.5 left). Between each click Number ceases to exist and its contents are lost.

4. Change the word **Dim** to **Static** and run the program again. This time the correct number of clicks is displayed (figure 3.5 right).

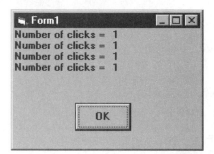 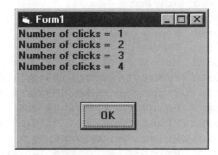

Figure 3.5: Program 3.3

end of Program 3.3

Constants

You can store a new value in a variable whenever this is appropriate. In program 3.3 the value of Number increased by 1 each time the user clicked the button. Instead of a variable use a **constant** when

- the user does not provide the value, and
- you don't want the value to change.

For example if the basic tax rate is 25p in the pound then you could declare it as a constant as follows:

```
Const TaxRate = 0.25          'use = sign when declaring a constant
```

If you try to assign to TaxRate another value such as 0.28 later in the program, an error results.

Arithmetic operations on data

Arithmetic can be done with variables belonging to all the data types listed at the start of this chapter except String.

Types of operation

There are 8 of these, as listed in figure 3.6.

Operator	*Visual Basic*	*Order of precedence*
Addition	+	6=
Subtraction	-	6=
Multiplication	*	3=
Division	/	3=
Integer division	\	4
Modulus	Mod	5
Negation	-	2
Exponentiation	^	1

Figure 3.6: The arithmetic operators

The program below would produce the output shown in figure 3.7:

```
Private Sub Form_Load()
   Const A = 6
   Const B = 4
   Form1.Show
   Form1.Print "A + B = "; A + B
   Form1.Print "A - B = "; A - B
   Form1.Print "A x B = "; A * B
   Form1.Print "A / B = "; A / B
   Form1.Print "A \ B = "; A \ B
   Form1.Print "A modulus B = "; A Mod B
   Form1.Print " A to the power B = "; A ^ B
End Sub
```

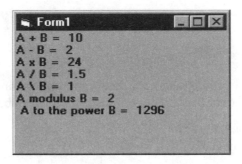

Figure 3.7

Note the following:

- Ordinary division (/) produces a number with a decimal place.
- Integer division (\) produces a whole number. The decimal part is removed.
- Modulus gives the remainder after the first number is divided by the second number, e.g. 6 Mod 6 = 0, 6 Mod 8 = 6, 12 Mod 5 = 2.

Order of precedence

This is shown in figure 3.6. It tells us the order in which Visual Basic carries out the operations. Look at the following program and the output in figure 3.8.

```
Private Sub Form_Load()
   Const A = 10
   Const B = 4
   Const C = 6
   Form1.Show
   Form1.Print "B + C * A = "; B + C * A
   Form1.Print "A / B * C / B = "; A / B * C / B
   Form1.Print "(A / B) * (C / B) = "; (A / B) * (C / B)
End Sub
```

In the first expression C * A is done first rather than B + C. In the second expression the three operations are done in the order written since division and multiplication have equal precedence. In the third expression the divisions are done before multiplication because of the brackets.

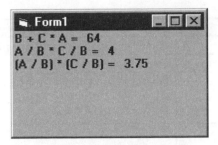

Figure 3.8

PROGRAM 3.4 *Calculating the average exam mark*

Specification Allow the user to enter as many exam marks as they wish and display them in a list box. The program finishes when the user clicks a button to show the average mark

Although the processing in this program is quite simple, we'll use this example as an opportunity to learn more about how the interface of a form can behave at run-time

1. Open a new project. Place on it the two labels, two text boxes, three command buttons and a list box as shown in figure 3.9.

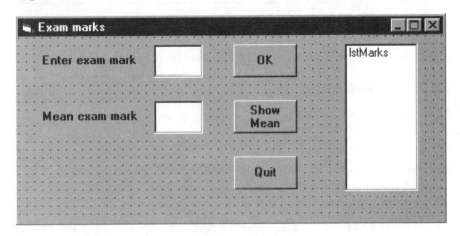

Figure 3.9: Design of program 3.4

2. Set the properties of these controls as listed in figure 3.10. Note:

- The OK button processes a mark but the user should not be able to click it until they have entered a mark. Setting its Enabled property to False does this. The same applies to the Show Mean button.
- Before the user enters a mark the text box (and label) to display the mean can be hidden. Setting its Visible property does this.

3. Two variables will hold the number of marks entered and the total of all the marks. These must be global because they will be used by the Click event procedures of two of the command buttons. Declare them as follows in the General section:

```
Option Explicit
Dim Total As Integer            'stores running total of marks
Dim NumberOfMarks As Integer    'stores number of exam marks entered
```

Control	Property	Property setting
Form	Caption	Exam marks
Label	Caption	Enter exam mark
Label	Name	lblMean
	Caption	Mean exam mark
	Visible	False
Text box	Name	txtMark
	Text	Blank
Text box	Name	txtMean
	Text	Blank
	Visible	False
Command button	Name	cmdOK
	Caption	OK
	Enabled	False
Command button	Name	cmdShowMean
	Caption	Show Mean
	Enabled	False
Command button	Name	cmdQuit
	Caption	Quit
List box	Name	lstMarks

Figure 3.10: Design-time property settings for controls in program 3.4

4.   Since these two variables store running totals **initialise** them to 0 in the form's Load event:

```
Private Sub Form_Load()
   Total = 0
   NumberOfMarks = 0
End Sub
```

Strictly speaking this is not necessary since Visual Basic initialises Integers to 0 when it creates them. It is a good practice to adopt, however, since you may wish to initialise numbers, or variables of other data types, to something other than 0.

When the OK button is clicked the following must happen:

- The Show Mean button must be enabled so the user can find the mean.
- The exam mark entered by the user must be removed.
- The cursor must be positioned ready for the next exam mark

5.   Type in the code below for the Click event of the cmdOK button.

```
Private Sub cmdOK_Click()
   Dim Number As Integer
   Number = txtMark.Text                 'read exam mark
   lstMarks.AddItem Number               'copy it to list box
   Total = Total + Number                'add it to running total of marks
   NumberOfMarks = NumberOfMarks + 1     'increase number of marks by 1
   cmdShowMean.Enabled = True            'enable the Show Mean button
   txtMark.Text = ""                     'clear out the old exam mark
   txtMark.SetFocus                      'place cursor ready for next mark
End Sub
```

Note in the second line that Visual Basic automatically converts the mark entered by the user in txtMark, which is stored as text in its Text property, into an Integer.

6. When the Show Mean button is clicked the text box (and label) to display the mean must be made visible. If the user clicks the OK button again there will not be a number to process and a run-time error will result. We should disable it. So type the following into the Click event of cmdShowMean:

```
Private Sub cmdShowMean_Click()
    Dim Mean As Single              'declare local variable
    Mean = Total / NumberOfMarks    'calculate mean mark and
    txtMean.Text = Mean             'display it
    txtMean.Visible = True          'show text box which displays mean
    lblMean.Visible = True          'and show its label
    txtMark.Enabled = False         'disallow more marks to be entered
    cmdOK.Enabled = False           'and disable OK button
End Sub
```

7. When the Quit button is clicked the program should close. In the Click event procedure for cmdQuit type in:

```
Private Sub cmdQuit_Click()
    Unload Form1                    'removes form from memory
End Sub
```

8. Run the program and enter an exam mark. There's a problem – the OK button is disabled so the mark cannot be processed! We disabled it at design time so that the user could not accidentally click it before a mark had been entered. The **Change** event for the text box where a mark is entered can handle this. This event occurs as soon as the first digit is typed in.

9. In the Change event procedure for txtMark enter the code below and then run the program again.

```
Private Sub txtMark_Change()
    cmdOK.Enabled = True
End Sub
```

The program outputs the mean with up to 6 decimal places. It's unlikely you'd want more than one decimal place displayed here. The next section tells you how to do this.

end of Program 3.4

Displaying output

In this section we'll look at formatting numbers and currency and at a method for joining strings together. Chapter 7 looks at formatting dates and times and reviews a number of string-handling functions.

The Format function

The **Format** function is used for formatting numbers and currency. Give it two arguments:

- The expression to be formatted. This would usually be a numeric constant such as 45.86 or a variable.
- An indication, inside quotation marks, of how to format the expression. This could be a **named numeric format** or a **user-defined numeric format**.

The program below uses a variety of named and user-defined numeric formats and it produces the output shown in figure 3.11. If you wish to run this program type it in the form's Load event procedure.

```
Const Number = 52478.3296
Form1.Show
Form1.Print "Using named numeric formats"
Form1.Print "    General Number    "; Format(Number, "General Number")
Form1.Print "    Fixed             "; Format(Number, "Fixed")
Form1.Print "    Standard          "; Format(Number, "Standard")
Form1.Print "    Percent           "; Format(0.175, "Percent")
Form1.Print "    Currency          "; Format(Number, "Currency")
Form1.Print
Form1.Print "Using user-defined numeric formats"
Form1.Print "0                     "; Format(Number, "0")
Form1.Print "0.00                  "; Format(Number, "0.00")
Form1.Print "###.00                "; Format(Number, "###.00")
Form1.Print "#,##0.0               "; Format(Number, "#,##0.0")
Form1.Print "###.00                "; Format(Number, "###.00")
Form1.Print "£#,##0.00             "; Format(Number, "£#,##0.00")
Form1.Print "0.0%                  "; Format(0.175, "0.0%")
```

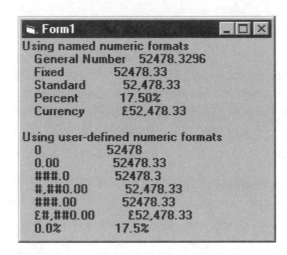

Figure 3.11

There are enough examples here for you to find or work out a format that covers any numeric output you are likely to require. Use this as a reference to return to when the need arises.

In program 3.4 to output the average exam mark with one decimal place, you could not use any of the named formats as these output at least two decimal places. The third user-defined format above shows how to display one decimal place. So in the Click event for cmdShowMean you would write:

```
txtMean.Text = Format(Mean, "0.0")
```

Joining strings together (concatenation)

To **concatenate** two or more smaller strings to form one larger one you use the ampersand operator (&). The code below concatenates two names into one.

```
FirstName = txtFirstName.Text
Surname = txtSurname.Text
lblFullName.Caption = FirstName & " " & Surname      '2 ampersands needed
                     'to produce a space between the two parts of the full name
```

Summary of key concepts

- A **variable** is a name made up by the programmer to identify the address in RAM where a particular piece of data is stored.

- Every variable must be of a particular **data type**. The main data types are **Integer**, **Long** (for storing whole numbers), **Single** (decimal numbers), **Currency** (monetary values or numbers with a fixed number of decimal places), **String** (text), **Date** (date and time) and **Boolean** (true or false).

- To declare a variable use the syntax **Dim** *identifier* **As** *data type*, e.g. Dim Number As Integer.

- Always use **Option Explicit** as this forces you to declare variables before using them.

- **Overflow** is caused by trying to store a number that is too large for its data type. It will result in a run-time error.

- The **scope** of a variable refers to the part of the program that can use it. **Global** variables on a form can be used by all procedures on a form. **Local** variables are declared inside a procedure and can only be used by code within that procedure.

- A good rule is always declare variables with as narrow a scope as possible.

- Form global variables exist until the form closes. Local variables exist until the procedure in which they are declared finishes. However a **Static** local variable keeps its contents between calls to the procedure in which it is declared.

- A **constant** holds a value that cannot be changed during the program. The declaration syntax is **Const** *identifier* = *value*, e.g. Const Number = 20.

- **Arithmetic operators** have an order of precedence. You can change the order by using brackets.

- Use the **Format** function to display numbers and currency.

- Joining strings together is called **concatenation**. Use the ampersand (&) operator to do this.

Take it from here...

1. Four data types not covered in this chapter are **Byte**, **Double**, **Object** and **Variant**. Investigate these.

2. Until Visual Basic 6 the Format function was the only one available for formatting numbers. This version introduced three more - **FormatCurrency**, **FormatNumber** and **FormatPercent**. If you have the appropriate version of Visual Basic investigate these functions.

3. There is a right and wrong way to declare two or more Integers (or any data type) on the same line:

```
Dim FirstNumber As Integer, SecondNumber As Integer      'correct way
Dim FirstNumber, SecondNumber As Integer                 'incorrect way
```

The incorrect way would not store FirstNumber as an Integer. Which data type would it be stored as, and how might you prove that is was not stored as an Integer?

4. You could replace the word Dim when declaring a form's global variable with **Public** or **Private**. Find out how these would affect the variable's scope.

5. There is an alternative concatenation operator to the ampersand – the plus sign (+). It usually works well but what would happen in the following situation? Explain the result.

```
Dim Number As Integer
Dim RoadName As String
Number = 10
RoadName = "The High Street"
Form1.Print Number & " " & RoadName
Form1.Print Number + " " + RoadName
```

6. Visual Basic has a range of functions to convert numeric variables from one data type to another. One of these is **CInt** which converts a non-Integer to an Integer (if possible). Investigate these.

Questions on the Programs

Program 3.1

*1. Change the program to add three numbers rather than two.

Program 3.2

*1. Change the output to a single line -**Your name is Joe Black**. The first name should be stored during the form's Load event and the surname during the button's Click event. You will need to use the concatenation operator for the output.

Program 3.3

*1. Using your knowledge of scope, there is another way of displaying the correct number of times the user has clicked the button without using the keyword Static. Change the code to do this.

Program 3.4

*1. If the user enters a lot of exam marks it can be tiresome having to click the OK button after each one. It would be easier to press Enter instead. Find out which property of the command button to set at design time to allow this.

**2. The user can enter one set of exam marks, find their average and then the program ends. Change it so that the user can enter as many sets of marks as they wish. Add a Clear command button to begin the new set of marks. Display only the current set of marks in the list box.

***3. The marks are displayed in a list box. Add a text box and display them here too. The problem is getting the marks displayed on separate lines. If you know about ASCII codes (covered in Chapter 6) use the Chr function with the code for a new line (you'll have to research into this). If you get the text box working, fill it with numbers and compare it with a list box for displaying output.

End of chapter exercises

Note: in questions 2 and 3 you will need to repeat code in some of the event procedures. This is not considered good programming, but the way of avoiding this is not covered until Chapter 7.

*1. Users are asked to enter the names and ages (whole numbers) of their two children. Display a message such as **Sally and Paul have an average age of 11.5 years**.

*2. Allow the user to enter a series of numbers in a text box (like the exam marks in program 3.4). Clicking a button between numbers displays their running total. Use a static variable for the running total.

**3. Figure 3.12 shows the program in action. Allow the user to enter the numeric values for A, B and C. They can then click one of three option buttons to display the result of an expression. Format the results of the first two expressions to two decimal places.

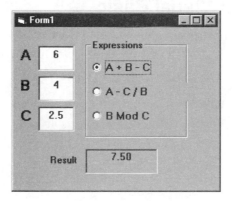

Figure 3.12: Exercise 3

***4. Build a simple calculator as shown in figure 3.13. The user enters two numbers and then clicks one of the four arithmetic operators to display the result. The whole calculation is also displayed in the list box. Clicking the Clear button allows all this to be repeated. Since the calculator has no memory, to calculate 6 + 8 – 2 for example, the user would need to look in the list box or at the displayed result of 6 + 8 to find the first number (14) to enter for the next calculation. In figure 3.13 the user is ready to click the subtraction button to complete this calculation.

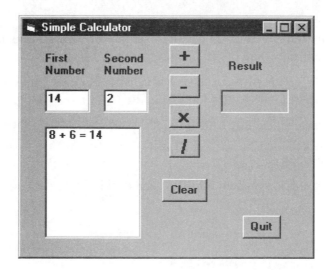

Figure 3.13: Exercise 4

Chapter 4 – Selection

What is selection?

Selection means that one or more lines of code may or may not be executed depending on whether a condition is true or false.

Types of selection in Visual Basic

Visual Basic has two selection constructs:

- **If**
- **Select Case**

The **If** construct has three variations:

- **If Then**
- **If Then…Else**
- **If Then…ElseIf**

If Then

Read the following code and then note the points made after it:

```
Dim Age As Integer
Age = txtAge.Text
If Age > 16 Then                              'age greater than 16?
   Form1.Print "You are old enough to drive"
End If
```

- The condition to test is *Age > 16*. If it is true the message is printed, and if false the message is skipped.

- The '>' sign means 'greater than' and is an example of a **relational operator**. Visual Basic has several of these, which are listed in the *Summary of key concepts*.

- Because the condition is either true or false it is called a **boolean** condition. (Boolean was one of the data types listed at the start of Chapter 3.)

- An **If** must always have a matching **End If** to tell Visual Basic where the construct ends.

If Then…Else

The **Else** part of the construct is executed if the boolean condition is false. For example:

```
If Age > 16 Then                              'age greater than 16?
   Form1.Print "You are old enough to drive"
Else                                          'age 16 or less
   Form1.Print "Sorry, you are too young to drive"
   Form1.Print "You must be 17 years old"
End If
```

If Then...ElseIf

In the previous example there were two routes through the **If** construct. With three or more possible routes you can use an **If Then...ElseIf**. For example:

```
If Age > 16 Then                                 'age greater than 16?
   Form1.Print "You are old enough to drive"
ElseIf Age = 16                                  'age 16 exactly?
   Form1.Print "Sorry, you are too young to drive"
   Form1.Print "You only have to wait less than a year though"
Else                                             'age 15 or less
   Form1.Print "Sorry, you are too young to drive"
   Form1.Print "You must be 17 years old"
End If
```

There are three routes through this example and two boolean conditions to test. If Age stores 16 the first condition *Age > 16* is false. The second one, *Age = 16*, is then tested, and since it is true the next two lines of code are executed. The Else part would be skipped.

PROGRAM 4.1 *Deciding exam grades*

Specification   Ask the user to enter an exam mark from 0 to 100. Display the grade it represents – Merit (60 or more), Pass (40 – 59), Fail (under 40)

In Chapter 3 you met the input box as a way of getting data from the user. Its output equivalent is the **message box**. We'll use both in this program.

1.   Open a new project, double-click on the form to bring up its Load event code template and type in:

```
Private Sub Form_Load()
   Dim Mark As Integer
   Mark = InputBox("Enter an exam mark from 0 to 100")
   If Mark >= 60 Then                            'mark 60 or more?
      MsgBox "Merit"
   ElseIf Mark >= 40 Then                        'mark 40-59
      MsgBox "Pass"
   Else                                          'mark under 40
      MsgBox "A mark of " & Mark & " is a Fail"
   End If
End Sub
```

Note that

- Mark is declared as a local variable (though it could have been a global one since there is only one procedure on the form).

- To display a message box use **MsgBox** followed by the message you wish to output in quotation marks. The third message uses two ampersands (&) to concatenate two strings inside quotes and the contents of Mark into one string.

- Another relational operator (>=) is used, meaning **greater than or equal to**. Note that the condition *Mark >= 60* is the same as *Mark > 59*.

1. Run the program three times and test each of the three routes through the **If** construct by entering, for example, marks of 70, 50 and 30.

end of Program 4.1

Testing multiple conditions

The boolean condition has so far consisted of one test. A multiple boolean condition has two or more tests and each one is either true or false. For this you need to use Visual Basic's **logical operators**. The two important ones are **And** and **Or**.

An AND condition

In the example below there are two conditions to test, *Age > 18* and *Gender = "F"*. Each of these is either true or false. **When you AND two or more conditions each one must be true for the overall condition to be true. If just one of them is false the overall condition is false.**

```
Dim Age As Integer
Dim Gender As String
Age = txtAge.Text
Gender = txtGender.Text
If (Age >= 18) And (Gender = "F") Then      'females 18 and over
   Form1.Print "Allow into nightclub"
Else                                        'everybody else
   Form1.Print "Do not allow into nightclub"
End If
```

The two conditions have brackets. This is optional, but as it can help readability the practice is used in this book.

An OR condition

Members of a ten-pin bowling club get an award if, during one season, they score at least 240 points on 5 or more occasions, or they score 200 points on 10 or more occasions:

```
Dim TwoForty As Integer     'VB does not allow identifiers 240 or 200
Dim TwoHundred As Integer   'since they must not start with a digit
'assume data input
If (TwoForty >= 5) Or (TwoHundred >= 10) Then
   Form1.Print "Give award"
End If
```

When you OR two or more conditions, then if at least one of them is true the overall condition is true. They must all be false for the overall condition to be false.

PROGRAM 4.2   *Selecting cutlery*

Specification   Write a program for a mail order cutlery company. The form should have a list of cutlery brands, a list of different cutlery items and a list of purchase quantities. The user must select one item from each of the three lists and then click a button for the price to be calculated. (N.B. the cost calculation is not relevant to the concept of multiple conditions and will not be coded.)

This program provides an opportunity to practice using some of the controls you covered in Chapter 2. Figure 4.1 shows the program in action. The user has selected a brand of cutlery but not the item(s) or quantity. If the Price button is then clicked the message in figure 4.2(a) appears. When all three things have been selected the satisfactory message in figure 4.2(b) appears.

The Items are selected using check boxes. If the Full Set check box is selected the other three should automatically be selected. The Quantity is selected using option buttons, but note that the mail order company has decided it does not want any of these selected by default.

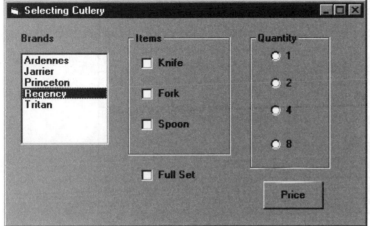

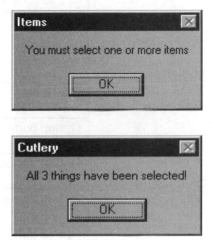

<table>
<tr><td>*Figure 4.1: Program 4.1*</td><td>*Figure 4.2 (a) above (b) below*</td></tr>
</table>

1. Open a new project and design the form using figures 4.1 and 4.3. Frames are used to contain three of the check boxes and the four option buttons. Recall that you must place the frame on the form first before placing the controls inside it if you want the controls to "belong" to it.

We don't need variables in this program and only two event procedures need to be coded:

- When the Full Set check box is clicked the other check boxes must be selected automatically.
- When the Price button is clicked an appropriate message must be displayed.

2. Double-click the Full Set check box to get its default Click event procedure. The **Value** property of a check box indicates whether or not it has been selected, so type in the following:

```
Private Sub chkFullSet_Click()
   If chkFullSet.Value = 1 Then      'Full Set selected
      chkKnife.Value = 1                 'select other 3 check boxes
      chkFork.Value = 1
      chkSpoon.Value = 1
   Else                               'Full set not selected
      chkKnife.Value = 0                 'deselect other 3 check boxes or
      chkFork.Value = 0                  'leave them deselected if in
      chkSpoon.Value = 0                 'that state already
   End If
End Sub
```

Control	Property	Property setting
Form	Caption	Selecting Cutlery
Label	Caption	Brands
List box	Name	lstBrands
	List	*See 5 brands in fig 4.1*
Frame	Caption	Items
Frame	Caption	Quantity
Check box	Name	chkKnife
	Caption	Knife
Check box	Name	chkFork
	Caption	Fork
Check box	Name	chkSpoon
	Caption	Spoon
Check box	Name	chkFullSet
	Caption	Full Set
Option button	Name	optOne
	Caption	1
Option button	Name	optTwo
	Caption	2
Option button	Name	optFour
	Caption	4
Option button	Name	optEight
	Caption	8
Command button	Name	cmdCalcPrice
	Caption	Price

Figure 4.3: Property settings for the controls in program 4.1

3. Get the event procedure for the command button and enter the code below. As there are three parts of the form for the user to make selections from, there are four routes through the **If** construct. Two **ElseIf**s and an **Else** handle this. Note that as **VB does not allow comments on the same line as a joining underscore character** the comments below on the ElseIfs are written on the previous line.

```
Private Sub cmdCalcPrice_Click()
  If lstBrands.Text = "" Then              'has a brand been selected?
    MsgBox "You must select a brand", , "Brand"
            'brand has been selected but has an item been selected?
  ElseIf (chkKnife.Value = 0) And _
         (chkFork.Value = 0) And _
         (chkSpoon.Value = 0) Then
    MsgBox "You must select one or more items", , "Items"
            'brand and item selected but has a quantity?
  ElseIf (optOne.Value = False) And _
         (optTwo.Value = False) And _
         (optFour.Value = False) And _
         (optEight.Value = False) Then
    MsgBox "You must select a quantity", , "Quantity"
  Else                                     'Everything has been selected
    MsgBox "All 3 things have been selected!", , "Cutlery"
  End If
End Sub
```

This code illustrates several things:

- The Value property of an option button is 1 if it is selected (unlike the check box which stores True).

- In program 4.1 we gave the MsgBox function only a message to display. You can also give it several other optional arguments or parameters One of these, used in the examples here, is a title (e.g. "Brand"). As this is the second optional parameter, and we are not supplying the first optional one, you must indicate this by having the two commas and nothing between them. The *Take it from here...* section asks you to explore these parameters further.

- The **ElseIf**s have several conditions to test and only if they are all true should the message be displayed. Therefore **And**s are needed. The conditions have been written on separate lines here because they will not fit on one line in this book. Recall from the Introduction that you use the underscore character (_) to join lines in Visual Basic code, and that there must be at least one space before the underscore.

4. Run the program and try out the four routes through the code.

end of Program 4.2

Nested If structures

A nested **If Then** is an alternative to using multiple AND conditions. Using our earlier example of the nightclub we could write:

```
If Age >= 18 Then                               'aged 18 or over
  If Gender = "F" Then                          'and female?
    Form1.Print "Allow into nightclub"
  Else                                          'all other people
    Form1.Print "Do not allow into nightclub"
  End If
End If
```

A nested **If Then...Else** could be used for the exam mark example. It looks very similar to the earlier code but note that the original **ElseIf** has been split over two lines and has become a nested **If** instead.

```
If Mark >= 60 Then                              'mark 60 or more
    MsgBox "Merit"
Else
  If Mark >= 40 Then                            'mark 40-59
    MsgBox "Pass"
  Else                                          'mark under 40
    MsgBox "A mark of " & Mark & " is a Fail"
  End If
End If
```

The common feature of both these examples is the pair of **End If**s to match the two earlier **If**s. It's for you to decide whether to use nested **If**s in your code. Again readability should probably be the deciding factor.

Complex multiple conditions

When you are coding a large program you might have to use quite complex multiple boolean conditions made up of a mixture of ANDs and ORs. In Chapter 3 you saw that arithmetic operators have an order of precedence. So do logical operators – AND is done before OR. Program 4.3 illustrates how you must take great care in writing more complex multiple conditions.

PROGRAM 4.3 *Rent a property*

Specification Illustrate the order of precedence of the AND and OR logical operators

Look at figure 4.4 showing the program in action. A customer wants to rent a holiday property which has 4 or more bedrooms, and it must be a cottage or a detached house. On the left a detached 5-bedroom property has been selected, the Correct button clicked and the appropriate message **Rent it** displayed. On the right, a one-bedroom cottage has been selected (not what the customer wants), but clicking Incorrect also says rent it. The Correct button has the properly coded multiple condition.

1. Open a new project and place two labels, two list boxes and two command buttons on the form. Set the captions of the labels and buttons to those shown in figure 4.4

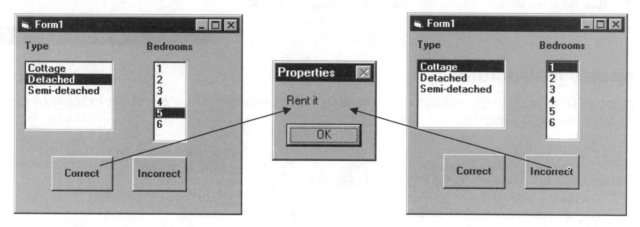

Figure 4.4: Program 4.3

2. Name the list boxes **lstTypes** and **lstBedrooms** and add the items shown in figure 4.4 using their List property.

3. Name the command buttons **cmdCorrect** and **cmdIncorrect**.

4. In the General part of the form's code declare two global variables:

```
Option Explicit
Dim PropType As String      'stores selected item from Type list box
Dim Bedrooms As Integer     'stores selected item from Bedrooms list box
```

5. In the Click event procedure for cmdCorrect enter the correct coding as follows:

```
Private Sub cmdCorrect_Click()
   PropType = lstTypes.Text
   Bedrooms = lstBedrooms.Text
   If (PropType = "Cottage") And (Bedrooms >= 4) _
                 Or (PropType = "Detached") And (Bedrooms >= 4) Then
      MsgBox "Rent it"
   End If
End Sub
```

If the user selects **Detached** and **5** from the list boxes the multiple condition becomes

(PropType = "Cottage") **And** (Bedrooms >= 4) **Or** (PropType = "Detached") **And** (Bedrooms >= 4)

False   **AND**   True   **OR**   True   **AND**   True

Since ANDs have precedence over ORs these are done first, which produces

False   **OR**   True

Finally the OR produces True, and the message **Rent it** is displayed.

6. In the Click event procedure for cmdIncorrect enter an example of incorrect coding as follows:

```
Private Sub cmdIncorrect_Click()
  PropType = lstTypes.Text
  Bedrooms = lstBedrooms.Text
  If (PropType = "Cottage") Or (PropType = "Detached") _
            And (Bedrooms >= 4) Then
    MsgBox "Rent it"
  End If
End Sub
```

If the user selects **Cottage** and **1** the multiple condition becomes

(PropType = "Cottage") **Or** (PropType = "Detached") **And** (Bedrooms >= 4)

True   **OR**   False   **AND**   False

Doing the AND first produces

True   **OR**   False

which produces a final True, and so the **Rent it** message is incorrectly displayed.

7. Run the program and try out a variety of types and bedrooms. You will find that a cottage with 1, 2 or 3 bedrooms incorrectly displays the message.

end of Program 4.3

Select Case

In the examples so far the largest number of routes through the **If** structure has been four. If you have more than this the **Select Case** structure is probably a better alternative.

Suppose you wished to output the name of the month corresponding to a number from 1 to 12 input by the user. If this value is stored in Month then you would code this as follows:

```
Select Case Month
  Case 1
    MsgBox "January"
  Case 2
    MsgBox "February"
  Case 3
    MsgBox "March"
            'and so on up to........
  Case 12
    MsgBox "December"
End Select
```

Visual Basic would look for the value of Month in one of the 12 **Case**s and execute the appropriate code. If it cannot find a match, because the user has entered 13 for example, nothing happens. You can cover this situation by adding an optional **Case Else**:

```
    Case 12
       MsgBox "December"
    Case Else
       MsgBox "You did not enter a valid month number"
  End Select
```

PROGRAM 4.4   *Wards and Patients*

Specification   Present the user with two list boxes. One of these lists the wards in a hospital. Clicking on one of the wards displays the names of its patients in the other list box.

Figure 4.6 shows the program. Selecting a ward changes the patient list on the right. This is a technique with many applications in computer projects. Examples include courses and students, departments and employees, authors and books and so on.

1.   Open a new project. Design the form using figures 4.5 and 4.6. Note that you only have to put items into the Wards list box, not the Patients list box too.

Control	*Property*	*Property setting*
Form	Caption	Wards and Patients
Label	Caption	Wards
Label	Caption	Patients
List box	Name List	lstWards *See the 3 wards listed in figure 4.6*
List box	Name	lstPatients

Figure 4.5: Property settings for the controls in program 4.4

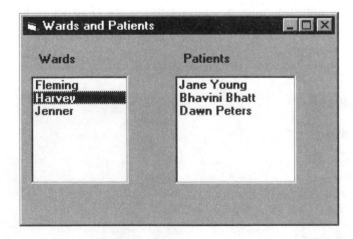

Figure 4.6: Program 4.4

2. Get the Click event procedure for the wards list box and type in the following code:

```
Private Sub lstWards_Click()
  Dim Ward As String
  Ward = lstWards.Text                'selected item from ward list box
  Select Case Ward
    Case "Fleming"
      lstPatients.AddItem "Fred Jones"    'AddItem method used to
      lstPatients.AddItem "John Green"    'populate patients list box
      lstPatients.AddItem "Imran Shah"
    Case "Harvey"
      lstPatients.AddItem "Jane Young"
      lstPatients.AddItem "Bhavini Bhatt"
      lstPatients.AddItem "Dawn Peters"
    Case "Jenner"
      lstPatients.AddItem "William Black"
      lstPatients.AddItem "Michael Jones"
      lstPatients.AddItem "Darren Campbell"
  End Select
End Sub
```

3. Run the program and click on two different wards. After clicking the second ward the list box has patients from both wards. We need to remove the patients from the first ward before the new names are added. Add the following line before each of the three AddItem lines in each Case:

```
lstPatients.Clear
```

Note that the method of populating the patients list box is not the way you'd do it in a real project. These names would be stored in a file. Files are covered in Chapter 10. With **Case** "Fleming", for example, the code would copy details of those patients in this ward from the file. However you would still need the AddItem method to get them into the list box.

end of Program 4.4

Extensions to Select Case

So far the **Case** values have all been simple single ones – months (1-12) and ward names. There are several extensions to this. Here are some examples:

A continuous range of values using *To*

```
Select Case Mark
  Case 0 To 39                          'value ranges from 0 to 39
    MsgBox "Fail"
  Case 40 To 59                         'value ranges from 40 to 59
    MsgBox "Pass"
  Case 60 To 100                        'value ranges from 60 to 100
    MsgBox "Merit"
End Select
```

A continuous range of values using *Is*

The code below does the same as the previous example. As relational operators are used the keyword **Is** must follow **Case**.

```
Select Case Mark
   Case Is < 40                    'value is under 40
      MsgBox "Fail"
   Case Is <= 59                   'value ranges from 40 to 59
      MsgBox "Pass"
   Case Is >= 60                   'value is 60 or over
      MsgBox "Merit"
End Select
```

A non-continuous range of values

```
Select Case Month
   Case 1, 3, 5, 7, 8, 10, 12
      MsgBox "This month has 31 days"
   Case 4, 6, 8, 11
      MsgBox "This month has 30 days"
   Case 2
      MsgBox "This month has 28 or 29 days"
End Select
```

Summary of key concepts

- Visual Basic has two selection constructs - **If** and **Select Case**. Both have several variations.

- With an **If** structure a boolean condition is tested. If it is true the associated code is executed, otherwise control passes to the optional **Else** if there is one.

- No matter how complex a multiple **If** condition is, it must reduce to an overall single true or false.

- Visual Basic supports the following **relational operators**:

=	equal to	<	smaller than
>	greater than	<=	smaller than or equal to
>=	greater than or equal to	<>	not equal to

- Visual Basic's two main **logical operators** are **And** and **Or**. The following rules apply:

  * When you AND two or more conditions each one must be true for the overall condition to be true. If just one of them is false the overall condition is false.

  * When you OR two or more conditions, then if at least one of them is true the overall condition is true. They must all be false for the overall condition to be false.

  * ANDs have precedence over ORs.

Take it from here...

1. In this chapter you gave the **MsgBox** function two parameters. It can accept more than this, and one of these refers to the type of buttons to display in the message box. Investigate some of the button types you can display.

2.   Visual Basic has an **IIf** function equivalent to If Then…Else and a **Switch** function equivalent to Select Case. Find out how you might use these functions in code.

3.   Only two logical operators, And and Or, were covered. Visual Basic has four more, although only one of these, the **Not** operator, is ever likely to be of use to you. Find out about this operator.

Questions on the Programs

Program 4.1

*1.   When you click to remove the message box, the empty form seems to appear. Add one line of code to stop it appearing.

*2.   Extend the code so that a mark of 80 or more gets a Distinction.

Program 4.2

*1.   Originally the mail order company did not want any of the Quantity options selected by default when the program runs. Now they have changed their mind. Change one of the properties of optFour to make quantity 4 selected when the program starts.

Program 4.3

*1.   Add a second Incorrect button so that if you select a Detached property with 3 bedrooms or less it will tell you (wrongly) to rent it.

Program 4.4

*1.   Add two more wards and write code to display three patients in each of them.

**2.   Rewrite the code using the ListIndex property of the wards list box rather than the Text property.

End of chapter exercises

*1.   Ask a salesperson to input the total value of their sales this year to the nearest whole pound. If it exceeds £100,000 their bonus is £10,000. If it is from £70,000 to £99,999 the bonus is £7,000 and if it is £50,000 to £69,999 the bonus is £4,000. Sales less than £50,000 receive no bonus. Output the salesperson's bonus.

*2.   A person wishes to attend an overnight conference. They cannot afford to pay more than £40.00 for their hotel, which must be no more than 3 km from the conference hall. Ask the user to input these two data items and then display a message to indicate whether they should book or not.

**3.   Write a program that calculates total weekly pay as shown in figure 4.7. The user enters the number of hours worked and selects the hourly rate of pay from a list box. If overtime has been done, the number of hours is also entered. Overtime hours are paid at double rate. A check box handles overtime. Clicking this should make visible the text box for inputting the number of overtime hours.

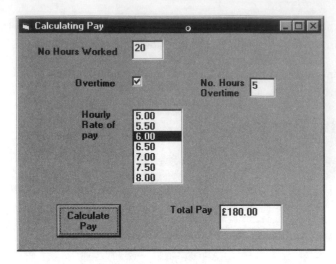

Figure 4.7: Exercise 3

**4. A sports club has three categories of membership charge. Juniors (aged up to 18) pay £60 per year, Seniors (19-49) pay £120 and Veterans (50 and over) pay £80. Juniors who have been a member for 2 years or more get a £20 reduction. Seniors and Veterans who have been members for 10 years or more get a £30 reduction. Write a program that asks for the member's age and the number of years they have been a member, and outputs their category of membership and how much they must pay. Use input boxes to get the data.

**5. The Shipshape Packing Company wants a program for their Orders Department to calculate and display the price of an order. The order clerks enter the number of units ordered, whether a customer is a wholesaler or retailer, and whether or not the customer is a special customer. Use a variety of controls for this data entry. The price the customer pays per unit depends on these three things. The prices are as follows:

	Wholesalers		Retailers	
No. units	Price per unit (£)		No. units	Price per unit(£)
1-5	50		1 – 3	60
6-10	45		4-8	55
11-20	40		9-15	50
21-50	35		16-40	45
over 50	30		over 40	40

Special customers get a 10% reduction on the prices above.

***6. Write a program to simulate the changes of a set of traffic lights. Use the Shape control in the toolbox to put three circles on a form. Set the BackColor property of the top one to red and the other two to white. With each click of a button the traffic lights should change continuously through the sequence: Red, Amber and Red together, Green and finally Amber You may need to look back at how you used the RGB function in program 2.4 in order to code the colour changes.

If you get this working now try to meet a different specification. When the button is clicked the traffic lights colour changes should go automatically through the cycle. For this you need to use a Timer control. Its default Interval setting is 0; change this to any positive value otherwise you may not get the colour sequence to start. A value of 1000 (i.e. 1000 milliseconds or 1 second) will be fine.

Chapter 5 – Loops

What is a loop?

A program loop is a section of code that may be repeatedly executed. The loop contains a boolean condition that will determine when it terminates.

Types of loop in Visual Basic

Visual Basic has six types of loop, but you only ever need to understand three of them. These are:

- **For…Next**
- **Do While…Loop**
- **Do…Loop Until**

The code, known as the **loop body**, is inserted in place of the three dots. Each loop works in a slightly different way and is useful in different circumstances.

For…Next

You use this type of loop when you know exactly how many times the code must be repeated. For example the code below prints the numbers 1 to 10, as shown in figure 5.1. Assume that Number has been declared as an Integer.

```
For Number = 1 To 10
    Print Number
Next Number
```

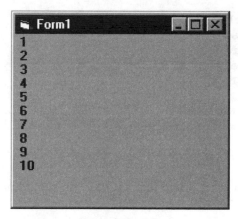

Figure 5.1

The first time the line

```
For Number = 1 To 10
```

is executed the value 1 is stored in Number. The statement in the loop body is then executed and the number 1 is printed. The line

```
Next Number
```

indicates the end of the loop and control passes back to the first line. Number is automatically incremented to 2 and the loop body executes again, this time printing 2. This process continues until the loop has been executed exactly 10 times, when control passes to the first statement after the loop.

The general form of a **For...Next** loop is

> **For** *variable identifier* = *start value* **To** *end value*
>   statement(s)
> **Next** *variable identifier*

Note that:

- Start and end values may be integer constants, variables or expressions.
- The variable identifier in the last line of the loop is optional, but it is good practice to include it.

PROGRAM 5.1   *Multiplication table*

Specification Ask the user to enter a number from 2 to 12 and then output the multiplication table for their number. If the user enters 5 then the output is

$$2 \times 5 = 10$$
$$3 \times 5 = 15$$
$$4 \times 5 = 20$$
$$......$$
$$12 \times 5 = 60$$

1. Open a new project and drop a label, textbox and command button on the form so that it looks like figure 5.2. Name the textbox **txtNumber** and the command button **cmdOK**.

2. Double-click on the command button to bring up the Code window. Type in code so that its event procedure is as follows:

```
Private Sub cmdOK_Click()
  Dim Number As Integer
  Dim Index As Integer
  Dim Result As Integer
  Number = txtNumber.Text
  For Index = 2 To 12
    Result = Index * Number
    Print Number & " x " & Index & " = " & Result
  Next Index
End Sub
```

3. Run the program and if you enter 5 into the text box you should produce the output shown in figure 5.3.

The first line in the loop

```
For Index = 2 To 12
```

stores the value 2 in Index. When Result is calculated by multiplying this by Number (e.g. 2 x 5), the concatenation operator **&** is used three times to output one line on the form (e.g. 2 x 5 = 10) with

```
Print Number & " x " & Index & " = " & Result
```

Next is then read and control returns to the first line of the loop. When Index has the value 12 the loop runs for the last time.

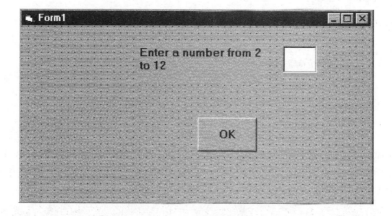

Figure 5.2: Design of program 5.1

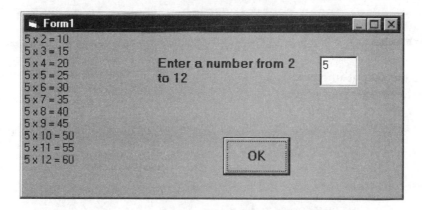

Figure 5.3: Output from Program 5.1

End of Program 5.1

The Step parameter

In the examples we've looked at so far, the value of the variable which controls whether or not the loop is executed has increased by 1 each time round the loop. However it doesn't have to increase by 1. For example, the code

```
For Index = 1 To 10 Step 2
    Print Index
Next Index
```

sets the values of Index to 1, 3, 5, 7 etc. by using the **Step** parameter and giving it a value of 2. The last execution of the loop occurs when Index has the value 9 because the next value, 11, would be bigger than the 10 allowed. You can even give **Step** a negative value. Thus

```
For Index = 20 To 0 Step -5
```

would successively store the values 20, 15, 10, 5 and 0 in Index and make the loop run five times.

A nested *For...Next* loop

A nested loop is when you have one loop inside another. The general structure of a nested **For...Next** loop is:

For.........	*start of outer loop*
For.......	*start of inner loop*
....	*body of inner loop*
Next	*end of inner loop*
Next	*end of outer loop*

Think of the outer loop as a large cog driving a smaller cog which is the inner loop. Every time the larger cog revolves once (one repetition of the outer loop), the inner cog usually revolves more than once. Have a look at the code which follows.

```
For OuterNumber = 1 To 4
   Print "Outer control variable is " & OuterNumber
   For InnerNumber = 1 To 2
      Print "        Inner control variable is " & InnerNumber
   Next InnerNumber
Next OuterNumber
```

This will produce the output in figure 5.4. The outer loop is run four times, and each time you go round the outer loop the inner loop runs twice.

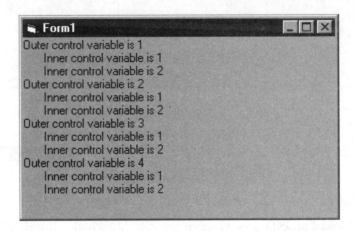

Figure 5.4

PROGRAM 5.2 *Addition Table*

Specification   Write a program to display the sum of row and column numbers

The running program is shown in figure 5.5.

1.   Open a new project and double-click on the form to get the form's Load event code template.

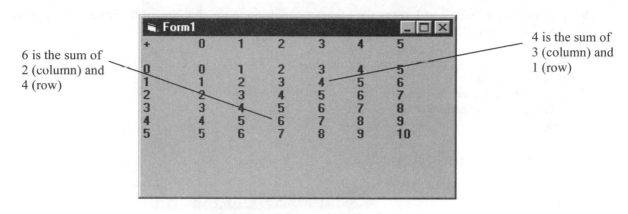

6 is the sum of
2 (column) and
4 (row)

4 is the sum of
3 (column) and
1 (row)

Figure 5.5: Program 5.2

2. Declare the following:

```
Const Max = 5
Dim ColNumber As Integer
Dim RowNumber As Integer
Dim Sum As Integer
```

3. In the form's Load event type in the following code to produce the addition table. Note the three new formatting commands **Space**, **vbNewLine** and **NewLine** and the use of the semi-colon (**;**). (Option Explicit must be Off for NewLine to be understood.)

```
Form1.Show
Print "+" & Space(12);                  'print table heading
For ColNumber = 0 To Max                'simple For…Next loop
   Print ColNumber & Space(8);          'print column value and 8 spaces
Next ColNumber
Print vbNewLine                         'print empty line
For RowNumber = 0 To Max                'start of outer loop
   Print RowNumber & Space(12);            'print first number in the row
   For ColNumber = 0 To Max                'start of inner loop
     Sum = ColNumber + RowNumber
     Print Sum & Space(8);                  'print addition
   Next ColNumber                         'end of inner loop
   Print NewLine                          'get to next line
Next RowNumber                          'end of outer loop
```

4. Run the program. Then remove one of the semi-colons and run it again. You should see that the semi-colon's job is to keep the cursor on the same line.

end of Program 5.2

Do While…Loop

The general form of **Do While…Loop** is

> **Do While** *condition* is true
> statement(s)   =   body of loop
> **Loop**

This type of loop executes as long as the boolean condition in the first line of the loop is true, otherwise it exits. Consider the following code:

```
Number = 5
Do While Number <> 10                    '<> means not equal to
   Print Number * Number
   Number = Number + 1
Loop
```

This will produce the output in figure 5.6.

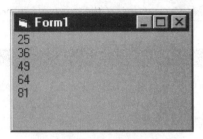

Figure 5.6

Note that:

- If you omitted the line

```
Number = Number + 1
```

the loop would never end, since Number would never equal 10. This is called an **infinite loop**. This is a common mistake and a good reason to always save your program before running it, because you will not be able to get out of an infinite loop without exiting Visual Basic and thus losing your code. However there is one way to escape an infinite loop - include the line **DoEvents** somewhere inside the loop. This tells Visual Basic to respond to events while the loop is executing; closing the program is the event you'll want it to respond to.

- If the first line of code was

```
Number = 10
```

then the condition *10 <> 10* would be false, and the loop would not be executed at all. This is one key feature of Do While…Loop which distinguishes it from Do…Loop Until.

PROGRAM 5.3   *Driving Test*

Specification	Ask the user to enter "Y", "N" or "Q" (quit) in response to the question "Has the person passed their driving test?" Continue asking this question until the user answers "Q". Output the number and percentage of people who have passed their test.

1.   Open a new project and design the form using figures 5.7 and 5.8.

Control	Property	Property setting
Label	Caption	Number who have passed driving test
Label	Caption	Percentage who have passed driving test
Text box	Name	txtNumberPassed
	Text	Blank
Text box	Name	txtPercentPassed
	Text	Blank
Command button	Name	cmdOK
	Caption	OK

Figure 5.7: Properties of the controls in program 5.3

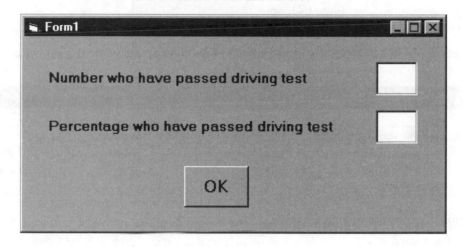

Figure 5.8: Program 5.3

2. Double-click the command button and type the following code into its click event procedure:

```
Private Sub cmdOK_Click()
  Dim TotalNumber As Integer
  Dim NumberPassed As Integer
  Dim Response As String
  TotalNumber = 0                     'initialise variables
  NumberPassed = 0
  Response = "Z"        'set to anything except Q so that loop is entered
  Do While Response <> "Q"
     Response = InputBox("Has person passed driving test?.Y/N " & _
                 "or Q to quit")
     If Response <> "Q" Then                  'user has entered Y or N
        TotalNumber = TotalNumber + 1
        If Response = "Y" Then           'person has passed driving test
          NumberPassed = NumberPassed + 1
        End If
     End If
  Loop
  txtNumberPassed.Text = NumberPassed
  txtPercentPassed = Format(NumberPassed / TotalNumber * 100, _
                     "###.00")
End Sub
```

3. Now for a really useful piece of advice mentioned earlier. Always save a program with an untested **While** or **Until** loop in it before you run it. If you have written your loop incorrectly so that it won't stop executing – the infinite loop – you will not be able to get back to the Visual Basic environment and you will lose your code. So save it now and then run it.

end of Program 5.3

Do...Loop Until

The general form of this loop is:

> **Do**
>   statement(s)   =   body of loop
> **Loop Until** *condition* is true

Since the condition is at the end of the loop the loop body must be executed at least once.

PROGRAM 5.4   *Password Entry*

Specification   Allow the user up to three attempts at entering the password "secret". Inform the user which attempt they are currently on (1, 2 or 3). Inform the user that the password is correct if they get it within the three attempts, otherwise inform them that their password is invalid.

1. Open a new project, drop a command button onto the form, set its Name to **cmdOK** and its Caption to **Enter Password**.

2. Double-click the button to bring up the Code window and enter the following code into its Click event procedure:

```
Private Sub cmdOK_Click()
  Dim Password As String
  Dim InputPassword As String
  Dim Attempt As Integer
  Password = "secret"                              'initialise variables
  Attempt = 0
  Do                                              'start of loop
    Attempt = Attempt + 1
    InputPassword = InputBox("Enter password. This is attempt " & _
               "number " & Attempt)
  Loop Until (Attempt = 3) Or (InputPassword = Password) 'end of loop
  If InputPassword = Password Then
    MsgBox ("This password is valid")
  Else
    MsgBox ("This password is invalid")
  End If
End Sub
```

The body of the loop asks the user for the password and then adds 1 to the number of attempts the user has had. The condition at the end of the loop is a multiple one:

```
Loop Until (Attempt = 3) Or (InputPassword = Password)
```

The condition is true if either the user has had three attempts or they have entered the correct password. It will also be true if they have entered the correct password at the third attempt since both parts of the multiple condition are true.

3. Run the program to check that it works.

end of Program 5.3

Summary of key concepts

- The general forms of the three loops covered in this chapter are:

For…Next	**For** *variable identifier = start value* **To** *end value* statement(s) **Next** *variable identifier*
Do While…Loop	**Do While** *condition* statement(s) = body of loop **Loop**
Do…Loop Until	**Do** statement(s) = body of loop **Loop Until** *condition*

- Use a **For…Next** loop when you know how many times the loop must be executed.

- Use **Do While…Loop** if there is the possibility that the loop body should not be executed.

- An **infinite loop** is one that never stops running. The program will just hang. It is caused by not allowing the condition tested in **Do While…Loop** to become false or the condition in **Do…Loop Until** to become true.

Take it from here…

1. It is possible to force a loop to terminate early by using the **Exit** statement. Find out how to exit early from the three types of loop covered in this chapter.

2. The beginning of this chapter said that Visual Basic has six types of loop, but that you only need to know three of these. Find out about the three that were not studied. These are **Do Until…Loop**, **Do…Loop While** and **While…Wend**. For each of these loops find out how the tested condition works. Also find out whether they must be executed at least once or whether they may be 'skipped' the first time.

3. There is a seventh type of loop called the **For Each…Next**. It has a special job in a Visual Basic program and is used only on arrays and collections (control arrays). Arrays are covered in Chapter 8. A collection is a set of related objects. For example if you had six text boxes and three command buttons on a form you would have a collection of text boxes and a collection of command buttons. Find out about how you might use the **For Each…Next** loop.

Questions on the Programs

Program 5.1

*1. In this program the user is expected to type in a number from 2 to 12. As the code stands they can type any number into txtNumber. Add a loop to the code in the event procedure cmdOK_Click to ensure that the user enters a value from 2 to 12. Making sure that input data satisfies certain conditions is called **validation**. All you are doing here is validating an inputted number. If the user entered one or more characters by mistake you would get a run-time error.

Program 5.3

*2. Rewrite this program using **Do...Loop Until** instead of Do While...Loop.

End of chapter exercises

In questions 2, 3 and 6 use an **input box** to get data from the user.

*1. Ask the user to input two different numbers. Print all the numbers between the two values they enter.

*2. A disco can hold 500 people. Allow the user to keep entering the number of people in each group as the group comes through the door. Display the running total and how many more people are allowed in before it becomes full. When the running total first reaches 500 display a message that the disco is full, or if 500 is exceeded, a message that the current group of people cannot go in.

*3. Allow the user to enter as many positive whole numbers as they wish, and to enter 0 to indicate they have finished. Then display the number of even values and number of odd values entered by the user. Use the **Mod** operator to work out whether a number is odd or even.

**4. Use nested loops to output the cell references found in the top upper left part of a spreadsheet, within the range A1 to E5, as shown in figure 5.8. You may wish to use two Visual Basic functions, Asc and Chr, to convert characters to their ASCII values and vice-versa.

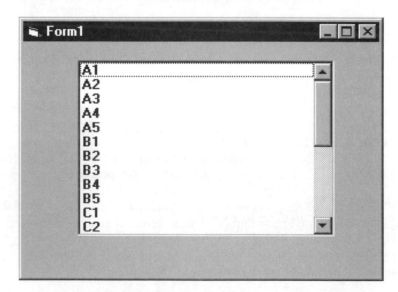

Figure 5.8: Output from Exercise 4

5.   Write a program that outputs all the dates in one year in a list box when the user clicks a button. The output is shown in figure 5.9. Use a **For...Next loop to handle the whole year and inside this a **Select Case** to handle each month. You will need to set the Column property of the list box at design time to allow multiple columns.

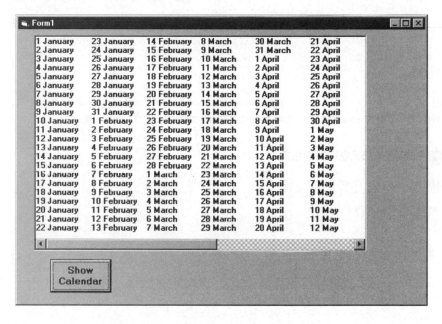

Figure 5.9: Output from exercise 5

***6.   People have been surveyed in a shopping centre about the main holiday they had in the past year. They were asked the following questions:

1. Have you had a holiday in the past 12 months?	Yes ☐	No ☐
2. If Yes, was it in Britain or abroad?	GB ☐	Abroad ☐
3. If Yes, how many weeks did it last?	Up to 2 weeks ☐	More than 2 ☐

Allow the user to enter data for as many respondents as they wish. Validate the items of data entered. When all the data has been entered display the number and percentage of respondents who

- did not take a holiday.
- took a holiday in Britain of up to 2 weeks.
- took a holiday in Britain of over 2 weeks.
- took a holiday abroad of up to 2 weeks.
- took a holiday abroad of over 2 weeks.

Chapter 6 – Handling Strings, Dates and Time

Introduction

String handing is probably the most common task in programming. Handling dates and time is less common, but when the need arises is very important to understand.

Declaring strings

Two types of string can be declared:

- **Variable length strings**
- **Fixed length strings**

The code below shows an example of each.

```
Dim Surname As String                    'variable length string
Dim EmployeeNumber As String * 6         'fixed length string
```

The examples in this book so far have been variable length strings. The size of the variable (in bytes) depends on how many characters are stored. If Surname above stores "Smith" it would be 5 bytes in size. With a fixed length string the variable is always the size you declare it to be. Use a fixed length string when you know exactly the number of characters needed. In the example above employees always have a 6-character employee number. However fixed length strings are optional - the only time you *must* use them is when storing records in a file (see Chapter 10).

ASCII

Most computers use the American Standard Code for Information Interchange (ASCII) for storing characters. Each character is stored as an integer from 0 to 255. The following are useful to know:

- Upper case letters ('A' to 'Z') are stored as numbers 65 to 90.
- Lower case letters ('a' to 'z') are stored as numbers 97 to 122.
- Numeric digits ('0' to '9') are stored as numbers 48 to 57.
- The space character is number 32.

Processing strings

Using relational operators

The code below outputs two strings, Name1 and Name2, in alphabetical order:

```
If Name1 < Name2 Then
   Print Name1 & "   " & Name2
Else
   Print Name2 & "   " & Name1
End If
```

Visual Basic does this by comparing the ASCII value of the first character in each string. A lower value indicates that this character comes alphabetically before the other one. If they are the same then the next character in each string is compared and so on. Note that since upper case letters have lower values than lower case letters, **Jones** is alphabetically before **brown**.

Searching for a substring using *Instr*

The **Instr** function returns the position in the main string of the substring being searched for. Thus the code below

```
MainString = "The man looked up and saw the moon"
SearchString = "man"
Position = InStr(MainString, SearchString)
```

would store the value 5 in Position. If the substring is not present the function returns 0. By default InStr is case sensitive. You must add a third parameter, 1, to make it case insensitive.

Processing individual characters using *Mid*

The **Mid** function returns a substring from the main string. Using the MainString variable in the previous example, consider the following:

```
Dim OneCharacter As String * 1
Dim Characters As String
MainString = "Keep on looking ahead"
OneCharacter = Mid(MainString, 9)          'returns 9th character i.e. 'l'
Characters = Mid(MainString, 9, 4)         'returns 4 characters starting
                                           'at position 9 i.e. 'look'
```

You need to state the position in the main string, and there is the option of specifying how many characters to return (4 in the example above).

PROGRAM 6.1   *Ensuring a person's name has only one space*

Specification   Ask the user to enter a person's surname and then their first name into a single text box. Check that only one space character has been used between the names.

1.   Open a new project and design the form using figure 6.1. Name the textbox **txtName** and the command button **cmdOK**

2.   In the Click event procedure for the command button enter the following code:

```
Dim Spaces As Integer
Dim EmployeeName As String
Dim Index As Integer
Dim Character As String * 1               'declare a one-character string
EmployeeName = txtName.Text
Spaces = 0
For Index = 1 To Len(EmployeeName)  'Len returns no of characters in string
   Character = Mid(EmployeeName, Index)   'extract one character
   If Character = " " Then                'is this character a space?
      Spaces = Spaces + 1                 'if yes, increment Spaces
   End If
Next Index
```

```
If Spaces >= 2 Then
  MsgBox "Too many spaces"
End If
```

The function **Len** returns the number of characters stored in the string passed to it. So the **For...Next** loop must be repeated that number of times in order to process each character.

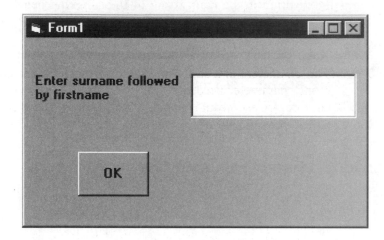

Figure 6.1: Program 6.1

3.   Run the program and test it several times by entering a name with one space between the surname and first name, more than one space, a space before the surname and between the names, and a space after the first name.

end of Program 6.1

Breaking strings up with *Left* and *Right*

The **Left** function returns a substring from the main string starting with the first character. One of its parameters is how many characters to return in the substring. **Right** is similar but returns a substring from the end of the string. In the example below each function is passed the string itself and the number of characters to extract. The result is shown in figure 6.2.

```
Dim Message As String
Message = "Printers are not expensive"
Form1.Print "The first 5 characters are    " & Left(Message, 5)
Form1.Print "The last 7 characters are   " & Right(Message, 7)
```

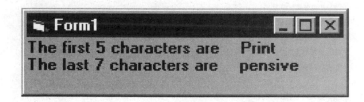

Figure 6.2

Removing spaces with *LTrim*, *RTrim* and *Trim*

The function **LTrim** removes any leading spaces at the left side of a string. **RTrim** does the same thing for trailing spaces on the right side of a string, and **Trim** does the job of both LTrim and RTrim. The only parameter each of these needs is the string itself. In program 6.1, where the user is asked to enter a surname and first name with one space between, you could use LTrim and RTrim to remove any accidental spaces before the surname and after the first name. Using Trim would (wrongly) get rid of the space between the two names also.

Changing case with *UCase* and *LCase*

The **UCase** function converts all characters in a string into their upper case equivalents. **LCase** converts them all into lower case. The only parameter needed is the string itself. If any of the characters are not letters they are ignored. Therefore UCase would change "Hello" into "HELLO" and "He**o" into "HE**O". The code below shows a possible use of UCase.

```
Dim Reply As String * 1
'user has just been asked to enter Y(es) or N(o) into a text box
Reply = txtReply.Text
Reply = UCase(Reply)          'ensure user reply is upper case
If Reply = "Y" Then
    'do something
End If
```

PROGRAM 6.2 *Extract the area telephone code*

Specification A telephone number is input in the form (01442)-12345, where the number in brackets is the area code. The area code may have a varying number of numeric digits. Output the area code without the brackets.

1. Open a new project and use figure 6.3 to design the form. Name the text box, command button and label for displaying the area code, **txtTelNumber**, **cmdDisplayAreaCode** and **lblAreaCode** respectively.

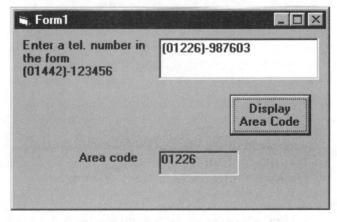

Figure 6.3: Program 6.2

2. Double-click the command button and make sure its code is as follows:

```
Private Sub cmdDisplayAreaCode_Click()
  Dim TelNumber As String
  Dim AreaCode As String
  Dim Index As Integer
  Dim Character As String * 1
  AreaCode = ""                         'initialise area code to blank
  TelNumber = txtTelNumber.Text
  Index = 1                  'set to 1 rather than 0 to skip first bracket
  Do
    Index = Index + 1
    Character = Mid(TelNumber, Index, 1)
    AreaCode = AreaCode & Character    'build up code character by character
  Loop Until Character = ")"           'stop when bracket found
  lblAreaCode.Caption = Left(AreaCode, Len(AreaCode) - 1)  'remove bracket
                                                           'from area code

End Sub
```

The first repetition of the loop processes the first digit after the opening bracket because Index has the value 2. Each repetition of the loop extracts a character using **Mid** and concatenates it to the area code. Because **Do…Loop Until** is used, in which the condition is tested at the end of the loop, the area code will have the closing bracket when the loop finishes. The first line of code after the loop uses **Left** to remove it.

3. Run the program to check that it works. Try it out with the brackets and then without an opening bracket. Without the bracket the first digit of the code is not displayed.

end of Program 6.2

Handling dates

Visual Basic has a wide range of functions for handling dates. The following are the most useful.

Date

The **Date** function simply returns the current date in the format set in Windows Control Panel. The UK format is day/month/year.

Month and Year

The **Month** function must be passed a date and it returns the number of the month from 1 to 12. **Year** returns an integer representing the year in the date passed to it as a parameter. Thus

```
MyDate = #16/04/1990#          'assign a date using # sign or "
Form1.Print Month(MyDate) & " " & Year(MyDate)
```

would print **04 1990**. Note that version 6 of Visual Basic introduced a **MonthName** function which returns the name of a month. However you can display this through the ordinary Format function (see below).

Formatting date output

In Chapter 3 you learned how to format numbers with named and user-defined formats using the **Format** function. You can use this function in a similar way with dates. Figure 6.4 shows the result of running the code below.

```
Const TheDate = "12/6/2001"    'date assigned using " rather than #
Form1.Show
Form1.Print "Using named date formats"
Form1.Print "    General Date   "; Format(TheDate, "General Date")
Form1.Print "    Long Date date   "; Format(TheDate, "Long Date")
Form1.Print "    Medium Date   "; Format(TheDate, "Medium Date")
Form1.Print "    Short Date   "; Format(TheDate, "Short Date")
Form1.Print "Using user-defined date formats"
Form1.Print "    d/mm/yy   "; Format(TheDate, "d/m/yy")
Form1.Print "    dd/m/yyyy   "; Format(TheDate, "dd/mm/yyyy")
Form1.Print "    dddd   "; Format(TheDate, "dddd")
Form1.Print "    dddddd   "; Format(TheDate, "dddddd")
Form1.Print "    dddd/dddddd   "; Format(TheDate, "dddd dddddd")
```

The full range of named formats is used above but only a small sample of possible user-defined ones are shown. The full range can be found by searching on **Format** in Help, clicking **See Also** and then selecting **UserDefined Date/Time Formats**.

Note that Visual Basic 6 introduced the **FormatDateTime** function but this provides no extra ways of displaying dates than Format.

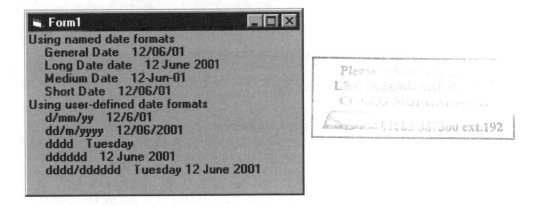

Figure 6.4

PROGRAM 6.3   *College Library issue desk*

Specification   Allow the issue and return of books in a school or college library. Books can be borrowed overnight, for 3 days, 10 days or 1 month. When a book is returned enter the date due back, select its loan period, and if it is overdue display how many days overdue and the fine. For the issuing of books select the loan period and display the date due back in the form Thursday 4 May 2000.

1.   Open a new project and design the form using figure 6.5. Set the captions of the four display labels to blank.

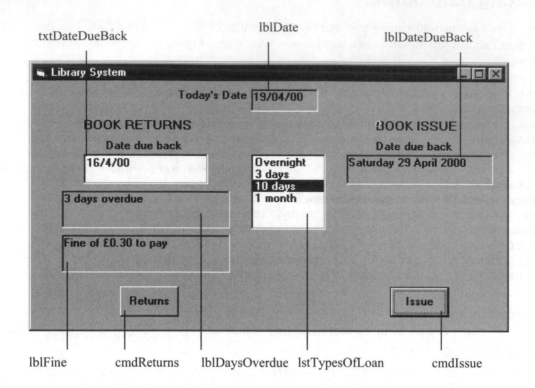

Figure 6.5: Program 6.3

2. In the General section declare a single global variable:

```
Dim DaysLoan As Integer
```

3. In the form's Load event procedure display the current date with:

```
lblDate.Caption = Date
```

4. In the Click event of cmdReturns declare the following local variables:

```
Dim DateDueBack As Date
Dim Overdue As Boolean
Dim DaysOverdue As Integer
Dim FineRate As Currency
Dim Fine As Currency
```

5. Complete the code for the Click event for cmdReturns:

```
DateDueBack = txtDateDueBack.Text
Select Case lstTypesOfLoan.ListIndex
  Case 0                              'overnight loan
    DaysLoan = 1
    FineRate = 0.5                    'fine is 50p per day
```

```
      Case 1                                  '3-day loan
        DaysLoan = 3
        FineRate = 0.25                       'fine is 25p per day
      Case 2                                  '10-day loan
        DaysLoan = 10
        FineRate = 0.1                        'fine is 10p per day
      Case 3                                  '1 month loan (=30 days)
        DaysLoan = 30
        FineRate = 0.05                       'fine is 5p per day
    End Select
    DaysOverdue = Date - DateDueBack          'eg of arithmetic on dates
    Overdue = Date - DateDueBack > 0          'if date due back is earlier than
                                              'today's date, set Overdue to True
    If Overdue Then                           'Does Overdue store True?
      Fine = FineRate * DaysOverdue
    Else
      Fine = 0
    End If
    lblDaysOverdue.Caption = DaysOverdue & " days overdue"
    lblFine.Caption = "Fine of " & Format(Fine, "currency") & " to pay"
```

Take note of the following:

- The item selected from the list box is stored in the control's ListIndex property and this is used to set the number of loan days and the fine rate in the **Select Case**.

- Because dates are stored as numbers one date can be subtracted from another to calculate the number of days overdue.

- Since Overdue is a Boolean data type, storing True or False, it can be assigned the result of a condition that yields a true/false result. The condition is *Date   DateDueBack > 0*.

- The **If** condition could be written as *If Overdue = True*, but writing just *If Overdue* makes it a little more readable.

6. Now for the code for the Click event of cmdIssue:

```
Dim DateDueBack As Date
Select Case lstTypesOfLoan.ListIndex
  Case 0
    DaysLoan = 1
  Case 1
    DaysLoan = 3
  Case 2
    DaysLoan = 10
  Case 3
    DaysLoan = 30
End Select
DateDueBack = Date + DaysLoan
lblDateDueBack.Caption = Format(DateDueBack, "dddd dddddd")
```

Note the user-defined formatting to display the full form of the date due back.

7. Run the program. Select a loan period from the list box and click the Issue button. Then enter a date due back in the Book Returns section earlier than today's date, click the Returns button and the number of days overdue and fine should be displayed.

end of Program 6.3

Handling time

Visual Basic has several functions to handle time. The most useful are:

Time and *Now*

The **Time** function is the counterpart of Date. It returns the current time e.g. 07:42:25. Depending on the time setting in Windows you may get AM or PM displayed after the time. **Now** returns both the date and time and is equivalent to using the Date and Time functions together.

Second, Minute and *Hour*

These functions return an integer in the range 0 to 60 for Second and Minute and 0 to 24 for Hour. For example if the current time is 10:45:12 then

```
Form1.Print Minute(Time)
```

would print 45.

Calculations with time

As with dates you can use the addition and subtraction operators. Consider the following examples which use the **Minute** function in calculating the number of minutes between two times. The output is shown in figure 6.6.

```
Dim Time1 As Date
Dim Time2 As Date
Dim Time3 As Date
Dim MinutesDiff As Integer
Form1.Show
Time1 = "6:10:30"
Time2 = "6:18:40"
Time3 = "8:30:10"
MinutesDiff = Minute(Time2) - Minute(Time1)
Form1.Print "Minutes difference between " & Time1 & " and " & Time2 & _
     " is    " & MinutesDiff
MinutesDiff = Minute(Time3) - Minute(Time1)
Form1.Print "Minutes difference between " & Time1 & " and " & Time3 & _
     " is    " & MinutesDiff
```

Figure 6.6

The first output in figure 6.6 is correct because the hour (06) is the same, but the second output, with different hours (06 and 08), does not show the correct total number of minutes difference. To calculate this you need to use the **Hour** function too. The following code would produce the correct answer of 140:

```
HoursDiff = Hour(Time3) - Hour(Time1)
MinutesDiff = (HoursDiff * 60) + (Minute(Time3) - Minute(Time1))
```

Summary of key concepts

- Strings can be declared as **variable length** or **fixed length**.

- Use the relational operators (>, < etc.) to compare strings.

- Use the **Mid** function to process individual characters in a string.

- Use the addition and subtraction operators to increase or reduce a date, or to find the number of days difference between two dates.

- Use the **Format** function to format the output of dates and times.

Take it from here...

1. Two string functions not covered are **StrComp** and **Like**. The former compares two strings to see if they are the same and the latter compares patterns of characters within strings. Find out how these functions work.

2. If you assigned the string "15 Jun 38" to a Date variable would Visual Basic store this as 15/06/1938 or 15/06/2038? Write a piece of code to demonstrate which century would be stored. Use this code to find out which is the boundary two-digit year for storing a date as 20th century or 21st century.

3. Find out about the following date functions not covered in the chapter – **DateSerial**, **DateAdd** and **DateDiff**.

Questions on the Programs

Program 6.1

**1. The program outputs only one message, if two or more spaces are found. Extend it to output appropriate messages if one or more spaces are found

- before the surname.
- after the first name.

Program 6.2

*1. Run the program but do not enter a closing bracket for the area code. Depending on the speed of your computer's processor the program may seem to hang. It may seem that you have an infinite loop because the loop condition cannot become true. After a short time you'll actually get a run-time error message displaying **overflow**. Click the **Debug** button and the offending line will be highlighted in yellow. Place the cursor over the word *Index* and you'll be given its current value. Can you explain the error?

*2. Assume that the area code always consists of 5 numeric digits. Use the Left and Right functions instead of Mid to extract the area code.

*3.   Rewrite the code using Do While…Loop instead of Do…Loop Until.

**4.   Extend the program so that if an area code without brackets is entered, an appropriate message is displayed.

Program 6.3

1.   The program uses the Format function to display the full date for the return of issued books. If you have a version of Visual Basic more recent than 5, use the **MonthName and **Month** functions to handle this instead of Format. If you have version 5 or earlier MonthName is not available, so use Month and a Select Case to convert Month's return value (1 to 12) to a month.

End of chapter exercises

*1.   Ask the user to enter a string and then display it in reverse using a function called **StrReverse** (available from Visual Basic version 6). For example "Hello there" would be displayed as "ereht olleH". There is a harder way to do this using **Mid**. If you use Mid count this as a two-star exercise.

**2.   Ask the user to enter a string and then tell them whether or not it is a palindrome. A palindrome is a string that is the same backwards and forwards. For example "level", "star rats", "eee" are all palindromes.

**3.   Write a program that reads a string from the user and displays only those words beginning with the letters 'd' or 't'.

**4.   Write a program that asks the user to input some text and to indicate which word to search for in the text. Output the number of times this word occurs.

5.   Ask the user to enter some text and change it into upper case without using the UCase function. You will need to use two functions not covered in the chapter, **Asc and **Chr**.

***6.   A manufacturer of sawn timber sells to a large number of timber yards and DIY shops. Assume the user is processing payments from these customers. Allow the user to input the date an invoice should have been paid by and the total value of the invoice. Calculate how many days late, if any, the payment has been made. If payment has been made 15 or more days before the due date give a 10% discount, otherwise give a 5% discount if it has been paid on time. Output details about whether payment has been made on time, any discount given and the total amount due.

***7.   Write a program that counts up and displays how many words the user can type in a minute. The running program can be seen in figure 1.1. Use a Timer control to display how many seconds have elapsed. At the simplest level you could count the number of spaces in the text to calculate the number of words. But for a 3-star exercise you should handle other possibilities. What if two or more spaces are entered by mistake between words? What if the user starts by accidentally pressing the space bar?

Chapter 7 – Procedures

What is a procedure?

A procedure is a separate section of code which performs one or more specific tasks and is identified by having a name.

Types of procedure in Visual Basic

Visual Basic has four types of procedure. These are:

- **Event** procedures
- **Sub** procedures
- **Function** procedures
- **Property** procedures

So far you have used only event procedures where code is executed in response to events such as click, change and so on. The other three types of procedure are not set off directly by events, but are **called** by code within an event procedure or from within another non-event procedure. Property procedures are only used when you adopt an object-oriented approach to programming (not covered by this book). Sub and function procedures are sometimes referred to as **general** procedures and are the subject of this chapter. Figure 7.1 illustrates how the different procedures may be linked. The click event procedure calls two general procedures, and one of these, procedure A, in turn calls another general procedure, function C. Note how control returns to the next line of code after the procedure call when the procedure is finished.

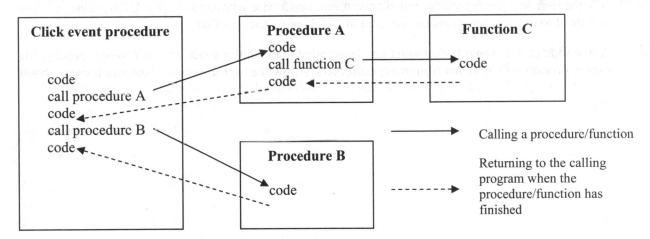

Figure 7.1: An example of how procedures may be linked

Sub and Function procedures

There are two key differences between these types of procedure:

- A function procedure always returns one piece of data to that part of the program which calls it. A sub procedure may return one or more items of data or no data at all. The way in which the two types of procedure return data is different.

- The way in which the procedure is called is different.

You can really only understand these by doing programs 7.1 and 7.2 (sub procedures) and 7.3 (function procedure).

Why use procedures?

Almost all programs you write inevitably use event procedures. You don't *have* to use sub or function procedures, but there are several good reasons why you should:

- **Avoid repeating code**. If you have identical code in two or more event procedures you may be able to write it just once in a procedure instead.

- **Make the code more readable**. An event procedure with many lines of code may be easier to understand if some of the code is put into procedures.

- **Help in debugging a program**. Splitting the program up into small logical units will make it easier to trace any errors in the program when it runs. This is called debugging a program.

- **Use a procedure in other programs**. Suppose you had written some code that validated a date. You could use this procedure in any other program that used a similar date.

- **Pass parameters**. All good programmers ought to pass parameters, where appropriate. Only by having procedures can you do this. Parameters are discussed later in this chapter.

What a procedure does is entirely up to you. There are no hard and fast rules, but as a guide use a procedure to carry out one specific task or a small number of related tasks.

PROGRAM 7.1   *Avoid repeating code*

Specification   Illustrate how procedures can make it unnecessary to repeat code in two or more event procedures.

Look back at program 2.4 which coloured a form according to the position of the scroll boxes in three scroll bars (figure 2.12). The code is shown in figure 7.2 – each of the three scroll bars has a single line of identical code for its Scroll event. In this program we will write this code only once, in a procedure.

```
hsbBlue                              ▼  Scroll                                 ▼

    Private Sub hsbBlue_Scroll()
        Form1.BackColor = RGB(hsbRed.Value, hsbGreen.Value, hsbBlue.Value)
    End Sub


    Private Sub hsbGreen_Scroll()
        Form1.BackColor = RGB(hsbRed.Value, hsbGreen.Value, hsbBlue.Value)
    End Sub


    Private Sub hsbRed_Scroll()
        Form1.BackColor = RGB(hsbRed.Value, hsbGreen.Value, hsbBlue.Value)
    End Sub
```

Figure 7.2

1. Open program 2.4 and delete the single line of code in each of the three Scroll event procedures shown in figure 7.2. (If you did not save this program earlier create it again now, but leave out steps 6 – 8 in program 2.4 as you don't need the event procedure code.)

2. There are two ways of adding a new procedure to the code window. You can write it all from scratch yourself or you can use the menu to provide a template. We'll use the second method in this example. Select **Tools/Add Procedure** and you'll get the Add Procedure dialog box shown in figure 7.3.

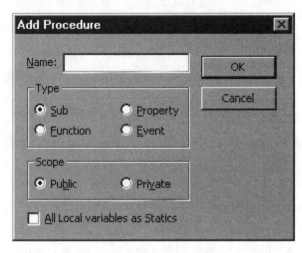

Figure 7.3: The Add Procedure dialog box

3. In the **Name** section type in the name of the procedure as **ShowFormColour**. As with variable names and names of objects Visual Basic does not allow any spaces in a procedure name.

4. The four types of procedure listed at the start of this chapter are offered in figure 7.3. The commonest is the **Sub** procedure which is the default. Accept this.

5. Two types of **Scope** are offered. **Public** means that the procedure can be used by all other procedures in a program (and some of these might be on another form). **Private** means that the procedure can only be used on the form on which it is declared. As we are only using one form it doesn't matter which of these we use so accept the default Public.

6. The check box at the bottom of the dialog box allows you to declare all local variables as static. Recall from Chapter 3, and in particular program 3.3, that a static variable retains its value between procedure calls. Normally you do not want variables to be static so again accept the default.

7. Click **OK** and you'll get the template for the new procedure. Write the code to set the form's colour:

```
Public Sub ShowFormColour()
   Form1.BackColor = RGB(hsbRed.Value, hsbGreen.Value, hsbBlue.Value)
End Sub
```

8. Now you have to tell each of the three Scroll event procedures to **call** this sub procedure. Their code should look as follows:

```
Private Sub hsbBlue_Scroll()
   Call ShowFormColour
End Sub
```

```
Private Sub hsbGreen_Scroll()
   Call ShowFormColour
End Sub

Private Sub hsbRed_Scroll()
   Call ShowFormColour
End Sub
```

The keyword **Call** is optional, but as it makes the code more readable we will use it throughout this book.

9. Run the program to check that it works.

end of Program 7.1

Passing parameters

A **parameter** is a piece of data that is sent to a procedure when it is called. The data is used by the procedure to help it carry out its task. Not all procedures need parameters; others may need one or more of them.

Actual and Formal parameters

Suppose the user has typed numbers into two text boxes and these are stored in variables FirstNumber and SecondNumber. You could write a procedure, FindSmaller, that works out which of the two numbers is the smallest, and call it with

```
Call FindSmallerNumber(FirstNumber, SecondNumber)
```

FirstNumber and SecondNumber are two parameters which are passed to the procedure. When you use the keyword Call you must list the parameters inside brackets. (If you don't use Call then the brackets aren't allowed.) Parameters passed to a procedure are called **actual parameters**.

When you declare the procedure FindSmallerNumber you must declare **formal parameters** to match the actual parameters you are sending it. You can use the same identifiers as the actual parameters or different ones. In this book we will always use different identifiers for the actual and formal parameters. When you declare a formal parameter it is optional whether you declare its data type too. However it makes the code a little easier to understand if you do, so we'll adopt the practice in this book. Thus all of the following declarations are correct:

```
Public Sub FindSmaller(NumberOne As Integer, NumberTwo As Integer) 'use
              'different identifiers for actual and formal parameters
Public Sub FindSmaller(NumberOne, NumberTwo) 'data types not declared
Public Sub FindSmaller(FirstNumber As Integer, SecondNumber As Integer)
                                             'use same identifiers
```

Figure 7.4 illustrates the matching of the actual and formal parameters. This example highlights three important rules:

- The number of actual and formal parameters must be the same.
- Parameters are matched according to their position, not according to their names.
- The data types of a matching pair of parameters must be the same.

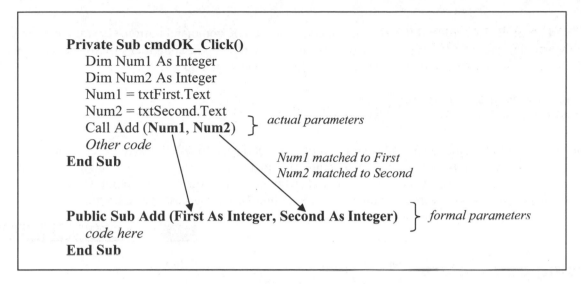

Figure 7.4: Matching actual and formal parameters

Value and Reference parameters

Formal parameters are divided into **value** and **reference parameters.** Reference parameters are used when you need to pass data back from a sub procedure to the calling program. The code inside procedure FindSmaller will find out which number is the smaller and since we need to get this information out it must be stored as a reference parameter. The two numbers themselves are not changed in any way, and do not need to be passed out again. Therefore they are **value parameters**. The complete code to call and declare the procedure now becomes:

```
Call FindSmaller(FirstNumber, SecondNumber, SmallerNumber)


Public Sub FindSmaller(ByVal NumberOne As Integer, _
          ByVal NumberTwo As Integer, ByRef Smaller As Integer)
```

Use the keywords **ByVal** and **ByRef** to declare value and reference parameters. When the procedure has found the smaller number it can be passed back to the calling code through Smaller, and this in turn is matched back onto the actual parameter SmallerNumber. Thus two further rules can be drawn up:

- A reference parameter is used when a piece of data needs to be passed out of the procedure.
- A value parameter is a piece of data used by the procedure. Any changes made to it inside the procedure are not passed back again.

PROGRAM 7.2 *Value and Reference parameters*

Specification   Write a program to illustrate the differences between value and reference parameters.

We'll reuse program 3.4 which calculates the average of a set of exam marks. Let's replace some of the code by two procedures as follows:

- Procedure **ProcessOneNumber**, which will be called from the click event of the OK command button.
- Procedure **CalcMean**, which will be called from the click event of the Show Mean command button.

1. Open program 3.4 and find the click event code for the OK command button. (If you have not saved this program create it again now.) Two of its tasks were to keep running totals of all the marks and of how many exam marks had been entered. Delete the code which does this:

```
Total = Total + Number
NumberOfMarks = NumberOfMarks + 1
```

We need to send the parameter Number *to* the procedure and to get back the two running totals *from* the procedure. Number should therefore be a value parameter and the other two should be reference parameters. Figure 7.5 shows what is going on. An arrow going into the procedure but without a matching one coming out represents a value parameter. Two matching arrows represent a reference parameter. Note that the identifiers for the outgoing reference parameters are first used in step 3 below.

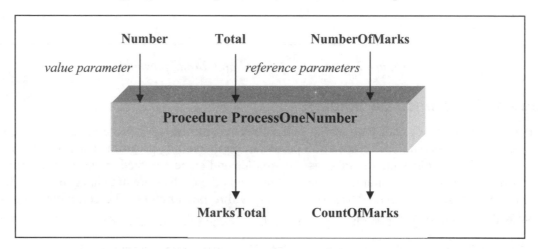

Figure 7.5: Parameters for procedure ProcessOneNumber

2. Replace the code you deleted in step 1 with a call to the procedure:

```
Call ProcessOneNumber(Number, Total, NumberOfMarks)
```

3. Get the code template for procedure ProcessOneNumber (see step 2 in program 7.1) and declare the formal parameters inside the empty brackets provided:

```
Public Sub ProcessOneNumber(ByVal ExamMark As Integer, _
             ByRef MarksTotal As Integer, ByRef CountOfMarks As Integer)
```

4. The code inside this procedure should be the same as the code you deleted in step 1, except that you must use the identifiers of the formal parameters:

```
MarksTotal = MarksTotal + ExamMark
CountOfMarks = CountOfMarks + 1
```

5. Now look at the code in the click event procedure for the Show Mean command button. The code which must be replaced by a procedure call is

```
Mean = Total / NumberOfMarks
```

We need to send two parameters, Total and NumberOfMarks, to be used by the procedure, and to get back from it the calculated mean. These two parameters should be value parameters and the returned mean must be a reference parameter. Figure 7.6 shows this diagrammatically.

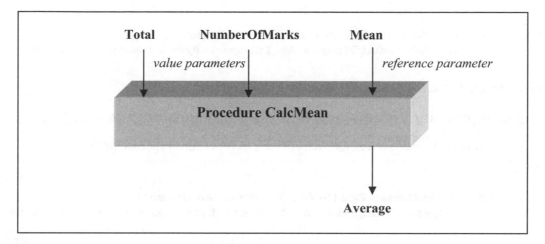

Figure 7.6: Parameters for procedure CalcMean

6. Replace the line of code in step 5 with

```
Call CalcMean(Total, NumberOfMarks, Mean)
```

7. Get the code template for the new procedure CalcMean (see step 2 in program 7.1) and declare its formal parameters as follows:

```
Public Sub CalcMean(ByVal MarksTotal As Integer, _
          ByVal CountOfMarks As Integer, ByRef Average As Single)
```

The parameter Average must be declared as Single because this is the data type of its matching actual parameter Mean.

8. Inside this procedure write the code to calculate the mean value:

```
Average = MarksTotal / CountOfMarks
```

9. Run the program.

end of Program 7.2

Practical work on using the correct formal parameters

Visual Basic does not insist that you identify formal parameters as value or reference by using the keywords ByVal and ByRef. If you omit these it treats all parameters as reference parameters. Although this won't produce errors, unless your code accidentally changes the content of a reference parameter, it is good practice to identify the parameter types. The purpose of the steps that follow is to give you a practical demonstration of how things can sometimes go wrong if you don't identify them correctly.

Pass a parameter by reference when it should be by value – no error

1. Open program 7.2 and change the first parameter, MarksTotal, in procedure CalcMean, from value to reference:

```
Public Sub CalcMean(ByRef MarksTotal As Integer, _
         ByVal CountOfMarks As Integer, ByRef Average As Single)
```

2. Run the program and everything should work fine.

Pass a parameter by value when it should be by reference – error!

3. Change the second formal parameter, MarksTotal, in procedure ProcessOneNumber, from reference to value:

```
Public Sub ProcessOneNumber(ByVal ExamMark As Integer, _
         ByVal MarksTotal As Integer, ByRef CountOfMarks As Integer)
```

4. Run the program. The mean mark will now be displayed as 0. The content of MarksTotal is not passed out of the procedure and therefore is not stored in its matching actual parameter Total. Total stores the value 0 because this is what Visual Basic by default initialises an Integer variable to. When procedureCalcMean is then called by

```
Call CalcMean(Total, NumberOfMarks, Mean)
```

a value of 0 is passed into the procedure through Total. This is matched onto CalcMean's formal parameter, MarksTotal, which in turn means that Average is calculated as 0 inside CalcMean. This 0 is passed back to the matching actual parameter Mean.

From steps 1 – 4 two further rules can be stated:

- a parameter declared as reference when it should be declared by value will **not** produce an error
- a parameter declared as value when it should be reference **will** produce an error

5. Close the program but don't save any of the changes. Program 11.2 uses the unchanged program 7.2.

Functions

Types of function

A function is a shorter name for a function procedure. Visual Basic has two types of function:

- **Built-in** functions which are supplied as part of the language
- **User-defined** functions which you write yourself

You have used a number of built-in functions in previous programs. Examples include Format, Mid and Date. Now you need to learn how to write your own.

Calling a function

There are several ways of calling a function. You have already used the two important ones in earlier chapters:

- **Assign its return value to a variable**. For example the following calls the function Left to store 'S' in the variable Character:

```
Name = "Smith"
Character = Left(Name, 1)
```

- **Display its return value directly**. For example the letter "S" can be printed directly by calling the function as part of the Print statement:

```
Name = "Smith"
Print Left(Name, 1)
```

PROGRAM 7.3   *Calculating interest*

Specification   Write a function to calculate the amount of interest earned on an investment. The amount invested, the interest rate and the number of years the investment lasts, are to be entered by the user.

If you invested £1000 over 2 years at an interest rate of 10% per year then the interest paid after one year would be £100 (i.e. 10% of £1000). In year 2 you would get 10% of (£1000 + £100), i.e. £110, and so the total interest paid would be £210. In this program a function named **CalculateInterest** will calculate and return this value.

1. Open a new project and design the form shown in figure 7.7. Name the controls needed in code as **txtAmountInvested**, **txtInterestRate**, **txtYears**, **lblInterest** and **cmdCalcInterest**.

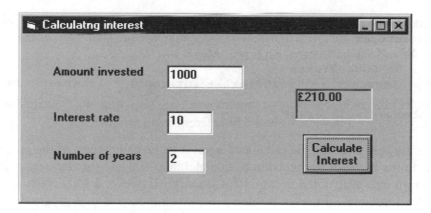

Figure 7.7: Program 7.3

2. Type the following code into the Click event of the command button:

```
Private Sub cmdCalcInterest_Click()
  Dim Interest As Currency
  Dim AmountInvested As Currency
  Dim RateOfInterest As Single
  Dim Years As Integer
  AmountInvested = txtAmountInvested.Text
  RateOfInterest = txtInterestRate.Text
  Years = txtYears.Text
  Interest = CalculateInterest(AmountInvested, RateOfInterest, Years)
  lblInterest.Caption = Format(Interest, "Currency")
End Sub
```

The function CalculateInterest is called as part of an assignment:

```
Interest = CalculateInterest(AmountInvested, RateOfInterest, Years)
```

Three actual parameters are passed, and the data item returned from the function is stored in the variable Interest.

3. Select **Tools/Add Procedure** and in the dialog box click the **Function** option button and enter its name **CalculateInterest**.

4. Declare the three formal parameters for function CalculateInterest as shown below.

```
Public Function CalculateInterest(ByVal Principal As Currency, _
                                  ByVal InterestRate As Single, _
                                  ByVal NumberYears As Integer) As Currency
```

Note the following:

- They are all value parameters since they are merely used by the function. Although you *could* use a reference parameter to return data as you did with sub procedures, this would not be considered good programming since the job of a function is really to return one item of data.

- The data type of the piece of data that *is* returned is declared after the last bracket. In this example it is Currency.

5. Write the code inside the function to calculate the interest:

```
Dim Interest As Currency
Dim Year As Integer
Interest = 0
For Year = 1 To NumberYears
   Interest = Interest + ((Principal + Interest) * InterestRate / 100)
Next Year
CalculateInterest = Interest
```

The last line is the way to return the calculated interest to the calling part of the program. Assign this data (Interest) to the name of the function (CalculateInterest). Note that Interest is of type Currency because the return data type noted in step 4 is Currency. (However Visual Basic is not always strict about this, which you will discover by doing the extra work on this program at the end of the chapter.)

6. Run the program and check that it works by using the sample data in figure 7.6 and other data of your choice.

End of Program 7.3

Form and Standard modules

So far all our general procedures have been written on the single form belonging to a project. There are two other places you could write them:

- On another form in the same project. This is called another **form module**.
- On a **standard module**, which cannot contain controls, only code.

In program 7.3 you could have put function CalculateInterest on Form2. You would call it with:

```
Interest = Form2.CalculateInterest(AmountInvested, RateOfInterest, Years)
```

You must indicate the form on which the function can be found followed by a '.' before calling it. Note that this call will only work because CalculateInterest was declared as Public. If you had declared it as Private then only code on Form1 could call it.

A standard module must be saved as a separate file to which Visual Basic gives a **bas** extension. You can then use this standard module in any program you write. Procedures in standard modules are often referred to as a **library**. You might write several procedures with a common theme and put them in the same library. An example might be several string-handling routines not provided by the language.

PROGRAM 7.4   *A standard module function*

Specification   Write a function that changes the first letter of a string to upper case. Write it in a standard module and use it in a program.

1.   Open a new project and build the form using the running program shown in figure 7.8. Name the controls **cmdNewName**, **txtName** and **lblNewName**.

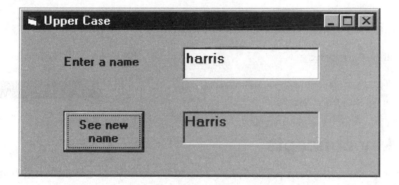

Figure 7.8: Program 7.4

2.   Select **Project/Add Module**, make sure the **New** tab is selected in the resulting dialog box, and click **Open**.

3.   The new module will be added to the Project Explorer. Save it as **StringLibrary** and Visual Basic will add a **bas** extension (see figure 7.9).

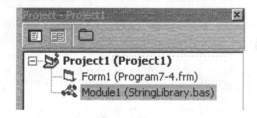

Figure 7.9: The standard module is added to the project

4. Open the Code window for this standard module. As an alternative to getting a template for your function write the template code yourself, and then the code which changes the first letter of the string passed to the function into upper case. (Note that Mid here is the Mid statement not the Mid function.)

```
Public Function UpperCaseFirstLetter(ByVal OldString As String) As String
   Dim FirstLetter As String
   Dim NewString As String
   FirstLetter = UCase(Left(OldString, 1))  'changes the first letter of
   Mid(OldString, 1, 1) = FirstLetter         'OldString to upper case
   NewString = OldString
   UpperCaseFirstLetter = NewString
End Function
```

5. In the Click event for the command button on Form1 enter the code:

```
Private Sub cmdNewName_Click()
   Dim Name As String
   Dim NewName As String
   Name = txtName.Text
   NewName = Module1.UpperCaseFirstLetter(Name)
   lblNewName.Caption = NewName
End Sub
```

Notice that the function call first states which module it is in (Module1).

6. Run the program.

end of Program 7.4

Summary of key concepts

- **General** procedures are non-event procedures. The two main types are **sub** and **function** procedures.

- General procedures are called from within an event procedure or from another general procedure.

- A function may be called in several ways. The commonest is by assigning its return value to a variable. You cannot call sub procedures in this way. Call them by using the **Call** statement.

- A function always returns one item of data.

- A **parameter** is a piece of data sent to a procedure when it is called. **Actual** parameters are passed to the procedure and matched to the **formal** parameters which are part of the procedure's declaration. The data type of a matching pair of actual and formal parameters must be the same.

- Formal parameters are divided into **value** and **reference** parameters. Any changes made to a reference parameter inside the procedure are passed out again. Changes to a value parameter cannot be passed out again.

- You do not have to declare formal parameters as value (**ByVal**) or reference (**ByRef**). If you don't, Visual Basic defaults to reference.

- If you pass a parameter by reference when it should be by value no error occurs, but if you pass by value when it should have been by reference, a serious error will occur.

- A **standard module** can only contain code. Its procedures can be used in any programs. Standard modules are sometimes used as **libraries**.

Take it from here...

1. Two methods of calling a function were covered. You could use a third method – call it in the same way as you call a sub procedure using the optional keyword Call. Investigate this method by trying it out in code. What do you think happens to the function's return value? What do you think of this method of calling a function?

2. One of the parameter rules is that the number of actual and formal parameters must be the same. Strictly speaking this is not a rule since Visual Basic does allow optional parameters. Search in Help on the keyword **optional** to find out about these parameters.

Questions on the Programs

Program 7.2

*1. The task of procedure CalcMean is simply to calculate the mean of the exam marks. Extend this to calculate *and display* the mean rather than sending it back to the event procedure to display it. Rewrite the code to handle this new specification.

**2. The chapter points out that parameter passing is not compulsory but that it is considered good programming to do so where appropriate. Rewrite this program so that no parameters are passed to the two procedures, but don't change what the procedures do. To do this some of the variables which would have been passed as parameters must be declared as global, but recall that in Chapter 3 you learned it is poor programming to use global variables when you don't need to. This exercise should show you that parameter passing reduces the number of global variables to a minimum.

Program 7.3

*1. The point was made in step 5 that the variable Interest is declared as Currency because this is the data type declared as the return data type (in step 4). Experiment by changing the data type of Interest, running the program, and then changing the return data type. What can you conclude about how strict Visual Basic is about the data types being the same?

Program 7.4

**1. Change the code in the Click event of cmdNewName so that it changes the first letter of each word in the string you enter into the text box. Your code will need to call the function UpperCaseFirstLetter each time a new word is encountered in the string.

**2. Write a second function in module StringLibrary which changes the first letter of every word in a given string into upper case. Name the function UpperCaseFirstLetters. Test it out by calling it from the Click event of the command button.

End of chapter exercises

*1. When the user clicks a single command button on a form display the message "This is a procedure call" in a message box. The message should be displayed by calling a sub procedure from the button's Click event.

*2. Ask the user to type a person's age into a text box and then to click a command button. Validate that the age lies in the range 18 – 40 by calling a function from the button's Click event. If the age is not valid the Click event procedure should display an appropriate message.

**3. Ask the user to enter two numbers into text boxes as shown in figure 7.10. Clicking the command button should call a sub procedure to swap the numbers, which are then passed back to the calling program. The Click event should then display them in the two labels on the right.

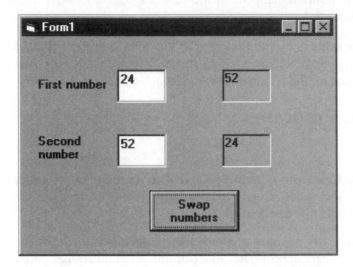

Figure 7.10: Exercise 3

**4. Write a function that is passed two parameters, a string and a character, and returns the number of times the character is present in the string. Ask the user to enter some text and a search letter in two text boxes, and then to click a command button. The button's event procedure should call the function and then it should output the number of occurrences.

***5. Write a program that processes invoices for a company selling a variety of products. Ask the user to enter the unit cost of the product, how many were sold and the date the invoice had to be paid by. A check box should be used to indicate if the product is VAT rated. When these details have been entered the user should click a command button. This event should call two general procedures. The first should calculate and return the basic cost of the invoice, including VAT. The second should reduce this basic cost by 10% if the invoice has been paid on time. The final cost should be displayed by the Click event of the command button. Allow the user to process as many invoices as they wish.

Chapter 8 – Arrays

What is an array?

To store a single number you would declare one Integer variable. To store three numbers you would need three variables:

```
Dim FirstNumber As Integer
Dim SecondNumber As Integer
Dim ThirdNumber As Integer
```

What about storing hundreds or even thousands of numbers? Clearly things get difficult if not impossible! An array is a **data structure** that stores as many items as you require using a single variable. All the items must be the same data type. Thus you can store an array of integers, an array of strings and so on. The only way to mix the data types is to store records in the array, but this is the subject of the next chapter.

You have already used the array data structure, probably without realising it. For example in program 2.1 you used the ListIndex property of a list box to identify which item in the list box is the currently selected one. Visual Basic numbers the items from 0. So if you had a list box named lstEmployees Visual Basic stores the 4th item as lstEmployees(3).

How to declare an array

To declare an array that can store 5 numbers you could write either of the following:

```
Dim Numbers(4) As Integer
Dim Numbers(1 To 5) As Integer
```

The first method numbers the items in the array from 0 to 4 and the second from 1 to 5, as shown in figure 8.1. The storage 'slots' in the array are called **elements**. The variable *Numbers* stores all the data. Numbers(4), for example, refers to the *contents* of element 4, i.e. 60 in the right-hand diagram.

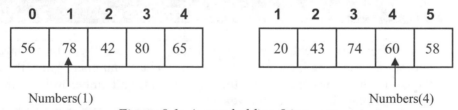

Figure 8.1: Arrays holding 5 integers

Which method you use may depend on what you are storing in the array. For example if you were storing the annual birth rate in the UK from 1880 to 1960 (81 years in total) you could use any of the following three declarations, but the third one is likely to be the most meaningful.

```
Dim BirthRates(80) As Single
Dim BirthRates(1 To 81) As Single
Dim BirthRates(1880 To 1960) As Single
```

Static and Dynamic arrays

A static array is one whose size is fixed throughout the program. A dynamic array can grow and shrink in size as the program runs. To change its size you must use **ReDim** at the point in your code where you want it to change. For example:

```
Dim Names() As String        'use empty brackets for first declaration
  'code to do something unrelated to the array goes here
ReDim Names(1 To 30) As String         'resize to store 30 items
  'code to add names to the array goes here
```

If we later ReDim the array again to hold more than 30 items, its contents will be lost unless we use the keyword **Preserve**:

```
ReDim Preserve Names(1 To 60) As String
```

Processing an array

Suppose you have declared an array to hold exam marks as follows:

```
Dim ExamMarks(1 To 40) As Integer
```

To store an exam mark in the 4th element of the array you could write:

```
Mark = txtExamMark.Text
ExamMarks(4) = Mark
```

Numeric literals, such as 4 in the above example, are not often used to identify an element in the array. More often you use a variable. Assuming NumberOfMarks stores how many numbers are in the array, the code below prints the array's contents:

```
For Index = 1 To NumberOfMarks
   Form1.Print ExamMarks(Index)
Next Index
```

PROGRAM 8.1   *Array to hold numbers*

Specification	Allow the user to enter up to 5 numbers and store them in an array. Output an appropriate message if the user attempts to store a 6th number. Allow the user to display the contents of the array at any time, and to enter a number to be searched for in the array. Display the result of this search.

1. Open a new project and design the form using figure 8.2. The form has three frames; recall that to make the controls 'belong' to a frame you must first put the frame on the form and then put the controls directly onto it from the toolbox. Name the command buttons **cmdAddToArray**, **cmdDisplay** and **cmdFindNumber**, the text boxes for input and searching **txtNumber** and **txtSearchNumber** respectively, the list box for output **lstNumbers**, and the label to display the result of the search **lblDisplaySearch**.

2. Declare global variables in the General section of the code. These must be globals because they are used in two event procedures.

```
Dim Numbers(1 To 5) As Integer
Dim Index As Integer                    'element of the array
```

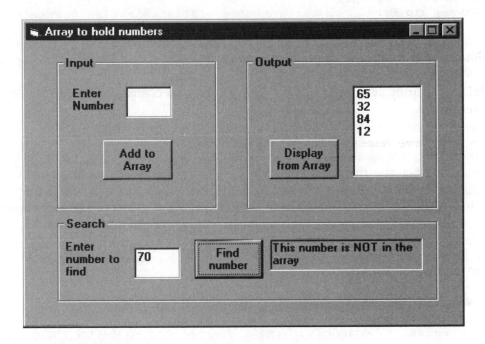

Figure 8.2: Program 8.1 – Four numbers have been stored and a number searched for

3. In the form's Load event procedure initialise Index:

```
Index = 0
```

Index is set to 0 because, as step 4 shows, the code to add an item to the array starts by adding 1 to the value of Index. The first time this is done it will set it to 1, which is the first element in the array.

4. In the Click event for the button to add a number to the array you need to check if the array is full. If it is not full store the number in Numbers(Index), i.e. in the current (free) element.

```
Private Sub cmdAddToArray_Click()
   Dim Number As Integer
   Number = txtNumber.Text
   If Index = 5 Then            'array is full (has 5 numbers in it)
     MsgBox "The array is FULL!"
   Else                         'array not full
     Index = Index + 1          'move to next free element in array
     Numbers(Index) = Number    'and store the number in it
     txtNumber.Text = ""        'clear text box ready for next number
     txtNumber.SetFocus         'and place cursor in it
   End If
End Sub
```

5. Because Index also stores how many numbers there are in the array, it can be used to control a **For...Next** loop to display the array's contents. In the Click event of the other command button type in:

```
Private Sub cmdDisplay_Click()
   Dim Element As Integer
   lstNumbers.Clear        'clear contents of list box else current numbers
                           'in array will be added to list box items
   For Element = 1 To Index  'go through each used element in array and
      lstNumbers.AddItem Numbers(Element) 'display its contents in list box
   Next Element
End Sub
```

6. Run the program and check that the storage and display of numbers works.

7. To search the array for the number entered by the user the content of each array element must be examined until either you find what you're looking for, or you reach the last number in the array without finding it. A Boolean value, Found, is initialised to false and switched to true if the number is found. It is used as part of the multiple condition to get out of the loop. The algorithm used here is the standard linear search, and is one that you might find very useful in your project.

```
Private Sub cmdFindNumber_Click()
   Dim Element As Integer
   Dim Found As Boolean
   Dim SearchNumber As Integer
   Element = 1
   Found = False       'searching hasn't started yet so Found should be false
   SearchNumber = txtSearchNumber.Text
   Do While (Found = False) And (Element <= Index)   'one repetition of
                                 'the loop processes one number in the array
      If Numbers(Element) = SearchNumber Then
         Found = True
      Else       'current element does not have number being searched for
         Element = Element + 1   'so go to the next element in the array
      End If
   Loop
   If Found Then                      'i.e. if Found = true
      lblDisplaySearch.Caption = "This number IS in the array"
   Else
      lblDisplaySearch.Caption = "This number is NOT in the array"
   End If
End Sub
```

8. Run the program and test the search code with a number that is present in the array and then with one that is not.

end of Program 8.1

Passing arrays to procedures

Some arrays can be very large. Since an actual parameter passed by value makes a copy of the contents of a parameter and passes this to the procedure, with a large array this can use up quite a lot of RAM. A parameter passed by reference involves just sending its RAM address. Whatever the size of the array this is simply where its storage in RAM starts from and is a very small overhead. Some languages only let you send arrays by reference. Others, like Visual Basic, allow passing by value as well.

Pass by value

Suppose you have declared an array to hold people's names as follows:

```
Dim Names(1 To 50) As String
```

To pass Names by value to a function FindName, which returns True if a particular name is present, you would write:

```
Found = FindName(SearchName, Names()) 'actual parameter in function call
...........
Public Function FindNumber(ByVal WantedName As String, _
                                ByVal NameArray) As Boolean
```

Note the empty brackets used for the actual parameter. This is optional but it does remind you that an array is being passed. The formal parameter NameArray must not have brackets nor a declared data type.

Pass by reference

One way to pass Names by reference is to use the same syntax as passing by value, but change ByVal to ByRef. Another way is to declare the formal parameter as follows:

```
ByRef NameArray() As String
```

PROGRAM 8.2   *Program 8.1 with a function to search the array*

Specification	Identical to program 8.1 but use a general procedure to search the array for the required number.

In program 8.1 several lines of code in the Click event for cmdFindNumber carried out the search of the array. This task could have been put into a general procedure. If we take the procedure's job as reporting whether or not the number is present (and let the event procedure handle displaying the result of the search), then we can use a function with a Boolean return value.

This program will also show you how to reuse an existing program and save it under another name.

1. Open a new project and select **Project/Remove Form1** to remove the default form from your program.

2. Select **Project/Add Form** and in the **Add Form** dialog click the **Existing** tab. Select the form you used in program 8.1 and click **Open**. This form is now added to the program.

3. Select **File/Save <form name> As** (where <form name> is the name of the form you added in step 2) and rename the form. You can now work on the renamed copy and change it to suit the new program specification.

4. Try running the program now and you'll get the error message shown in figure 8.3.

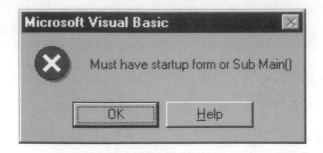

Figure 8.3: The error message

When a program first runs it must either load a named form or execute the code inside a procedure called Main. By default it is set up to load the form you get when you start a new project, i.e. Form1. In step 1 you removed this form and so Visual Basic defaults to the procedure Main. As you haven't written one with this name the program cannot start.

5. Click **OK** to remove the error message (and if you get a further one saying *Out of memory* simply remove it). Select **Project/Project 1 Properties…** and in the **Startup Object** box change Sub Main to **Form1**. Click **OK**. Now try running the program.

6. Next we need to change the code in the Click event for cmdFindNumber (step 7 of program 8.1). Since its task is now to call the function to search for the required number and to output an appropriate message, any code which contributes to the searching itself can be removed. This means we can remove the variable Element and the loop. The new code should look as follows:

```
Private Sub cmdFindNumber_Click()
  Dim Found As Boolean       'stores function FindNumber's return value
  Dim SearchNumber As Integer
  SearchNumber = txtSearchNumber.Text
  Found = FindNumber(SearchNumber, Numbers()) 'call the function and pass
                                              'it two parameters
  If Found Then
    lblDisplaySearch.Caption = "This number IS in the array"
  Else
    lblDisplaySearch.Caption = "This number is NOT in the array"
  End If
End Sub
```

The return value from the function FindNumber is stored in the Boolean Found and this is used to output the message. Two parameters must be passed to the function – the number to look for (SearchNumber) and the array itself (Numbers).

7. Write the function's declaration directly, or by selecting **Tools/Add Procedure** and clicking the Function option button, as shown below:

```
Public Function FindNumber(ByVal WantedNumber As Integer, _
                          ByVal NumberArray) As Boolean
```

Both formal parameters can be passed by value because we do not need to change their contents. Note that the array parameter does not declare a data type. Since the function must return whether or not the number is present, the return value is declared, outside the parameter brackets, as Boolean.

8. Complete the code to carry out the search and return a true or false value as shown below. The search code is the same as that in program 8.1, except that the formal parameter, WantedNumber, is used.

```
Dim Found As Boolean
Dim Element As Integer
Found = False
Element = 1
Do While (Found = False) And (Element <= Index)
   If NumberArray(Element) = WantedNumber Then
      Found = True
   Else
      Element = Element + 1
   End If
Loop
If Found Then
   FindNumber = True     'to return a value from the function assign
Else                     'it to the function's name
   FindNumber = False
End If
End Function
```

9. Run the program.

end of Program 8.2

Two-dimensional arrays

All the arrays so far have been one-dimensional. Suppose you wished to store a firm's quarterly sales figures for the decade 1990 - 1999. This requires 4 (quarters) x 10 (years) = 40 pieces of data. You could declare a two-dimensional array to hold this data as follows:

```
Dim SalesFigures(1990 To 1999, 1 To 4) As Currency
```

After running the following code

```
SalesFigures(1990, 3) = 56800
SalesFigures(1998, 4) = 96400
```

the array would look like the matrix shown in figure 8.4. The years are the rows and the quarters the columns because they are declared in that order.

You can have arrays with more than two dimensions, but it's unlikely you would ever need to use one. Two-dimensional arrays are useful for storing data for some mathematical problems, but in 'business' type problems they are less useful because all their data items must be of the same data type. An array of records (covered in the next chapter) is a more convenient data structure.

Control arrays

A control array is a group of controls which are all of the same type. You can have a control array of text boxes, of command buttons and so on. There are two main advantages in grouping controls this way:

- They all share the same name. For example five text boxes used for inputting numbers could be named txtNumber(1), txtNumber(2) and so on. If they were not part of a control array each text box would need a different name. Name sharing can often reduce the amount of code you have to write, as program 8.3 illustrates. This technique is used to great effect in the sample project in Part Three.

- Each control array element has its own properties but, as program 8.4 shows, shares its event procedure code with the other control array elements.

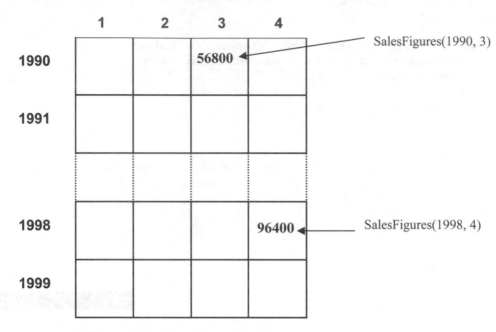

Figure 8.4: A two-dimensional array

PROGRAM 8.3   *A control array of text boxes*

Specification   Use a control array to store five numbers entered by the user. When all the numbers have been entered copy them to an 'ordinary' array and display the contents of this array in a second control array.

Figure 8.5 shows the program in action. Five numbers have been entered into a control array of text boxes on the left and then copied to an 'ordinary' array. The control array of labels on the right displays the contents of this ordinary array.

There are two ways of building a control array. Steps 1 and 2 build the text box array using one method, and steps 3 and 4 use the other method to build the array of labels.

1.   Open a new project and place the first text box on the form. Name it **txtNumbers**. Set its **Index** property to **1**. The Properties window now shows this control is stored as **txtNumbers(1)**, i.e. element 1 of a control array of text boxes called Numbers.

2.   Position four more text boxes. Set their names to **txtNumbers** and their Index property to **2, 3, 4, 5** as appropriate.

3.   Position the first display label and name it **lblNumbers**.

4.   Copy and paste this label and Visual Basic will display a dialog box asking you if you want to create a control array. Click **Yes**.

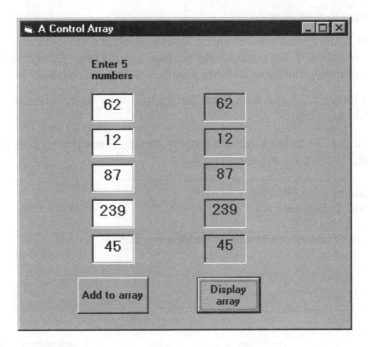

Figure 8.5: Program 8.3

5. In the Properties window you can see that Visual Basic stores these two labels as lblNumbers(0) and lblNumbers(1). When you create a control array using this method the element numbering starts from 0. To keep it in line with the numbering of the text box elements change the Index property of lblNumbers(1) to **2** and of lblNumbers(0) to **1**. Then place three more labels, name them lblNumbers and set their Indexes from **3** to **5** as appropriate.

6. Add the label instructing users to enter 5 numbers and the two command buttons. Name the buttons **cmdAddToArray** and **cmdDisplayArray**.

7. Declare the 'ordinary' array in the General section:

```
Dim Numbers(1 To 5) As Integer
```

8. Type in the following code for the Click event of the command button to copy the numbers from the control array to the ordinary array.

```
Private Sub cmdAddToArray_Click()
  Dim Index As Integer
  If (txtNumbers(1).Text = "") Or (txtNumbers(2).Text = "") _
       Or (txtNumbers(3).Text = "") Or (txtNumbers(4).Text = "") _
       Or (txtNumbers(5).Text = "") Then
    MsgBox "You have not entered 5 numbers"
  Else
    For Index = 1 To 5
      Numbers(Index) = txtNumbers(Index).Text 'eg number in element 3
                'of control array copied to element 3 of ordinary array
    Next Index
  End If
End Sub
```

There are two things to note here:

- A multiple OR condition is used to check that the control array contains 5 numbers. If there had been 20 or 30 text boxes this code would become cumbersome. The question on this program at the end of the chapter points you towards a simpler solution to such a situation.

- A **For...Next** loop copies the data from the control array to the ordinary array by matching the elements of the two arrays.

9. The Click event of the command button to copy from the ordinary array to the control array of labels uses a similar **For...Next** loop to the previous one:

```
Private Sub cmdDisplayArray_Click()
   Dim Index As Integer
   For Index = 1 To 5
      lblNumbers(Index).Caption = Numbers(Index)
   Next Index
End Sub
```

10. Run the program. Try it out with less than 5 numbers and then with the required number.

end of Program 8.3

PROGRAM 8.4   *A control array with a shared event procedure*

Specification	Represent the 4 tennis courts owned by a small tennis club by labels on a form. They should be coloured green when the program starts. Clicking any of these should colour it red to show that the court is now in use. The name of the club member responsible for the court should be displayed next to it.

Figure 8.6 shows the program in action. Courts 2 and 3 are in use.

1. Open a new project and build a control array of 4 labels. Name each one **lblCourts** and set their Index property to **1, 2, 3, 4** as appropriate so that they are stored as lblCourts(1) to lblCourts(4). Set their Font to **14 bold**. Set the Alignment of each to **2 – Center** and the BorderStyle to **1 – Fixed Single**. Set their BackColor to green by clicking the small button in this property, clicking the **Palette** tab and selecting a green colour of your choice.

2. Put 4 further labels to the right of the tennis court labels and name them **lblNames**. Set their Index properties to **1** to **4** as appropriate so that the control array consists of lblNames(1) to lblNames(4).

3. Position the text box for inputting a member's name and name it **txtName**. Add the other two labels and set their captions as shown in figure 8.6.

4. Double-click any of the tennis court labels and you'll get the following declaration in the code template:

```
Private Sub lblCourts_Click(Index As Integer)
```

Visual Basic has supplied a single parameter, Index. Because the four labels share this procedure, Index is used to identify which one has been clicked.

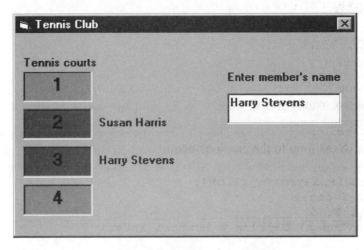

Figure 8.6: Program 8.4

5. Complete the code for this Click event as follows:

```
Dim Name As String
Name = txtName.Text
lblCourts(Index).BackColor = vbRed     'change tennis court to red and
lblNames(Index).Caption = Name         'display member's name next to it
```

The new thing here is the use of **vbRed**. This is one of 8 **color constants** that you can use to set the colour of an object rather than using the RGB function that you used in Chapter 2.

6. Run the program, enter a member's name and click one of the tennis courts to check that it works.

end of Program 8.4

Summary of key concepts

- An **array** can hold any number of items of the same data type.

- A **static** array cannot change in size at run-time. A **dynamic** array can grow or shrink in size. To change its size redeclare it with the **ReDim** keyword, followed by **Preserve** if you wish to retain the array's contents.

- The storage 'slots' in an array are called **elements**. Thus Numbers(5) and Numbers(24) are two elements of an array called Numbers. Any array element can be read or written to directly.

- When a Visual Basic program runs, the first thing it does is look for a named startup form or a sub procedure named Main.

- Arrays can have two or more dimensions. A **two-dimensional array** can be viewed as a matrix with rows and columns.

- A **control array** is a group of controls or objects which are all of the same type. The controls share the same name and event procedures. For example a control array of text boxes might be stored as txtNumbers(1) to txtNumbers(10).

Take it from here...

1. If you declare an array with

```
Dim Numbers(9) As Integer
```

Visual Basic numbers the elements from 0 to 8. Find out about **Option Base** and how you can change the lower default boundary.

2. Two functions not used in the chapter are **UBound** and **LBound**. Find out what these do and how you might use them when handling arrays. Also find out about the **UBound** and **LBound** *properties* of a control array.

Questions on the Programs

Program 8.1

*1. When a number is added to the array a check is made to see if it is full. Remove this check by commenting out all the code in the If statement body except the four lines which currently belong to Else. Run the program and enter 6 numbers. Try to understand the error message you get when you try to store the 6th number.

*2. Allow the user to store more than 5 numbers in the array. Declare it as a dynamic array and increase its size by 1 each time the *Add to Array* button is clicked.

**3. Add command buttons to do two things:

- Find and display the highest number in the array. Hint: store the first number in the array into a variable *Highest* and then loop through the rest of the numbers comparing each with the current value of *Highest*.

- Calculate and display the mean value of the numbers in the array.

Program 8.2

***1. If you have done question 3 for program 8.1, put the code for finding the highest number in the array and for calculating the mean of the numbers in the array, into two general procedures. Call these from the Click event procedures of the command buttons. Allow these event procedures to display the results. Note that the general procedures can be functions because each of them returns a single value.

Program 8.3

1. A compound If statement is used in the Click event for cmdAddToArray to check if any of the five text boxes have not got a number. Rewrite this using a **For Each...Next statement. You may have found out about this special loop in doing question 3 of *Take it from here...* in Chapter 5. It allows you to process each element in a control array. Visual Basic has a range of data types to handle controls or objects in your program, and you will need to use one of these here. Declare a variable of a TextBox data type, for example:

```
Dim MyTextBox As TextBox
```

End of chapter exercises

*1. The purpose of this exercise is to demonstrate the point made after step 4 of program 8.2 that when a program starts running it looks for a named form or a sub procedure called Main. Write a program which does nothing except display a message box with the message *This is all this program does.* Put the code in a procedure named Main, and this in turn should be in a standard module (see Chapter 7).

*2. In a program you could have a control array of command buttons instead of using option buttons. Build a simple program to illustrate this. Use an array of three command buttons to represent how much a person is satisfied with a particular service on a scale of 1 to 3. When one of the buttons is clicked an appropriate message should be displayed, e.g. for button 3 display the message *You are very satisfied with the service.*

**3. Exercise 4 at the end of Chapter 3 asked you to build a simple calculator. You will have needed separate event procedures for each of the four arithmetic operator command buttons. Now group these buttons into a control array and rewrite the program using a single event procedure.

**4. Write a program to store product codes in an array. Product codes have 6 characters and each code must be different from all the other codes. After the user enters a product code check that the code has not been used already, and output an appropriate message if it has.

**5. Write a program to help children learn their capital cities. Use two arrays – one for country names and one for their capitals. Store about 6 items in each array (or more if you wish) in the form's Load event procedure, and use two list boxes to display the contents of the arrays when the program starts. The child should select a country from one list box and its corresponding capital from the other. When a command button is clicked tell the child if the answer is correct. If the answer is wrong display the correct one.

***6. Write a program to input, for up to 20 students, their name and the marks they achieved on each of three exams. Store this data in a two-dimensional array. Because the names must be stored as Strings, the marks must also be of this data type rather than Integer, since all items in an array must be of the same data type. Allow the user to display all the names and marks at any time (in a list box). This part of the program is shown in figure 8.7.

When you have this working extend the program so that the user can select one of the exams and see its average mark. Use option buttons for selecting the exam.

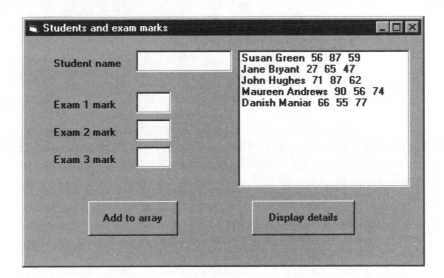

Figure 8.7: Program for the first part of exercise 6

***7**. Write a program to build a more realistic calculator than the one in exercise 3, as shown in figure 8.8. Use two control arrays of labels. One of these has the 10 digits plus the decimal point. The other has the 4 arithmetic operators and the '=' sign. Clicking any of the labels in the arrays sets off the relevant control array's Click event procedure. The C button clears the display and allows a new calculation to start. The Off button simulates switching the calculator off, i.e. the program closes. Use Unload to close the program (see step 7 in program 3.4).

Figure 8.8: The calculator for exercise 7

***8**. A stack is an extremely useful data structure in computing systems and can be implemented using an array. Copy the file Stack.exe from the web site. It is an executable file which means you can run it from Windows but you can't get at the Visual Basic code. The stack can hold six single characters and these are stored in a control array. Now create this program yourself in Visual Basic.

Chapter 9 – Records

What is a record?

When a credit card company holds details about its customers it stores many items of data about each one. Four of these items are shown in Figure 9.1. Each item is stored in a column or **field** and all the items for a particular customer are stored in one row or **record**.

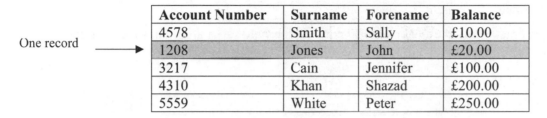

One record →

Account Number	Surname	Forename	Balance
4578	Smith	Sally	£10.00
1208	Jones	John	£20.00
3217	Cain	Jennifer	£100.00
4310	Khan	Shazad	£200.00
5559	White	Peter	£250.00

Figure 9.1: Records

An array of records

You could store the data in figure 9.1 in a two-dimensional array provided that each field is the same data type. This is not always possible and, even if it is, not always desirable. A record allows you to mix data types. If you have many records you can store them in an array; each array element has one record. Figure 9.1 shows an array of records, which is really the same as a table in a database.

How to declare an array of records

There are two stages:

- Declare a single record.
- Declare an array of this single record.

To declare a single record to hold the data for one customer in figure 9.1 you would write:

```
Private Type CustomerType        'declare data type for one record
   AccountNumber As Integer      'declare the 4 fields
   Surname As String
   Forename As String
   Balance As Currency
End Type
Dim Customer As CustomerType      'declare variable to hold one record
```

Each field is declared separately, sandwiched between the keywords **Type** and **End Type**. The code defines a new data type called CustomerType, similar to the standard data types such as Integer and String. The choice of identifier is yours but it is a good idea to finish it with the word 'Type' so that you can recognise it as a data type in your code. Because you have defined it yourself a Type declaration is often called a **user-defined** data type. The last line declares a variable, Customer, of data type CustomerType that is capable of storing four items of data.

To store details of 1000 customers you would extend the declaration as follows:

```
Dim Customers(1 To 1000) As CustomerType
```

Now the variable Customers can store 4 items about 1000 customers, i.e. 4000 items of data.

Processing an array of records

Look carefully at figure 9.2 which shows how to visualise an array of records. The elements are numbered along the base and one element holds one record, i.e. one customer's details. You can refer to any of the 4000 items of data using the syntax

Customers(Element).Fieldname

The dot between the bracket and the field name is known as the **field separator**. Thus the data item *Jones* is stored in Customers(2).Surname and the item *112.60* stored in Customers(999).Balance.

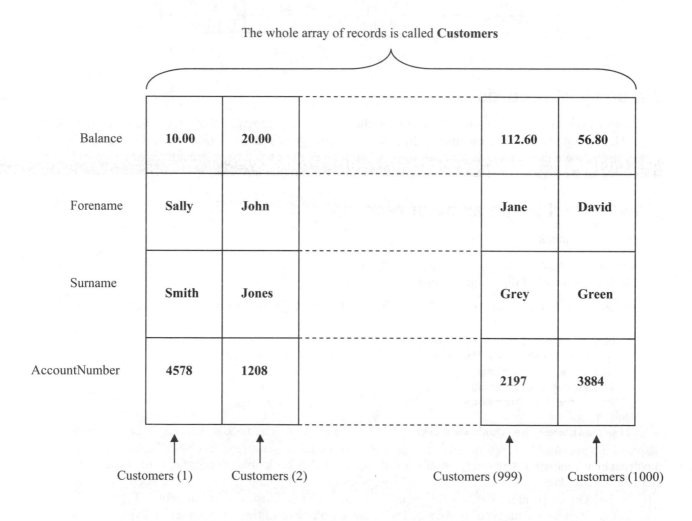

Figure 9.2: An array of records

Think of the syntax as made up of three things that get smaller in size from left to right, as shown in figure 9.3.

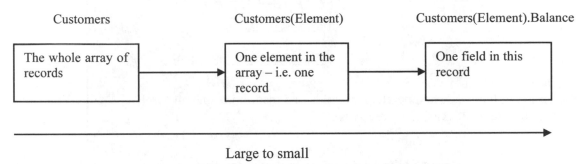

Figure 9.3: Different sized parts of an array of records

If you have a text box named txtSurname then you would store what the user types in by writing

```
Customers(Element).Surname = txtSurname.Text
```

If Element currently has the value 60 then the item of data is stored in the 60th record. To output the same piece of data you would write

```
Form1.Print Customers(Element).Surname
```

PROGRAM 9.1   *Football Team Players*

Specification	Write a program to store the following details about players in a football league for one season:

> Name
> Team
> Number of times played
> Number of goals scored
> Whether ever sent off or not

> Store these details in an array of records and display details of one player by using back and forward buttons to navigate through the array. Also allow the user to select a given player and display their details.

The finished program can be seen in figures 9.4 and 9.5. It has two forms, one for entering data and the other for displaying it. In figure 9.4 clicking Add stores the player's details in an array, and clicking New clears the contents of the input controls ready for the next player's details. In figure 9.5 clicking Previous displays the previous player's details (i.e. the previous record in the array), and clicking Next displays the next player's details.

Apart from using an array of records the program uses a standard module and a general procedure with parameter passing (both covered in Chapter 7).

Designing the forms

1. Open a new project and name the form **frmEnterData**.

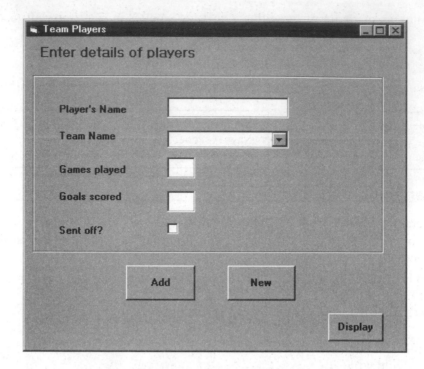

Figure 9.4: Program 9.1 – the opening form

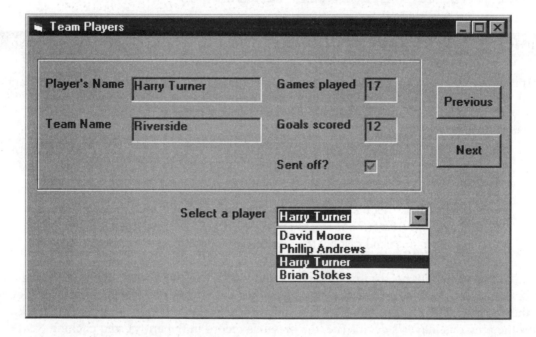

Figure 9.5: Program 9.1 – the second form

2. Design the form using figure 9.4. The controls for entering data are on a frame. The Team Name control is a combo box and the Sent Off control is a check box. Name the data entry controls **txtPlayer**, **cboTeams**, **txtGames**, **txtGoals** and **chkSentOff**. Set the Text property of the combo box to blank and write several team names of your choice into its List property. You'll need to delete the check box caption and use a separate label.

3. Name the command buttons **cmdAddRecord**, **cmdNewRecord** and **cmdDisplay**.

4. To add the second form select **Project/Add Form**. Make sure the **New** tab is selected and that **Form** is selected in the window. Click **Open**. Name this form **frmDisplayData**.

5. Design the form using figure 9.5. The controls for displaying data are on a frame. Name the display controls **lblPlayer**, **lblTeam**, **lblGames**, **lblGoals** and **chkSentOff**. Set the Enabled property of the check box to **False** since it is used for display only. Name the command buttons **cmdPrevious** and **cmdNext**. Name the combo box (for selecting a player) **cboPlayers** and set its Text property to blank.

Declaring variables

6. In the General section of frmEnterData declare two global variables. Since we will need to use Number on both forms we must declare it in a different way. Omit Dim and declare it with the Public keyword:

```
Dim Element As Integer        'current element of the array
Public Number As Integer      'number of players' details in array
```

7. In the General section of frmDisplayData declare:

```
Dim Element As Integer        'current element of the array
```

Although this variable has the same name as one of those in frmEnterData, it is a *different* variable.

8. In step 6 you declared a variable to be used by both forms. The array of records must also be used by both but you cannot use this method for declaring a user-defined type. Instead you must declare it on a standard module (covered in Chapter 7). Select **Project/Add Module**. With the **New** tab selected and **Module** highlighted, click **Open** and you'll get a standard module. A standard module cannot have any controls, only code. You have to save it as a separate file and Visual Basic will give it a '.bas' extension. Save it now.

9. In this standard module declare a type, and a variable of this type using the keyword Public:

```
Public Type PlayerType      'data type for one record. Public IS optional
  PlayerName As String              'declare the 5 fields
  TeamName As String
  Games As Integer
  Goals As Integer
  SentOff As Boolean
End Type
Public Players(1 To 20) As PlayerType      'stores details of 20 players
                                           'Public keyword is not optional
```

Entering data

10. In the Load event of frmEnterData initialise the two global variables:

```
Element = 0
Number = 0
```

11. When details of one player are stored in the array we need to increment these two global variables. The complete code for the Click event of cmdAddRecord is:

```
Private Sub cmdAddRecord_Click()
  Element = Element + 1
  Number = Number + 1
  Players(Element).PlayerName = txtPlayer.Text
  Players(Element).TeamName = cboTeams.Text
  Players(Element).Games = txtGames.Text
  Players(Element).Goals = txtGoals.Text
  If chkSentOff.Value = 0 Then     '0 means check box is NOT checked
    Players(Element).SentOff = False
  Else                             'holds 1 - check box IS checked
    Players(Element).SentOff = True
  End If
End Sub
```

An **If** statement is needed to convert the Value property of the check box to the Boolean value needed for the SentOff field of the record.

12. The Click event of cmdNewRecord sets all the fields to blank and positions the cursor in the text box ready for the next player's name. The check box can be set to unchecked by default since a player is more likely never to have been sent off (hopefully!).

```
Private Sub cmdNewRecord_Click()
  txtPlayer.Text = ""
  cboTeams.Text = ""
  txtGames.Text = ""
  txtGoals.Text = ""
  chkSentOff.Value = 0             'set check box to unchecked
  txtPlayer.SetFocus
End Sub
```

13. The cmdDisplay button simply opens frmDisplay.

```
Private Sub cmdDisplay_Click()
  frmDisplayData.Show
End Sub
```

Displaying data

When frmDisplayData loads there are several things that must happen:

- The combo box must show the players' names;
- Details of the first player in the array should be displayed;
- The Previous button should be disabled because the current record is the first one;
- The Next button should be disabled if the user hasn't entered any data or has entered only one player's details.

14. The code to handle this is:

```
Private Sub Form_Load()
  Dim Index As Integer
  Element = 1
  cmdPrevious.Enabled = False
  If frmEnterData.Number = 0 Then              'no data yet entered
    cmdNext.Enabled = False
  ElseIf frmEnterData.Number = 1 Then 'details of only 1 player entered
    cmdNext.Enabled = False
    Call DisplayPlayer(Element) 'procedure call with 1 parameter
  Else                                'details of 2 or more players entered
    cmdNext.Enabled = True
    Call DisplayPlayer(Element) 'procedure call with 1 parameter
  End If
  For Index = 1 To frmEnterData.Number  'populate combo box with names
    cboPlayers.AddItem Players(Index).PlayerName
  Next Index
End Sub
```

Note:

- There is a call to procedure DisplayPlayer, but we haven't written it yet.
- When the variable Number is used, it is prefixed by the name of the form on which it is declared and a dot separator is placed between the two (frmEnterData.Number).

15. When the Previous or Next button is clicked the current element of the array must be changed, and the previous or next player's details displayed by calling procedure DisplayPlayer. If the Previous button is in a disabled state when you click Next, it must be enabled to be able to go back one record.

```
Private Sub cmdNext_Click()
  Element = Element + 1
  Call DisplayPlayer(Element)
  cmdPrevious.Enabled = True      'ensure user can go back one record
End Sub

Private Sub cmdPrevious_Click()
  Element = Element - 1
  Call DisplayPlayer(Element)
End Sub
```

Note that there is more that can be done on enabling and disabling the Previous and Next buttons, but this is left for you to do in question 4 on the program later.

16. When the user selects a player's name from the combo box their details should be displayed. Recall that the ListIndex property of list and combo boxes holds the index of the selected item, and that indexing starts at 0. For example the third name in the combo box has a ListIndex value of 2, but this name in our array of records is in element 3 (because we numbered the array from 1). Therefore you must add 1 to the ListIndex value.

```
Private Sub cboPlayers_Click()
  Dim RecordNumber As Integer
  RecordNumber = cboPlayers.ListIndex + 1
  Call DisplayPlayer(RecordNumber)
End Sub
```

17. The procedure DisplayPlayer has been called in five places in the code above. One parameter is passed to it – the current element in the array. Since this parameter is only used and not changed by the procedure, it can be passed by value rather than by reference.

```
Public Sub DisplayPlayer(ByVal Index As Integer)
  With Players(Index)
    lblPlayer.Caption = .PlayerName
    lblTeam.Caption = .TeamName
    lblGames.Caption = .Games
    lblGoals.Caption = .Goals
    If .SentOff = True Then
      chkSentOff.Value = 1          'set check box to checked
    Else
      chkSentOff.Value = 0          'set check box to unchecked
    End If
  End With
End Sub
```

The new thing in the code above is the use of **With...End With**. You can use this with a user-defined type simply to cut down on code. Instead we could have written

```
lblPlayer.Caption = Players(Index).PlayerName
lblTeam.Caption = Players(Index).TeamName
'etc
```

which requires writing *Players(Index)* on each line.

18. Run the program and check that everything works. Recall that the Previous and Next buttons have intentionally not been made to work fully. Question 4 on this program asks you to take this further.

end of Program 9.1

Reflections on program 9.1

If you run program 9.1 a few times you will realise that one drawback is having to enter all the players' details each time. In real-world programs this data would be kept as records on file and read from the file as appropriate. If only one player's details have to be read then a single record variable could be used. If several players' details, or perhaps the whole file, have to be read and copied into RAM then an array of records would be used. Files are studied in the next chapter.

Summary of key concepts

- A **record** is a data structure in which you can mix data types. It is made up of one or more **fields**.

- To declare a record use **Type...End Type**. You build a **user-defined** data type and then declare a variable of this type.

- To use a variable on all the forms in a program declare it in the General section as **Public** and omit the keyword Dim, e.g. Public Number As Integer. When the variable is used on a form other than the one on which it is declared, it must be prefixed by the name of the form and a dot separator used, e.g. frmEnterData.Number.

- To use a **user-defined type** on more than one form in a program, declare it in a standard module.

- **With…End With** can be used when assigning or reading data to a given record. It saves having to write out part of the syntax when processing individual fields.

Questions on the Program

*1. Rewrite the code in the Click event for cmdAddRecord using **With…End With**.

*2. Set the Sorted property of the combo box on frmDisplayData to True. Enter several players' names not in alphabetical order. Make a note of the order you entered the names. Try selecting these players from the combo box on frmDisplayData. Can you explain why the wrong player's details are usually displayed? (Change the Sorted property back to False when you've finished.)

*3. Run the program and enter three records. Then click the Next button on the second form three times or more. Nothing appears in the Player's Name, Team Name or Sent Off controls, but the other two controls show 0 values. Explain why. Then keep clicking the Previous button until you get an error message. Can you explain what it is saying?

**4. There is some enabling/disabling of the Previous and Next buttons in the code but it doesn't cover all situations. Extend the code so that the buttons are enabled only when necessary. For example if the array is full the Next button should be disabled, (though in a real program you would either make sure the array is large enough or use a dynamic array).

***5. Extend the program to do the following:

- allow the user to select a team and scroll through only details of players in this team;

- in a list box display the name and team of all players who have been sent off;

- in a list box display the name and team of all players who have scored at least a given number of goals. Allow the user to input the number of goals to search on.

End of chapter exercises

**1. Store the following details of a member of a health club in a record – name, weight (in kilograms), height (in metres and centimetres, e.g. 1.86) and age. Have two command buttons on the form. Clicking one of them should ask the user for these details by using a series of input boxes. Clicking the other should print details of the member on the form.

***2. Students on a two-semester course take an exam at the end of each semester. Allow the user to enter student names and their mark (out of 100) in each exam. Store all the data in an array of records. Display:

- the average mark in each exam;
- the name of the student with the highest mark in each exam;
- the names of those students who passed the course. At least 50 marks in both exams are needed for a pass.

Design the form appropriately. Use a general procedure to validate the mark (i.e. to only accept a value from 0 to 100).

Chapter 10 – Files

What is a file?

In all the programs covered so far, any stored data is lost when the program closes, and would have to be entered again when the program next runs. For a program like 9.1, where a lot of data might be stored in an array of records, this is clearly a waste of time. The solution is to store the data permanently – in a file.

Types of file in Visual Basic

Visual Basic supports three types of file. You are likely to use only two of these:

- Text files
- Random access files

There are several key differences between these files:

- A text file stores all its data as characters, represented by their ASCII codes. For example it would store the number 25 as character 2 (ASCII code 50) and character 5 (ASCII code 53). In binary these two ASCII codes are 0110010 (50) and 0110101 (53). A random access file would store this number differently. Assuming it is stored as a 2-byte integer it would be stored as 0000000000011001.

- A random access file stores only records. In a text file there is no naturally built-in structure to the data since it is simply stored as a sequence of characters.

- You cannot open a text file to be both read from and written to, but you can with a random access file.

- With a random access file you can read and write to any position within the file. For example you can read the 5th record or overwrite the 8th record. This is also called **direct access**. You cannot directly change the data in a text file. To change some data you would have to read all the data before the data you wish to change and write this to a new file. Then write the changed data to the new file. Finally read all the data after the changed data and write this to the new file too. Because the data must be read from the beginning of the file a text file is often called a **sequential** file.

Opening/closing a file

You must always open a file before you can use it. To open a **text** file use one of the following;

```
Open Filename For Input As #1      'to read from the file
Open Filename For Output As #1     'to write to the file
Open Filename For Append As #1     'to write to the end of the file
```

- The **Open** statement opens a file if it exists. If it doesn't exist, Open first creates it and then opens it.

- Filename is a String variable that holds the name of the file. You need to tell Visual Basic the full path to the file too, e.g. "c:\My VB Work\Programs\Students.txt".

- The **Input**, **Append** and **Output** statements indicate how you wish to read/write. If you open a file for Output, Visual Basic deletes the contents of the file (even if you don't write anything to it). To add data to an existing file you must use Append, which adds the data after the existing data.

- **As #1** assigns the file the number 1. All files are identified by a number, not by their name. If you have two or more files open at the same time they must have different numbers.

To open a **random access** file you must tell Visual Basic the length (in bytes) of the records it stores. This means that you must state the length of any String fields in your defined data type. For example if you were storing records from program 9.1 on file, the PlayerName and TeamName fields (step 9 in program 9.1) must have defined lengths. If these were 20 and 14 bytes then the total length of a record would be 40 bytes since the other three fields need only 6 bytes. Assuming a variable, OnePlayer, has been declared to hold one record, you could write either of the following to open the file:

```
Open Filename For Random As #1 Len = 40
Open Filename For Random As #1 Len = Len(OnePlayer)
```

The second method is more convenient as it uses the **Len** function to find the length of the record for you. Note that the first use of the word 'Len' is just part of the syntax and not a function call.

When you have finished using a file always close it. To close either a text or random access file is very easy:

```
Close #1
```

Reading from a file

Visual Basic keeps an imaginary file pointer as it reads through a file. When the file is opened it points to the first line of a text file or the first record of a random access file. Suppose a text file holds a series of whole numbers, one on each line in the file. Assuming Number has been declared as an Integer, the following code would display these on a form:

```
Do While Not EOF(1)          'EOF means End Of File. NB pass it just the
    Input #1, Number         'number of the file, not # sign too
    Form1.Print Number
Loop
```

The **EOF** function returns True when the end of a file has been reached. The While condition uses the **Not** logical operator and is saying *continue until the end of the file is reached*. The **Input** statement reads the item of data on the current line in the file and stores it in Number. After reading the single item of data on the line, the file pointer points to the next line.

With a random access file you can only read (and write) one record at a time. You cannot read or write individual fields within a record. To read and display the whole of a random access file you would write:

```
Do While Not EOF(1)
    Get #1, , OneTeam          'OneTeam is a record variable
    'code to display the contents of the record
Loop
```

The middle argument for the **Get** statement above is missing, indicated by the pair of commas. Visual Basic numbers the records in a random access file from 1 onwards, and the missing argument here is this record number. In the code above the file pointer is moved to the next record each time round the loop, so there is no need to state the record number. Visual Basic will process the current record.

When you wish to go directly to a particular record you *do* need to state the record number. The next example reads a record from the file at record position *RecordNumber*. It uses the **Seek** statement, whose second argument is the record number where the file pointer should be positioned.

```
    Seek #1, RecordNumber
    Get #1, , OneTeam
```

Seek is not always needed before Get. In the example above you could read the record directly with Get if you provide the record number:

```
    Get #1, RecordNumber, OneTeam
```

Writing to a file

For text files use the **Write** or **Print** statements. (Program 10.1 illustrates the slight difference between these.) So

```
    Write #1, Number
```

writes the contents of Number to the current file pointer position.

With a random access file use the **Put** statement. This works in the same way as the Get statement to read from a file. It may need to know the record number and must be passed one whole record to write to the file:

```
    Put #1, , OneTeam                    'write to current file pointer position
    'or
    Put #1, RecordNumber, OneTeam        'write to RecordNumber record number
```

Getting the file name

When you open an existing file you must supply its name. There are three ways of doing this:

- Hardcode the full path and file name
- Use App.Path
- Use the CommonDialog control

Hardcode the full path and file name

Assuming Filename has been declared as a String you might write:

```
    Filename = "c:\My Visual Basic Work\Members.dat"
```

The disadvantage of this method is that the file must be in the folder specified by the path. If you move the file to another folder you have to change the code.

Use App.Path

App is a Visual Basic object that gives information about your application or program. The **Path** property stores the application's path. The example below adds the file name to the path.

```
    Filename = App.Path & "\Members.dat"
```

The file must be in the same folder as your program, but this method is more flexible than hardcoding the full path and file name since you can move the program and file into any folder and the code will work.

Use the CommonDialog control

The CommonDialog control can be added to the toolbox. Let's have a practical demonstration of how it works.

1. Open a new project. Select **Project/Components** and in the Components dialog box check the item called **Microsoft Common Dialog Control** as shown in figure 10.1. (If it is not there click **Browse** and select the file **Comdlg32.ocx**.) Click **OK**.

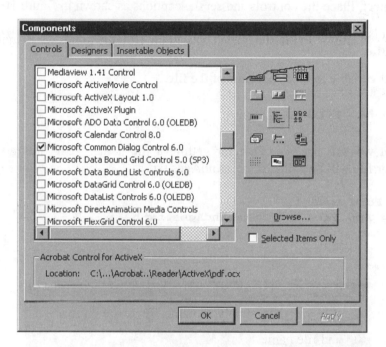

Figure 10.1: Selecting the CommonDialog control

2. The control will be added to the toolbox. Like the Timer control it is invisible at run time and can be placed anywhere on the form. Place this control and a command button on the form, and keep their default names CommonDialog1 and Command1.

3. Code the Click event of the command button as follows:

```
Private Sub Command1_Click()
   CommonDialog1.ShowOpen
   Form1.Show
   Print CommonDialog1.FileName
End Sub
```

The ShowOpen method will display the same dialog box (window) you get when you select File/Open from a Windows application. The FileName property stores the full path and name of the file you select from this dialog box.

4. Run the program. Click the button and you'll get the very familiar Open dialog box. Select any file you want, or even type in a file that isn't listed, click **Open** and you'll see the path and file name printed on the form.

It is important to realise that all the ShowOpen method of this control has done is to get a path and the file name. It has not opened the file. You still need to use the Open statement to do this.

PROGRAM 0.1   *Text file to hold names nd ages*

> **Specification**   Allow the user to enter people's names and ages and store these in a text file. Allow the user to display the contents of the file at any time.

Figure 10.2 shows the program after two sets of names and ages have been stored in the file.

1.   Open a new project. Place the controls and set the captions as shown in figure 10.2.

2.   Name the controls **txtName**, **txtAge**, **cmdAddToFileWrite**, **cmdAddToFilePrint**, **cmdDisplayFile** and **lstDisplayFile**.

3.   Declare a global variable to hold the name of the file:

```
Dim Filename As String
```

4.   In this program we will use App.Path for getting a file name. Text files normally have a '.txt' extension, so our file will be called NamesAndAges.txt.

```
Private Sub Form_Load()
    Filename = App.Path & "\NamesAndAges.txt"
End Sub
```

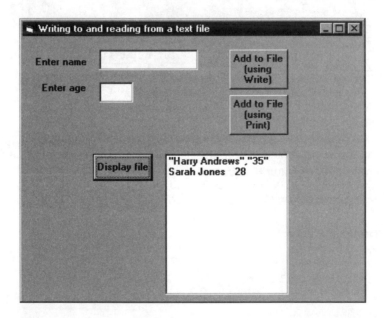

Figure 10.2: Program 10.1 after two names and ages have been stored

5.   The code for the Click event of the upper Add command button is:

```
Private Sub cmdAddToFileWrite_Click()
    Dim Name As String
    Dim Age As String
    Name = txtName.Text
    Age = txtAge.Text
```

```
      Open Filename For Append As #1     'open the file,
      Write #1, Name, Age                'write two items of data to it, then
      Close #1                           'close it
      txtName.Text = ""
      txtAge.Text = ""
      txtName.SetFocus
   End Sub
```

6. The code for the lower Add command button is the same but uses Print rather than Write. Type the code in now.

7. In the Click event to display the file, write:

```
Private Sub cmdDisplayFile_Click()
   Dim DataToDisplay As String
   Open Filename For Input As #1
   lstDisplayFile.Clear
   Do While Not EOF(1)
      Line Input #1, DataToDisplay
      lstDisplayFile.AddItem DataToDisplay
   Loop
   Close #1
End Sub
```

Rather than reading the two items of data on each line in the file into two variables, the **Line Input** statement is used to read the whole line into one variable. But if we had wanted to display people aged over 20 for example, we would need to read in the items separately, in order to test the age data.

8. Run the program. Enter a name and age and click the upper command button. Enter another name and age and click the lower button. Click the button to display the file and you'll see how Write and Print store the data differently in the file. Write puts quotation marks around each piece of data and separates them with a comma. Print simply puts spaces between the two pieces of data.

end of Program 10.1

PROGRAM 10.2   *Random access file of Garden Centre products*

Specification   A garden centre stores the following details about each of its 800 products:

- ID
- Description
- Price
- Quantity in stock
- Reorder level (i.e. number to which stock has to fall before it is reordered)

Write a program which stores details of products in a random access file. The number of products in the file should always be displayed. The program should allow the user to search for a product both by record number and by product ID. It should also display the entire contents of the file in a list box in product ID order. Use the CommonDialog control to retrieve the name of the file.

You can see the program in figure 10.3. though in a real program you wouldn't display the file name; it's displayed here simply to demonstrate that the CommonDialog control has worked. Since the products were not entered into the file in product ID order, the display in the list box does not reflect their physical order in the file. The details at the bottom left are of record number 3. In a real application you are unlikely to search for a given record number (unless the key field contains values which are the same as the record number values, e.g. membership numbers from 1 upwards). It is included here to illustrate direct access to a given record.

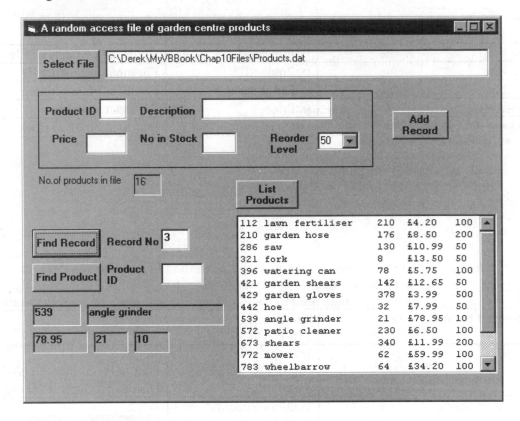

Figure 10.3: Program 10.2

1.   Open a new project and design the form using figures 10.3 and 10.4. As usual the Text property of all the text boxes should be set to blank. The 5 input text boxes are enclosed by a Shape control whose Shape property is set to **0 – Rectangle**. The 5 labels in the bottom left of the form should have their Border Style property set to **1 – Fixed Single**.

2.   Place a CommonDialog control anywhere on the form.

3.   Declare the following in the General section:

```
Private Type OneProduct
   ProductID As Integer          '2 bytes storage needed
   Description As String * 18    '18 bytes
   Price As Currency             '8 bytes
   QuantityInStock As Integer    '2 bytes
   ReorderLevel As Integer       '2 bytes
End Type                         'total 32 bytes to store 1 record
Dim Filename As String
Dim NumberOfRecords As Integer   'no. records currently stored in file
```

Since random access files store records, and we must read and write whole records to the file, we need to declare a type to hold details of one product. A variable of type OneProduct has *not* been declared here. Since several event procedures will need to use this variable it is much safer to declare it locally when needed. Note that the length of the Description field is declared. **You must always state the length of String fields when using random access files.**

Control	Property	Property setting	Comment
Command button	Name Caption	cmdSelectFile Select File	
Text box	Name	txtFilename	Holds path + name of file
Text box	Name	txtProductID	For input of product ID
Text box	Name	txtDescription	For input of description
Text box	Name	txtPrice	For input of price
Text box	Name	txtQuantityInStock	For input of no. in stock
Combo box	Name List Text	cboReorderLevel 10 50 100 200 50	There are 4 reorder levels 50 is commonest reorder level, so set as default
Command button	Name Caption	cmdAddRecord Add Record	
Label	Name	lblNumberOfRecords	Displays no. of records in file
Command button	Name Caption	cmdDisplayFile List Products	
List box	Name Font Sorted	lstDisplayFile Courier New size 8 True	Font to keep output in columns Display products in ID order
Command button	Name Caption	cmdFindRecord Find Record	
Text box	Name	txtFindRecord	To enter record number to search for
Command button	Name Caption	cmdFindProduct Find Product	
Text box	Name	txtFindProduct	To enter product ID to search for
Label	Name	lblProductID	At bottom left of form
Label	Name	lblDescripton	At bottom left of form
Label	Name	lblPrice	At bottom left of form
Label	Name	lblQuantityInStock	At bottom left of form
Label	Name	lblReorderLevel	At bottom left of form

Figure 10.4: Properties of the controls in program 10.2

4. In the Click event for cmdSelectFile we'll use the CommonDialog control to get the file name, then open the file and display how many products it holds. To calculate the number of products (records) divide the total size of the file in bytes by the size of one record. The LOF (**L**ength **O**f **F**ile) function is used to get the size of an open file.

```
Private Sub cmdSelectFile_Click()
   Dim Product As OneProduct            'one record
   CommonDialog1.ShowOpen             'display the Open (file) dialog box
   txtFilename.Text = CommonDialog1.Filename 'display selected file name
   Filename = txtFilename.Text
   Open Filename For Random As #1 Len = Len(Product)       'open file
   NumberOfRecords = LOF(1) / Len(Product) 'calculate no. records in it
   lblNumberOfRecords.Caption = NumberOfRecords
   Close #1
End Sub
```

5. Clicking the Add Record button writes the record to the file, updates the number of products in the file, and clears the text boxes ready for the next product:

```
Private Sub cmdAddRecord_Click()
   Dim Product As OneProduct                 'one record
   Filename = txtFilename.Text
   Product.ProductID = txtProductID.Text 'store input data into one record
   Product.Description = txtDescription.Text
   Product.Price = txtPrice.Text
   Product.QuantityInStock = txtQuantityInStock.Text
   Product.ReorderLevel = cboReorderLevel.Text
   Open Filename For Random As #1 Len = Len(Product)    'open file
   Put #1, NumberOfRecords + 1, Product  'write record after current record
   Close #1
   NumberOfRecords = NumberOfRecords + 1
   lblNumberOfRecords.Caption = NumberOfRecords 'update no.products in file
   txtProductID.Text = ""                      'clear input for next product
   txtDescription.Text = ""
   txtPrice.Text = ""
   txtQuantityInStock.Text = ""
   txtProductID.SetFocus
   cboReorderLevel.Text = "50"            'set reorder level to default value
End Sub
```

6. To display the contents of the file in the list box use a **For…Next** loop. Each execution of the loop processes one record. Although you earlier set the font of the list box to Courier New to display the output in columns, this only works properly for strings of a specified length. Three of the fields are Integers and only by storing them as Strings can we make them occupy a given amount of space.

```
Private Sub cmdDisplayFile_Click()
   Dim Index As Integer
   Dim DataToDisplay As String        'details of one product
   Dim Quantity As String * 4         '3 fields to store as fixed-length
   Dim Price As String * 6            'Strings
   Dim ReorderLevel As String * 3
   Dim Product As OneProduct          'one record
   Filename = txtFilename.Text
   lstDisplayFile.Clear
   Open Filename For Random As #1 Len = Len(Product)
   For Index = 1 To NumberOfRecords   'loop through all records in file
      Get #1, , Product               'read one record
      Quantity = Product.QuantityInStock
      Price = Format(Product.Price, "currency")
      ReorderLevel = Product.ReorderLevel
```

```
            DataToDisplay = Product.ProductID & " " & Product.Description _
                    & " " & Quantity & " " & Price & " " & ReorderLevel
        lstDisplayFile.AddItem DataToDisplay
    Next Index
    Close #1
End Sub
```

7. Use Get to display the contents of a record from the file using its record number. The code checks that the record number entered by the user is a valid one.

```
Private Sub cmdFindRecord_Click()
    Dim RecordNumber As Integer
    Dim Product As OneProduct        'one record
    Filename = txtFilename.Text
    RecordNumber = txtFindRecord.Text
    If (RecordNumber > 0) And (RecordNumber <= NumberOfRecords) Then
        Open Filename For Random As #1 Len = Len(Product)
        Get #1, RecordNumber, Product          'read required record
        lblProductID.Caption = Product.ProductID     'and display its fields
        lblDescription.Caption = Product.Description
        lblPrice.Caption = Product.Price
        lblQuantityInStock.Caption = Product.QuantityInStock
        lblReorderLevel.Caption = Product.ReorderLevel
        Close #1
    Else
        MsgBox "Invalid record number"
    End If
End Sub
```

8. Finding a product with a given product ID involves a linear search through the file from the first record using **Do While...Loop**. A Boolean value is switched to True if the record is found and the loop stops.

```
Private Sub cmdFindProductID_Click()
    Dim RecordNumber As Integer
    Dim Found As Boolean
    Dim ProductID As String
    Dim Product As OneProduct
    ProductID = txtFindProduct.Text
    RecordNumber = 0
    Found = False
    Filename = txtFilename.Text
    Open Filename For Random As #1 Len = Len(Product)
    Do While (Not EOF(1)) And (Found = False) 'loop until no more records
                                              'or record is found
        RecordNumber = RecordNumber + 1
        Get #1, RecordNumber, Product
        If Product.ProductID = ProductID Then          'record found?
            Found = True
            lblProductID.Caption = ProductID
            lblDescription.Caption = Product.Description
            lblPrice.Caption = Product.Price
            lblQuantityInStock.Caption = Product.QuantityInStock
            lblReorderLevel.Caption = Product.ReorderLevel
        End If
```

```
      Loop
      Close #1
      If Not Found Then
         MsgBox ("Product ID " & ProductID & " is not in the file")
      End If
   End Sub
```

9.   Run the program. Click Select File and enter a file name of your choice, e.g. Products.dat. Enter details of several products, display them and then try looking for a given product by record number and by ID. Enter valid and invalid record numbers.

end of Program 10.2

Summary of key concepts

- The two main types of file are **text** files (**sequential** files) and **random access** files (**direct access** files). Data in text files is stored as a sequence of characters but in random access files it is stored as records.

- In code files are referenced by an integer number, e.g. #1.

- The **Open** and **Close** statements open and close a file. A text file can be opened for input or output, but not both at the same time. A random access file *can* be opened for both.

- Use the **Input** statement to read from a text file and the **Get** statement to read from a random access file.

- Use the **Write** or **Print** statements to write to a text file and the **Put** statement to write to a random access file.

- Use the **Seek** statement to position the file pointer at a particular record in a random access file. Get and Put can also do this.

Take it from here...

1.   Only the ShowOpen method of the CommonDialog control was used in this chapter. Experiment with the **ShowSave**, **ShowPrinter** and **ShowColor** methods.

2.   When using the CommonDialog control to get a file name you can state which folder or directory you wish the Open dialog box to display by setting one of the control's properties. Try this out.

3.   In program 10.2 the LOF function is used to find the size of an open file in bytes. Find the name of the function that is used to do the same for a file that is not open.

4.   The number that identifies a file has been coded as '#' followed by an integer number (e.g. #1) in the programs. Visual Basic provides an alternative way by using the **FreeFile** function. Find out how this works.

Questions on the Programs

Program 10.1

*1.   Delete the word **Line** from the line of code

`Line Input #1, DataToDisplay`

and run the program. How is the data displayed in the list box? What can you conclude about what Visual Basic stores in DataToDisplay when Line is omitted?

**2. Add a command button which calculates and displays the average age of the people stored in NamesAndAges.txt. You will have to read the name and age for each person into two separate variables and then process the age variable. (Note: write the data to the file with Write not Print.)

Program 10.2

**1. Add three option buttons to display in the list box details of those products:

- which cost more than a given price – the user enters the search price in a text box;
- whose number in stock exceeds a given value – the user enters this stock value in a text box;
- whose reorder level is the same as or greater than a given level – user selects level from combo box.

End of chapter exercises

**1. Write a program which displays the names of students on a selected GNVQ course by reading from a text file, as shown in figure 10.5. The text file, GNVQStudents.txt, has the names and course codes for 125 students and can be found on the web site. The names are unsorted in the file but should be displayed alphabetically in a list box. The course codes are:

HC-F	Foundation Health & Social Care	HC-N	Intermediate Health & Social Care
IT-N	Intermediate ICT	IT-V	Advanced ICT Year 1
IT-VU	Advanced ICT Year 2		

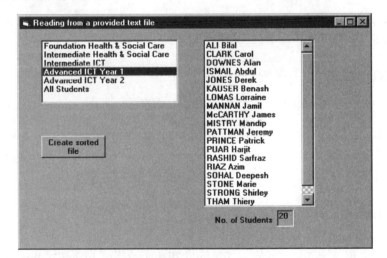

Figure 10.5: Exercise 1

When you have this working, add a command button to create a second file with the names in alphabetical order. Do this by copying the contents of the list box to the new file.

**2. Programmers working on new business applications sometimes have to convert text files into random access files. Write a program which does this for the file in exercise 1, GNVQStudents.txt. Include a list box to display the contents of the new file. If you allow strings of 20 and 5 for the student name and course code fields the total size of the random access file should be 3125 bytes (125 records x 25 bytes).

3. Write a program that generates a random number from 0 to 100 every second and stores it in a text file as shown in figure 10.6. (Search Help for the Rnd function to find out about producing random numbers.) Use the CommonDialog control for getting the file name. The contents of the file are displayed in figure 10.6 both in a text box and in a list box. To display the contents of a text file in a text box you should read the entire contents into a single String variable and simply display the contents of this variable at one go. If the variable is *FileContents* then you would write:

```
FileContents = Input(LOF(1), #1)
TxtRandomNumbers.Text = FileContents
```

This uses the Input function which is different from the Input statement you use when opening a file. This function returns a string of characters and its first parameter states how many to return. This parameter is the LOF (**L**ength **O**f **F**ile) function, which in turn returns the size of the file in bytes. To display the numbers on separate lines in the text box you must set its MultiLine property to True.

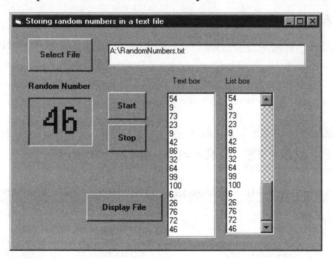

Figure 10.6: Exercise 3

4. Write a program to store the following details about second-hand cars for sale:

- registration number
- make (e.g. Ford)
- model
- year of manufacture
- price

Store the details in a random access file and display them in a list box. Do not allow duplicate registration numbers. Allow the user to search for the following (and display the results in the list box):

- a particular car using the registration number to search on – the user should select the registration number from a combo box;
- all cars of a given make and model entered by the user;
- all cars less than a given number of years old – allow the user to enter the number of years.

Part Two – Further Topics

Chapter 11 – Debugging and Error Handling

Introduction

A **bug** is some sort of error in the code which can prevent your program from running properly. When you write a substantial program always assume that it contains bugs. When you discover a bug you may or may not know how your code has caused it. **Debugging** is about finding these causes. Visual Basic has a variety of debugging tools, which are discussed in the first part of this chapter. The later part of the chapter looks at how your code might handle run-time errors, for which the normal process of debugging is not relevant.

It makes sense to know about Visual Basic's debugging tools reasonably soon after beginning the language. Handling run-time errors in code is a more advanced topic and probably only one you would consider applying to a program of 'A' level project standard.

Types of error

There are three types of error:

- Syntax error
- Run-time error
- Logic or semantic error

A **syntax error** is a mistake in the grammar of Visual Basic. Examples include misspelling keywords (e.g. Lop rather than Loop), forgetting an End If and so on. They are usually simple to fix since the compiler can pick them out for you. A **run-time error** causes the program to stop working. An example was shown in figure 3.3, where trying to store too large a number into an Integer variable caused overflow. A **logic** error results from a mistake in the logic of your code. Examples are using the wrong logical operators (AND/OR) in loop conditions or assigning an incorrect value to a variable. They are usually the hardest type of error to track down.

The topic of debugging in this chapter is not concerned with syntax or run-time errors, but with tracking down logic errors. The topic of error handling is concerned with run-time errors so that your program won't crash.

Visual Basic's Debug toolbar and menu

The Debug toolbar and menu are shown in figures 11.1 and 11.2. You'll be using most of these items in this chapter.

Stepping through code

The Debug toolbar and menu have three options for stepping through code – executing it one line at a time. The first two are the most useful:

Step Into Runs the current line of code. If this line calls a general procedure this procedure is entered.

Step Over Runs the current line, but if this is a general procedure call the procedure is executed without stepping through its code.

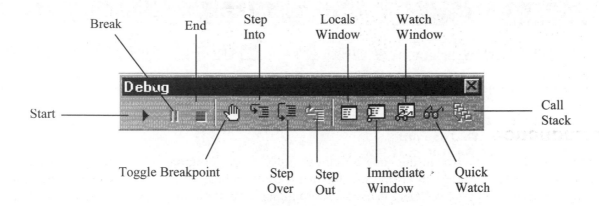

Figure 11.1: The Debug toolbar

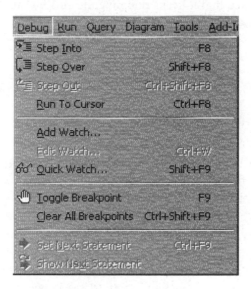

Figure 11.2: The Debug menu

Watches

A watch allows you to see the value of a variable or expression as the program runs. As you step through the code this value is displayed in the Watch window. You can only add a watch through the **Debug** menu, which brings up the Watch window.

PROGRAM 11.1   *Stepping through code and setting Watches*

Specification   Demonstrate how to step through code and set watches on variables

1.   Open a new project and type the following into the form's Load event procedure:

```
Private Sub Form_Load()
   Dim Number As Integer
   Dim Counter As Integer
   Form1.Show
   Number = 2
   For Counter = 1 To 10
      Form1.Print "2 to the power " & Counter & " is " & Number
      Number = Number * 2
   Next Counter
End Sub
```

2.   Run the program and confirm that it keeps doubling the current number as shown in figure 11.3.

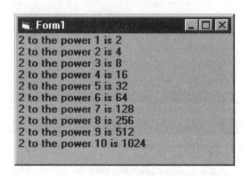

Figure 11.3: Output from program 11.1

3.   Select **Debug/Add Watch** from the menu and set a watch on the variable Number by typing it into the Expression box as shown in figure 11.4. Click **OK**. The Watch window will appear with details of the current state of the variable as shown in figure 11.5. Since the program hasn't yet started these indicate an <Out of Context> Value and an Empty (data) Type.

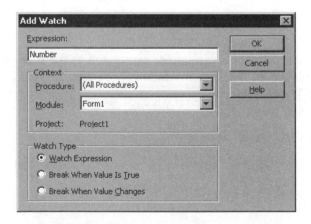

Figure 11.4: The Add Watch dialog box

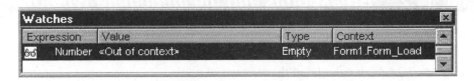

Figure 11.5: The Watch window

4. Select **View/Toolbars/Debug** to bring up the Debug toolbar. Click the **Step Into** icon and the first line of code will be highlighted in yellow. If the Watch window disappears click the Watch Window icon on the Debug toolbar. Number will have the value 0 in it because Visual Basic initialises Integers to 0 when they are declared.

5 Click the **Step Into** icon again (or simply press the F8 key) and the next line of executable code will be highlighted (Form1.Show). Two more clicks and Number has the value 2.

6. Keep stepping through the code and watch the value of Number increase as you go round the loop. Select **Run/End** or click **End** on the Debug toolbar to stop the program.

7. Select **Debug/Add Watch** and this time enter an expression. Type in **Number > 500**. We want to know when Number holds a value greater than 500. The Watch window should look like figure 11.6. (You may need to widen the Expression column to see the full expression.)

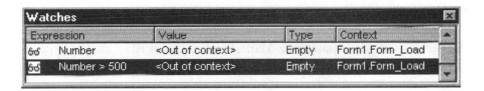

Figure 11.6

8. Run the first line of code (step 5 above) and the Value of the expression will be shown as False. Keep stepping through until it changes to True when Number holds 512. Stop the program as in step 6.

End of Program 11.1

Using Breakpoints

A **breakpoint** is a place in the code where the program will temporarily stop. You can set as many of these as you like. When the program stops at a breakpoint you can examine the contents of variables and expressions in the Watch window if you have set watches, or you can use the Immediate window.

The Immediate Window

The Immediate window lets you do a variety of things such as look at and change the contents of variables, carry out commands and so on.

PROGRAM 11.2 *Breakpoints and the Immediate Window*

Specification Demonstrate the use of breakpoints and the Immediate Window

We will use program 7.2 which calculated the average of a series of exam marks entered by the user. The code relevant to program 11.2 is shown below. When the cmdOK button is clicked the procedure ProcessOneNumber is called and sent three parameters, Mark, Total and NumberOfMarks. As Total and NumberOfMarks match onto reference parameters, these store new values when the procedure has been executed.

```
Private Sub cmdOK_Click()
   Dim Mark As Integer
   Mark = txtMark.Text
   lstMarks.AddItem Mark
   Call ProcessOneNumber(Mark, Total, NumberOfMarks)
   cmdShowMean.Enabled = True
   txtMark.Text = ""
   txtMark.SetFocus
End Sub


Public Sub ProcessOneNumber(ByVal ExamMark As Integer, _
             ByRef MarksTotal As Integer, ByRef CountOfMarks As Integer)
   MarksTotal = MarksTotal + ExamMark
   CountOfMarks = CountOfMarks + 1
End Sub
```

1. Change the declaration of the parameter MarksTotal so that it is a value parameter. The second line of the procedure declaration should now look as follows:

```
             ByVal MarksTotal As Integer, ByRef CountOfMarks As Integer)
```

This is now a serious error which you may remember demonstrating in the practical work immediately after program 7.2.

2. Set a breakpoint on the first line of code after ProcessOneNumber is called. There are two ways to do this.

- Position the cursor in the line of code and then click the Toggle Breakpoint button on the Debug toolbar, or select **Toggle Breakpoint** on the **Debug** menu or press the F9 key.
- Click in the grey vertical column to the left of the code where you want the breakpoint to come.

A brown circle will appear to the left of the line of code and the code itself will be highlighted as shown in figure 11.7

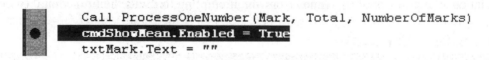

Figure 11.7: Setting a breakpoint

3.   Run the program. Enter a mark of 46 and click the OK button. The program will stop and the line of code with the breakpoint will be highlighted in yellow.

4.   Select **View/Immediate Window** or click the **Immediate Window** button on the Debug toolbar. In the window type in **?Total** and press Enter as shown in figure 11.8. Type in **?NumberOfMarks** and press Enter again. The Immediate window shows their values are 0 and 1 respectively. Total's value should be 46 so we know there is a logic error here.

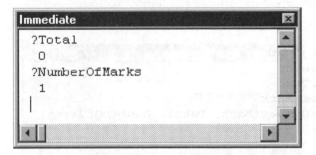

Figure 11.8: The Immediate Window

5.   Select **Run/End** to finish the program and change the MarksTotal parameter back to **ByRef**. Repeat step 4 and you will get the correct running total shown for Total in the Immediate window.

6.   Remove the breakpoint by clicking on the brown circle in the grey column or positioning the cursor in the breakpoint line and pressing the F9 key.

end of Program 11.2

The Debug Object

Visual Basic supplies the **Debug** object to help you debug a program directly from the code itself. It has no properties and only two methods. The **Print** method is the useful one. In program 11.2 we could have written

```
Debug.Print Total
```

after the call to ProcessOneNumber. The value of Total would be displayed in the Immediate Window.

Handling run-time errors

You have seen that debugging is about tracking down logic errors which will probably produce incorrect results but won't stop the program running. Handling errors at run time which *will* crash the program requires special code. Examples of run-time errors are attempting to divide a number by 0 (which can't be done) and trying to open a file which is already open. Let's go straight into a practical demonstration.

PROGRAM 11.3   *Simple Error Handling*

Specification	Ask the user to enter a number into a text box. Write an error routine to handle a number with one or more characters entered by mistake.

1. Open a new project and construct the form shown in figure 11.9. Name the text box **txtNumber** and the command button **cmdOK**.

2. In the Click event procedure for the command button enter the following code:

```
Private Sub cmdOK_Click()
   Dim Number As Integer
   Number = txtNumber.Text
End Sub
```

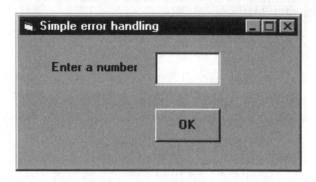

Figure 11.9: Program 11.3

3. Run the program and enter a character instead of a number in the text box. Click the OK button and you'll get Visual Basic's default error message window for this type of error, as shown in figure 11.10. Click **End**.

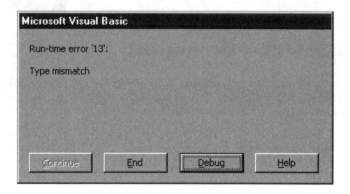

Figure 11.10: Run-time error

4. Now change the code so that it handles the type mismatch error, as shown next.

```
Private Sub cmdOK_Click()
   Dim Number As Integer
   On Error GoTo TypeMismatchHandler     'if there is an error pass control
                                         'to label TypeMismatchHandler

   Number = txtNumber.Text
   MsgBox ("You entered a number")
   Exit Sub                              'quit procedure
TypeMismatchHandler:                     'label to handle error
   MsgBox ("Numbers do not have characters")
End Sub
```

There are several key things in this error-handling routine:

- The code **On Error GoTo** is part of the Visual Basic syntax, and if an error happens control passes to the label which is listed next, **TypeMismatchHandler**. You can name the label anything you like. Note that this label has nothing to do with the Label control.

- The label itself must be followed by a colon (:). Visual Basic will not let you indent a label. If the user enters one or more characters in the text box, control passes to the code immediately after the label and outputs an appropriate message.

- If the user does enter an acceptable number this part of the procedure must not be executed. The **Exit Sub** takes care of this.

5. Run the program twice. First enter a small number and check that the first message appears. Then enter one or more characters to check that the error-handling routine works.

6. Run the program again but this time enter a number that is too big to store as an Integer – any value over 32767 (see figure 3.1). The error-handling code is executed but this time the error message about numbers not having characters is inappropriate. Without the error handling code you would get Visual Basic's default message for this type of run-time error (see figure 3.3).

end of Program 11.3

The Err Object

Step 6 in program 11.3 showed that you need to make your error-handling code appropriate for the type of error that triggers it off. Visual Basic supplies the **Err** object for this, with of course a number of properties and methods. The **Number** property is the only one you are likely to need.

PROGRAM 11.4   *More advanced error handling using the Err object*

Specification	Ask the user to enter numbers into two text boxes. The result of dividing the first number by the second should be displayed. Use the Err object to display different messages for different input errors.

1. Open a new project and design the form using figure 11.11. Name the text boxes **txtFirstNumber** and **txtSecondNumber**, the label for output **lblResult** and the command button **cmdDivide**.

2. Type the following code into the Click event of the command button:

```
Private Sub cmdDivide_Click()
   Dim FirstNumber As Integer
   Dim SecondNumber As Integer
   Dim Result As Single
   On Error GoTo ErrorHandler
   FirstNumber = txtFirstNumber.Text
   SecondNumber = txtSecondNumber.Text
   Result = FirstNumber / SecondNumber
   lblResult.Caption = Result
   Exit Sub
```

```
ErrorHandler:
    Select Case Err.Number
        Case 6
            lblResult.Caption = "One or both of the numbers is out of range"
        Case 11
            lblResult.Caption = "Cannot divide by zero"
        Case 13
            lblResult.Caption = "Numbers do not contain characters"
    End Select
End Sub
```

The Number property of the Err object is used to control the **Select Case**. Visual Basic would accept just **Err** instead of **Err.Number**. Three error codes are used in this example:

- Error code 6 is triggered if the user enters a value outside the Integer range of -32768 to +32767.
- Dividing a number by 0 is mathematically impossible and triggers error code 11.
- Look back at figure 11.10 and you'll see that number 13 is indeed the code for type mismatches.

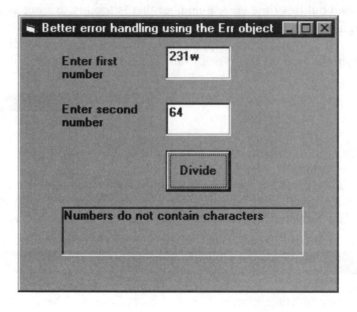

Figure 11.11: Program 11.4

3. Run the program and enter test data to cover the three types of error and to cover acceptable numbers.

end of Program 11.4

Summary of key concepts

- A **bug** is an error in a program. **Debugging** is the process of finding and removing errors.
- The **Debug toolbar** and **Debug menu** provide aids in tracking down **logic** errors.
- To **step** through code is to execute it line by line.

- A **watch** on a variable or expression allows you to see how its value changes during a program. The **Watch Window** displays watches.

- A **breakpoint** is a place in the code where the program temporarily stops.

- **Debug.Print** <variable identifier> in your code displays the contents of a given variable in the **Immediate Window**.

- The **Err** object's **Number** property can be used to trap different types of error.

Take it from here...

1. Investigate the **Quick Watch** button on the Debug toolbar.

2. The Immediate Window and Watch Window were covered in the chapter. Investigate a third window used in debugging, the **Locals Window**.

3. Figure 11.4 shows there are three Watch Types available when setting a watch. Only the first of these was covered in the chapter. Explore the other two.

4. Only the **Step Into** option of stepping through a program was used in the chapter. Use any program you have written with one or more general procedures and try out **Step Over**.

5. One of the things you can do in the Immediate window is change the contents of variables. Using any suitable program you have written, set an appropriate breakpoint, run the program, and in the Immediate window confirm the contents of one of your program's variables. Then assign a new value to the variable in the Immediate window (e.g. Number = 75) and press Enter. Confirm that the variable holds this new value.

6. You met several error codes belonging to the Err object. Search Help for Trappable Errors and find out more about the numbering of errors.

7. Sometimes you may wish to tell Visual Basic where to begin execution after an error has been dealt with. Investigate the **Resume** statement which handles this.

Questions on the Programs

Program 11.4

*1. Error code 13 is used in this program to trap any characters in the number but it will also trap the case where the user forgets to enter a number. Extend the code to display a different message for this situation.

Chapter 12 – Sending Output to the Printer

Printing to a form

In earlier programs we often used the Print method of a form to display output. We did this as a quick method of confirming that our code was doing what it was supposed to do. Most of these programs, 3.1 to 3.3 for example, simply printed the result of something at the left margin of the form. Program 5.2, however, used one or two other ways to position the printed output on a form. Whatever the display looks like, in real applications it is unlikely that you will wish to print much data on a form.

Printing to a file

In Chapter 10 you learned how to store data in a text file. Sometimes this might be more appropriate than sending output to the printer. For example if a business wishes to keep a permanent record of its weekly sales these would be stored on file and perhaps printed out when required from Notepad. The disadvantage of using a text file over printing a report directly is that you can do little to format it. Of course you *could* open it in Word or another word processing package and format it there.

The code below stores details of three employees in a text file. It uses Print rather than Write because we don't want quotation marks around the data in the file. It also uses the Tab function to position the data into columns. Tab takes one argument – the column number to move to before the next item is printed. Figure 12.1 shows the contents of the file. The 'J' in John is in column 1 and the 'A' in Andrews in column 12.

```
Filename = App.Path & "\Staff.txt"
Open Filename For Output As #1
Print #1, "List of employees"
Print #1,                                    'to produce a blank line
Print #1, "John"; Tab(12); "Andrews"; Tab(25); "Senior programmer"
Print #1, "Sarah"; Tab(12); "Matthews"; Tab(25); "Programmer"
Print #1, "Jane"; Tab(12); "Lewes"; Tab(25); "Project manager"
Close #1
```

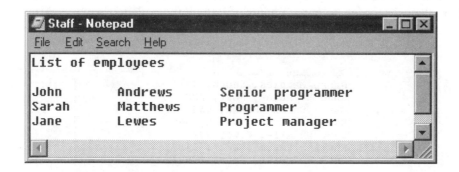

Figure 12.1: Contents of the text file

Printing to a printer

To send output to a printer you need to use the Printer object. Like all objects it has a range of properties and methods. The most important ones are:

Properties

Orientation   The page orientation. Use the constants **vbPRORPortrait** and **vbPRORLandscape**.

Page   Visual Basic keeps track of how many pages have been printed.

Methods

EndDoc   Terminates a print operation sent to the Printer object. For safety call this method at the end of a print operation.

Font   FontSize, FontBold, FontUnderline, FontItalic are the important varieties. Set FontSize to a number and the others to True or False (e.g. Printer.FontSize = 15).

NewPage   Forces output to a new page, Increments the Page property by 1.

Print   Prints the listed item(s) after this method call and moves the printing position to the next line. To get a blank line call the method alone.

PROGRAM 12.1   *Printing reports on sales staff*

Specification   Use an existing text file that holds, for each salesperson, their name, the region they work in and the annual value of their sales. Print this data on the form and to the printer. Two printed reports should be made. One should output the details by salesperson and the other should group these details by region.

1. Download the file **Sales.txt** from the web site. Its contents are shown in figure 12.2. (If you cannot download it you can create the file in Notepad in a few minutes). The numbers refer to the value of sales in thousands of pounds. Thus the first value represents £250,000.

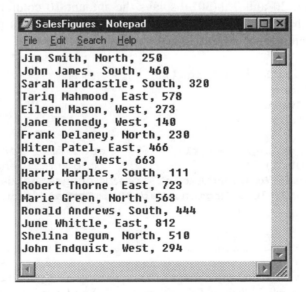

Figure 12.2: Contents of Sales.txt

2. Open a new project and place three command buttons on it as shown in figure 12.3. Name them **cmdPrintToForm, cmdReportBySalesperson** and **cmdReportByRegion** and set their captions as in the figure. Set the form's Font to an even spaced font – **Courier New 8 point bold**.

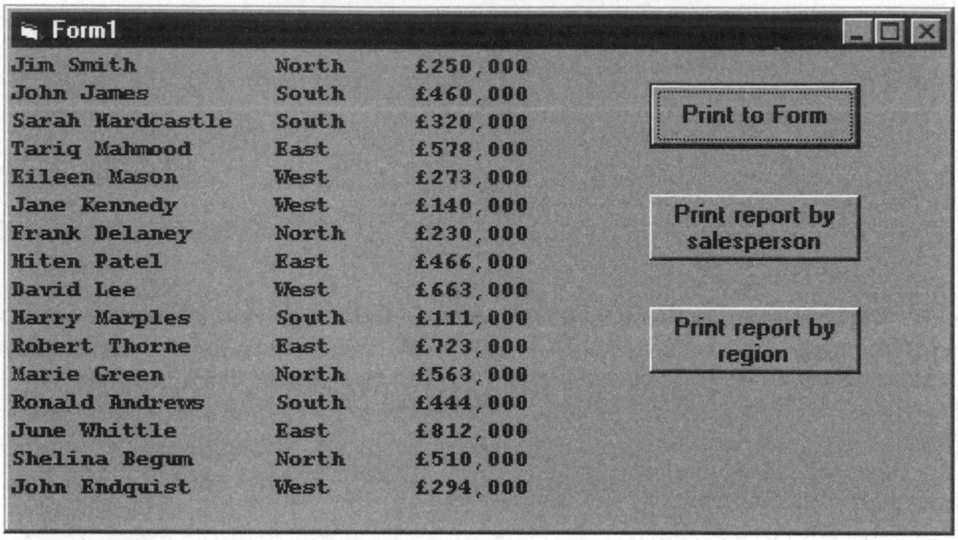

Figure 12.3: Program 12.1 when the Print to Form button has been clicked

3. Declare a global variable to hold the file name and assign it a value in the form's Load event:

```
    Dim Filename As String


Private Sub Form_Load()
    Filename = App.Path & "\Sales.txt"
End Sub
```

4. Figure 12.3 shows the contents of the file printed on the form. Tab(20) in the code below displays the sales region in column 20 and Tab(30) displays the amount 10 columns further on from the first character of the region. Note that the sales value stored in the file is converted to thousands and formatted to whole pounds.

```
Private Sub cmdPrintToForm_Click()
    Dim Name As String
    Dim Region As String
    Dim Amount As Long
    Form1.Show
    Open Filename For Input As #1          'open file for reading
    Do While Not EOF(1)                    'loop until end of file reached
        Input #1, Name, Region, Amount 'read 3 items of data for one person
        Print Name; Tab(20); Region; Tab(30); Format(Amount * 1000, "£#,##0")
    Loop
    Close #1                               'close file
End Sub
```

5. Run the program and check that your output looks like that in figure 12.3. Then experiment to see how the Tab function works. Change Tab(20) to Tab(14) and run it again. The data for two people, Sarah Hardcastle and Ronald Andrews, is now displayed over two lines, and in six cases the region is displayed after the name with no space between the two items. The reason for the two-line display is because these names are 14 or more characters long and Tab(14) needs to display the sales region in column 14. If the column is "occupied" like this then printing resumes on the next line, in column 14 in this example. Change the 14 back to 20 when you've tried this out.

6. The report we want to produce by clicking the *Print report by salesperson* button is shown in figure 12.4. The code is essentially the same as for printing to the form except that the Print method of the Printer object is used. The point made in step 5 about setting the Tab positions in unoccupied spaces applies equally to the Printer object.

```
Private Sub cmdReportBySalesperson_Click()
  Dim Name As String
  Dim Region As String
  Dim Amount As Long
  Printer.Print "Report on annual sales made by sales staff"
  Printer.Print                          'produce blank line on report
  Printer.Print "Salesperson"; Tab(20); "Region"; Tab(30); _
                                "Value of sales"

  Printer.Print
  Open Filename For Input As #1
  Do While Not EOF(1)
    Input #1, Name, Region, Amount
    Printer.Print Name; Tab(20); Region; Tab(30); _
                      Format(Amount * 1000, "£#,##0")
  Loop
  Close #1
  Printer.EndDoc                         'safely terminate printing
End Sub
```

```
Report on annual sales made by sales staff

Salesperson          Region      Value of sales

Jim Smith            North       £250,000
John James           South       £460,000
Sarah Hardcastle     South       £320,000
Tariq Mahmood        East        £578,000
Eileen Mason         West        £273,000
Jane Kennedy         West        £140,000
Frank Delaney        North       £230,000
Hiten Patel          East        £466,000
David Lee            West        £663,000
Harry Marples        South       £111,000
Robert Thorne        East        £723,000
Marie Green          North       £563,000
Ronald Andrews       South       £444,000
June Whittle         East        £812,000
Shelina Begum        North       £510,000
John Endquist        West        £294,000
```

Figure 12.4: Report on sales by salesperson

7. Run the program and check that the report is printed correctly.

8. Figure 12.5 shows the report by region. The sales region names make up what is called a **group header**. To process one sales region each line in the file must be read to see if its sales region matches the one being processed. To get the file pointer back to the start of the file ready for the next sales region you have to close the file and open it again. This explains why the Open and Close statements are *inside* the For…Next loop. If we had been using a random access file we would only need to open and close it once, and reposition the file pointer with Seek or Get. The other thing to note here is the **Space** function. The group header name is printed 3 spaces from the left; we could also have written Tab(3).

```vb
Private Sub cmdReportByRegion_Click()
   Dim Name As String
   Dim Region As String
   Dim Amount As Long
   Dim Index As Integer
   Dim RegionGroup As String
   Dim NumUnderscores As Integer
   Printer.FontSize = 13               'larger point size and
   Printer.FontBold = True             'bold too for report header
   Printer.Print "Report on annual sales made by sales staff"
   Printer.FontSize = 11               'back to normal for rest of report
   Printer.FontBold = False
   For NumUnderscores = 1 To 60        'put line across most of page
      Printer.Print "_";
   Next NumUnderscores
   Printer.Print
   Printer.Print
   For Index = 1 To 4                  'loop 4 times - once per sales region
      Select Case Index
        Case 1
           RegionGroup = "East"
        Case 2
           RegionGroup = "North"
        Case 3
           RegionGroup = "South"
        Case 4
           RegionGroup = "West"
      End Select
      Printer.Print Space(3); RegionGroup 'print region 3 columns from left
      Open Filename For Input As #1
      Do While Not EOF(1)                 'go through whole file
        Input #1, Name, Region, Amount
        If Region = RegionGroup Then      'is region the required one?
           Printer.Print Tab(10); Name; Tab(40); _
                              Format(Amount * 1000, "£#,##0")
        End If
      Loop
      Printer.Print
      Close #1
   Next Index
   Printer.EndDoc
End Sub
```

```
Report on annual sales made by sales staff
_____

    East
            Tariq Mahmood                £578,000
            Hiten Patel                  £466,000
            Robert Thorne                £723,000
            June Whittle                 £812,000

    North
            Jim Smith                    £250,000
            Frank Delaney                £230,000
            Marie Green                  £563,000
            Shelina Begum                £510,000

    South
            John James                   £460,000
            Sarah Hardcastle             £320,000
            Harry Marples                £111,000
            Ronald Andrews               £444,000

    West
            Eileen Mason                 £273,000
            Jane Kennedy                 £140,000
            David Lee                    £663,000
            John Endquist                £294,000
```

Figure 12.5: Report on sales by region

9. Run the program and check that the report is printed correctly.

end of Program 12.1

Summary of key concepts

- Both a form and the printer are objects, and they share the same Print method for displaying output.

- Use the **Tab** and **Space** functions to position output.

Questions on Program 12.1

*1. When printing the file to the form you could use the Visual Basic constant **vbTab** instead of the Tab function as follows:

```
Print Name & vbTab & Region & vbTab & Format(Amount * 1000, "£#,##0")
```

Try this out. It seems to work except for Sarah Hardcastle. What change could you make to the declaration of the local variable to hold the salespersons' names to keep the region and sales value data in columns?

*2. The role of the EndDoc method will not have been clear from the program as it stands. Comment out Printer.EndDoc in cmdReportBySalesperson, run the program and then click the button to print the report by salesperson. Nothing is printed. Now click to produce the other report. Examine what comes out of the printer. Now remove the commenting and then comment out the same line in cmdReportByRegion, run the program and click both buttons (report by salesperson first). What is printed? Close the program and the other report will be printed. What can you conclude about the way EndDoc works from all this?

**3. Extend the report by region to include:

- A group footer (i.e. at the end of each sales region) to show the total value of the sales for that region.
- Use the Page property and NewPage method of the Printer object to print the details of each region on a separate page and to print the page number on each page. The report header should now be a page header so that it is repeated on each page. You may wish to make its font smaller.

***4. Extend the report by salesperson to include:

- The total value of all sales.
- The average value of all sales.
- A 4th column indicating how much the salesperson's value of sales exceeds or is below the average, expressed as a percentage.

End of chapter exercises

*1. Write a program to accept student names and their exam mark (0-100) from the user and store these in an array. Send a report to the printer showing the names of those who passed the exam. Assume a mark of 50 or more is a pass.

2. Use the random access file **GardenCentreProducts.dat from the web site. It was produced by running program 10.2 and contains details of 16 products. (If you completed this program you may wish to use your own file.) You will need to look at step 3 in program 10.2 to see how the record for one product is declared. Produce the following reports:

(a) The report shown in figure 12.6 (N.B. this only shows details of the first two products).
(b) A report displaying the same information as figure 12.6 but grouped according to the price of the products. Use 3 groups – under £10.00, £10.00 to under £50.00 and £50.00 and over.

```
Report on Garden Centre stock

Product ID  Description          Price      Qty in stock    Stock value

421         garden shears        £12.65         142         £1,796.30
783         wheelbarrow          £34.20          64         £2,188.80
............
                                          Total stock value £24,445.01
```

Figure 12.6: The report for exercise 2(a)

***3.** You may have done exercise 1 at the end of Chapter 10 and used the text file **GNVQStudents.txt**, which stores the name and course code for 125 GNVQ students. Use a similar file, **GNVQStudents2.txt** that stores the same data plus the gender (M or F) of each student. The file can be downloaded from the web site.

(a) Produce a printed report from this file that is grouped on the course as shown in figure 12.7.

(b) Produce a report which groups on gender *within* each course group. Separate totals of the number of male and of female students on each course should be shown, as well as the total number of students on each course. The total number of male and of female students and the total number of students on all courses should be displayed at the end of the report. Look back at exercise 1 in Chapter 10 to see what the course codes mean.

```
                                            Page 1
               Report on GNVQ students

        Foundation Health & Social Care

            Shabana Masih
            Neeta King

            ............

            No. students   19
        _____


        Intermediate Health & Social Care

            Husna Begum
            Edith Teacher

            ............

            No. students   35
        _____


            ..............


        _____

        Total no. students   125
```

Figure 12.7. Report for exercise 3(a)

Chapter 13 – Menus

Introduction

The graphical interfaces you have designed so far have covered many of the typical features of a Windows environment, but not menus. Menus only have one event, the Click event, and when a user clicks the menu its code is run in the usual way. To create the menus themselves, though, requires no code. In this chapter we are concerned only with building menus, not with what happens when a menu item is selected.

Types of menu

Visual Basic supports two types of menu. The **drop-down** menu is the commonest Windows menu. Figure 13.1 shows the drop-down menu when you select **File** in the Visual Basic programming environment. A **pop-up** menu often appears when you right-click the mouse over an appropriate part of the screen. Figure 13.2 shows the pop-up menu which appears when you click on a Visual Basic form in design view.

Figure 13.2 : An example pop-up menu

Figure 13.1: An example drop-down menu

Features of a menu

Figure 13.1 illustrates the following features:

- A menu item can have one underlined letter, which acts as a hot key. As an alternative to being clicked the item can be selected by pressing the Alt and hot keys together.
- A menu item may have an ellipsis (…) meaning that a dialog box will appear when it is selected.
- A menu item can be greyed out, meaning that it is currently not available.
- Menu items can be grouped using separators – horizontal lines. In figure 13.1 there are 6 separators.

The one feature that figure 13.1 does not illustrate is a nested or submenu. This is where you click a menu item and another menu appears. The first menu item has a small triangle to inform you that it leads to a nested menu.

PROGRAM 13.1   *A drop-down menu*

Specification   Create a drop-down menu containing a selection of its features.

Figure 13.3 shows the menu we're going to create. It is taken from Microsoft Photo Editor. We will build the main menu bar of 7 items and then only those drop-down items associated with the View item.

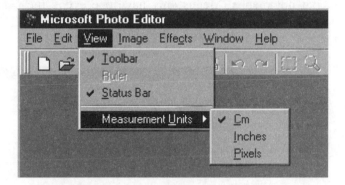

Figure 13.3: The drop-down menu for program 13.1

1.   Open a new project. Select **Tools/Menu Editor** to bring up the **Menu Editor** dialog box. This is where you set the properties of the various menu items.

2.   For the first menu item, **File**, set its Caption property to **&File** and its Name to **mnuFile** (as shown in figure 13.4). The ampersand character (&) means that the next letter acts as a hot key.

3.   Press Enter and &File will appear in the bottom part of the dialog box. Repeat step 2 for the other six main menu items. Note that they all have an ampersand before their first letter except Effects, whose Caption should be **Effe&cts**. Name them **mnuEdit, mnuView** etc. If you make a mistake use the buttons in the middle part of the dialog box to correct it.

Figure 13.4: The Menu Editor after the main File menu has been added

4. Now for the nested menus. As we are only doing these for View, select **&Image** in the bottom of the dialog box and then click **Insert** to get a blank entry after View.

5. Enter **&Toolbar** for the Caption and **mnuToolbar** for the Name. Figure 13.3 shows this menu item as checked (the tick to its left), so click in the **Checked** box. Then click the right-pointing arrow button to make Toolbar nested within View. The ellipsis (…) shows the nesting as you can see in figure 13.5.

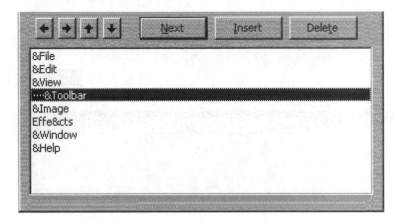

Figure 13.5: The nested Toolbar menu

6. Repeat step 4 and then enter **&Ruler** and **mnuRuler** for the properties of the next submenu. Figure 13.3 shows this is disabled so uncheck the Enabled property. Click the right-pointing arrow to nest it.

7. Now add the other two submenus in figure 13.3 (Status Bar and Measurement Units). The bottom part of the Menu Editor should now look like that in figure 13.6.

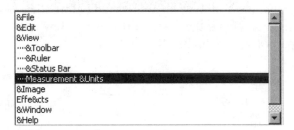

Figure 13.6: The completed first level of nesting

8. Figure 13.3 shows that the submenu Measurement Units in turn has three submenu items. Insert these after Measurement &Units and click the right arrow twice for each to nest it to the correct level.

9. Figure 13.3 shows that the Status Bar and Measurement Units have a separator. Insert an item between the two by selecting Measurement &Unit and clicking **Insert**. This item will have an ellipsis. In the Caption property enter a single dash (-). Name it **mnuSeparator1**. There are no more separators in this example menu but if you had more than one you would have to give them different names. Click **OK** in the Menu Editor to finish with it.

10. We'll add code to one of the menu items just as a check that its Click event gets fired off. In Design view click **View/Measurement Units/Cm** and you'll get the code template for mnuCm's Click event. Just type in

```
Private Sub mnuCm_Click()
   MsgBox ("You chose to measure in centimetres")
End Sub
```

11. Run the program. Confirm that you can get to the **View** submenus by clicking the main item and by pressing the **Alt** and **V** keys together. Click the **Cm** submenu to check that the message box appears.

end of Program 13.1

PROGRAM 13.2   *A pop-up menu*

Specification   Create a pop-up menu.

Figure 13.7 shows the program. Clicking the File button produces a small pop-up menu with two items. To produce a pop-up menu you must first create a drop-down one using the Menu editor, and then add a line of code to the event that will cause the pop-up menu to appear.

1. Open a new project. Select **Tools/Menu Editor** and create an ordinary menu with **File** and **Exit**. Name them **mnuFile** and **mnuExit**. Nest two submenus inside File – **Open** and **Save**. Name these as you please.

2. Put a command button on the form. Name it **cmdFile** and set its caption to **File**.

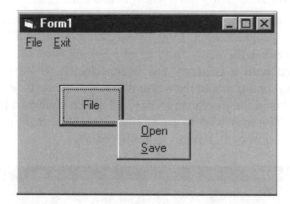

Figure 13.7: The pop-up menu in program 13.2

3. In the command button's Click event procedure type in

```
Private Sub cmdFile_Click()
   PopupMenu mnuFile
End Sub
```

This uses the PopupMenu method (or procedure) and you pass it the name of the menu to pop up.

4. Run the program and click on the button. Note that contents of the pop-up menu are also produced by clicking **File** in the main menu.

end of Program 13.2

Summary of key concepts

- Visual Basic supports two types of menu – **drop-down** and **pop-up**.

- Drop-down menus are permanently displayed and have only one event – the Click event. Pop-up menus appear only in response to an event somewhere else.

Questions on the Programs

Program 13.1

**1. One of the properties shown in the Menu Editor (figure 13.4) is Index. This allows you to create two or more menu items as a control array. Change the three submenu items Cm, Inches and Pixels so that they form a control array named mnuUnits. Write code for the control array's Click event so that a different message is displayed when each is selected at run time.

Program 13.2

*1. Having the **File** menu available on the main menu and as a pop-up menu doesn't seem like very good design. Make one small change to the program so that it appears only as a pop-up.

End of chapter exercises

**1. Write a program to handle the buying and selling of foreign currencies in exchange for pounds. Figure 13.8 shows the program when Euro is selected from a menu of currencies. The Transaction menu has a nested menu with items Buying and Selling (not shown in figure 13.8). This menu should not be enabled until a currency has been selected. If buying, then an amount of foreign currency is entered in *Amount in* and the amount to pay is in £s. If selling the amount entered is in £s and the amount to pay is in the foreign currency. Make up your own buying and selling rates (or find out the current rates). You may wish to create one or both the main menus as a control array (see the question on program 13.1 above), but this is not necessary.

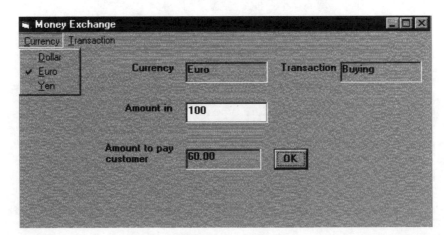

Figure 13.8:
Exercise 1

Chapter 14 – Graphics

Graphical controls and methods

The standard toolbox has four **graphical controls** – **Line**, **Shape**, **PictureBox** and **Image**. In this chapter we'll use only the Shape control. Like all controls, graphical controls have properties and methods.

Graphical methods allow you to draw directly on the form at run time. Visual Basic supplies **Circle**, **Line**, **Cls**, **Pset** and **Point**. The first three of these are covered in this chapter.

Form measurement

If you look at the ScaleMode property of any form you've used you'll see its default value is 1 – Twip. There are 567 twips in one centimetre and so most of the forms you have designed are many thousands of twips in height and length. A form's **Height** and **Length** properties hold the exact values.

Visual Basic lets you use several other units of measurement – inches, centimetres and so on – by setting the **ScaleMode** property. One of these options is to use your own measurement and this approach is used in two of the three programs in this chapter. You set the **ScaleHeight** and **ScaleWidth** properties to the number of units required. It means, for example, that you can set the vertical and horizontal sizes of the form to be 100 units (or whatever number you choose). So if you wish to print something starting in the centre of the form you need to go to position 50 across and position 50 down.

Form co-ordinates

You can't get far in graphics without understanding the form's co-ordinate system. Figure 14.1 shows the basic arrangement assuming you have set the form's ScaleHeight and ScaleWidth values to 100. Note that the title bar is not part of the co-ordinate system.

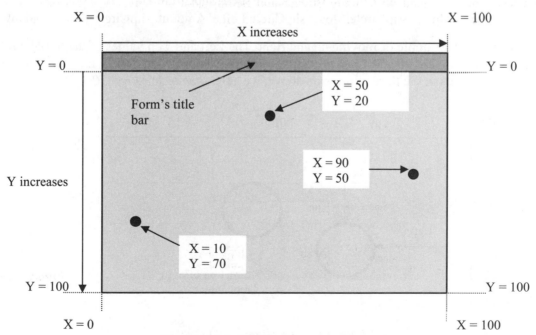

Figure 14.1: The form's co-ordinates

The most important thing to learn from figure 14.1 is that **X values increase from left to right and Y values increase from top to bottom**. Two more very useful form properties, not available at design time, are **CurrentX** and **CurrentY**. These return or set the horizontal (X) or vertical (Y) co-ordinates for the next printing or drawing method.

The Move method

Use the Move method to move any control on a form. Its syntax is

NameOfObject.Move left, top, width, height

where *left* is the X co-ordinate of the left edge of the object and *top* is the Y co-ordinate of the top edge of the object. *Width* and *height* are the new width and height you want the moved object to have. If you don't wish to alter the object's size leave these two parameters out. The only parameter you *have* to supply is *left*. Figure 14.2 summarises what to do to move vertically or horizontally. *Amount* refers to the number of units of movement required.

Movement	Reset **left** parameter	Reset **top** parameter	No. parameters needed
Up		Subtract Amount	2
Down		Add Amount	2
Left	Subtract Amount		1
Right	Add Amount		1

Figure 14.2: Summary of how to use Move's parameters

Amount must be added or subtracted to the **Left** and **Top** properties of the object. Left stores the distance between the left edge of an object and the left edge of its container, and Top stores the distance between the top edge of an object and the top edge of its container. The following examples show how to move a circle named shpCircle:

- Move it right   shpCircle.Move shpCircle.Left + Amount
- Move it up   shpCircle.Move shpCircle.Left, shpCircle.Top – Amount
- Move it up *and* right shpCircle.Move shpCircle.Left + Amount, shpCircle.Top - Amount

Figure 14.3 shows an example of moving up and right. The Left and Top values of the initial circle are 30 and of the moved circle are 50 and 15. It needs to be moved 20 units right and 15 units up. So substituting values for the variables in the third expression above, we have *shpCircle.Move 30 + 20, 30 - 15*.

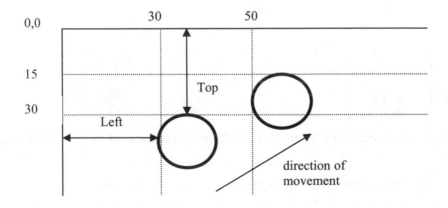

Figure 14.3: An example of movement

PROGRAM 14.1 *Moving a Shape control by button clicks*

Specification Allow the user to move a small circle a given amount by clicking command buttons. The circle should move directly up, down, left or right.

Figure 14.4 shows the program. The left diagram shows the circle in the middle of the screen when the program first runs, and the right diagram shows its position after the Up and Right buttons have been clicked a few times.

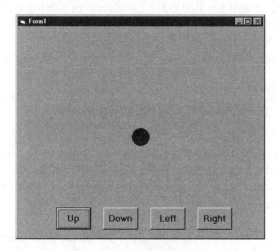
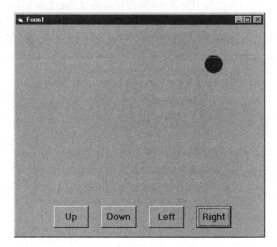

Figure 14.4: Program 14.1

1. Open a new project, place a Shape control anywhere on the form and name it **shpCircle**. By default this is a rectangle but change it to a circle by setting its Shape property to **3 – Circle**. Set its FillColor property to a colour of your choice.

2. Replace the default unit of measurement (twip) and divide the form into 100 vertical and horizontal units by setting its ScaleHeight and ScaleWidth properties to **100**. Notice that Visual Basic automatically changes the ScaleMode property to 0 – User (from 1 – Twip). Note also that if you resize the form *after* setting these property values, Visual Basic recalculates them.

3. Place the four command buttons, set their captions as shown in figure 14.4 and name them **cmdUp**, **cmdDown**, **cmdLeft** and **cmdRight**.

4. Declare a global constant to hold the number of units the circle will move when one of the command buttons is clicked. If we set this to 10 then the circle can be in one of ScaleWidth/10 = 10 horizontal positions. It also has the same number of possible vertical positions. So declare:

```
Const Amount = 10
```

5. To position the circle in the centre of the form when the program runs set its Left and Top properties in the form's Load event.

```
Private Sub Form_Load()
    shpCircle.Left = (Form1.ScaleWidth / 2) - (shpCircle.Width / 2)
    shpCircle.Top = (Form1.ScaleHeight / 2) - (shpCircle.Width / 2)
End Sub     'NB could replace (Form1.ScaleWidth / 2) by value 50 above
```

6. Using figure 14.2 and the examples below it, we can code the Click events of the four command buttons as:

```
Private Sub cmdUp_Click()
   shpCircle.Move shpCircle.Left, shpCircle.Top - Amount '2 parameters
End Sub                                                  'needed to move up

Private Sub cmdDown_Click()
   shpCircle.Move shpCircle.Left, shpCircle.Top + Amount '2 parameters
End Sub                                                  'needed to move down

Private Sub cmdLeft_Click()
   shpCircle.Move shpCircle.Left - Amount               '1 parameter needed
End Sub                                                  'to move left

Private Sub cmdRight_Click()
   shpCircle.Move shpCircle.Left + Amount               '1 parameter needed
End Sub                                                  'to move right
```

7. Run the program. Click the Up button 5 times and the circle should reach the top edge of the form. This is because the ScaleHeight property of the form was set to 100 (in step 2), and since the circle's initial position is in the centre of the form it has 50 units to move to reach the top edge (or any other edge). Since Amount is 10 it takes 50/10 = 5 clicks to get there.

end of Program 14.1

Drawing circles

Program 14.1 used a Shape control to display a circle. Instead you can get Visual Basic to draw one using the form's **Circle** graphical method at run time. The basic syntax is

   Circle (x, y), radius

where x and y are the X and Y co-ordinates of the centre of the circle and *radius* is its radius. Thus

```
Circle (50, 50), 10
```

would draw a circle 10 units in radius in the centre of the form (assuming the ScaleHeight and ScaleWidth properties had been set to 100).

PROGRAM 14.2   *Animate a circle moving across the screen*

Specification   Use the Circle method to make a circle move across the screen.

The program is shown in figure 14.5. The circle has moved from the top left towards the opposite corner. So that you can see the direction of movement, successive positions of the circle are shown, but it is easy to remove these so that at any one time only the current circle is shown. We'll use a Timer control to determine when the circle should be redrawn and the form's Paint event to carry out the redrawing.

1.   Open a new project and resize the form so that it is a square.

2. Drop a Timer and a command button on the form. Leave the default name of the Timer, set its Enabled property to **False** and its Interval property to **100**. This value will set the Timer off every 100 milliseconds (one-tenth of a second). Name the button **cmdStart** and set its caption to **Start**.

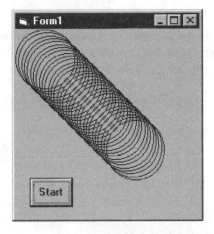

Figure 14.5: Program 14.2

3. Declare two global variables, to hold the X and Y co-ordinates of the centre of the circle, and initialise them to 500 when the program first runs. As we haven't set the form's ScaleHeight and ScaleWidth properties (like we did in program 4.1), our unit of measurement is the default twip. Since our circle will have a radius of 500 twips, setting these values to 500 will draw the first circle against the top left corner of the form. We also need a constant declaration to hold how much to add to the circle's co-ordinates before each redrawing.

```
Dim XCent As Integer
Dim YCent As Integer
Const Amount = 50

Private Sub Form_Load()
   XCent = 500
   YCent = 500
End Sub
```

4. Switch the timer on when the button is clicked by changing its Enabled property to **True**:

```
Private Sub cmdStart_Click()
   Timer1.Enabled = True
End Sub
```

5. Use the form's Paint event to draw the circle using the Circle method:

```
Private Sub Form_Paint()
   Circle (Xcent, YCent), 500
End Sub
```

6. Each time the timer executes we need to alter the X and Y co-ordinates of the centre of the circle and to redraw it by calling the Paint event:

```
Private Sub Timer1_Timer()
    XCent = Xcent + Amount
    YCent = Ycent + Amount
    Form_Paint
End Sub
```

7. Run the program and you should get the pattern shown in figure 14.5. To get rid of the trail effect of the previous circle positions, remove the current circle from the form by calling the form's **Cls** (clear screen) method as the first thing inside the Timer event:

```
Cls
```

end of Program 14.2

Drawing lines

To draw a line use the form's **Line** method. The basic syntax is:

Line (x1, y2) – (x2, y2)

where x1 and y2 are the X and Y co-ordinates of the line's starting point and x2 and y2 the co-ordinates of its finishing point. The x1 and y2 parameters are optional; if you omit them the line begins at the position of the form's CurrentX and CurrentY values.

1. Open a new project and set the form's ScaleHeight and ScaleWidth properties to **100**.

2. In the form's Load event type in the following, run it and you'll get the lines in figure 14.6.

```
Form1.Show
Line (0,0) - (70, 30)
Line (70, 30) - (20, 90)
```

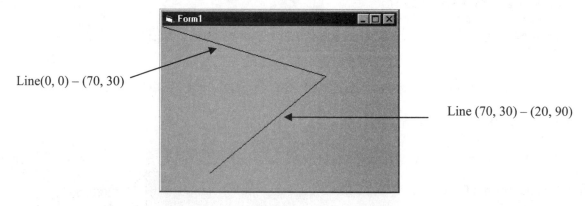

Figure 14.6: Using the Line method

The second Line statement could have been coded in two other ways:

```
Line Step (0, 0) - (20, 90)      'using the Step parameter
Line - (20, 90)                  'omitting the first set of co-ordinates
```

Step specifies that the starting or finishing point co-ordinates are relative to the values of CurrentX and CurrentY. Since these values are 70 and 30 after the first line has been drawn, Step (0, 0) means that the next line should start from this point.

3. Replace the two lines of code with the following and run the program. Figure 14.7 shows the result.

```
Line (50, 0)-(50, 100)
Line (0, 50)-(100, 50)
```

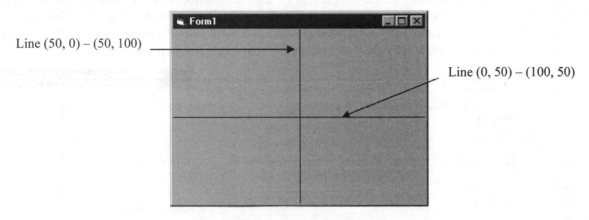

Figure 14.7: Using the Line method

4. Replace the two lines of code with the line below, which includes an optional parameter **B** (standing for **B**ox). Figure 14.8 shows the result. It draws a box shape with the two sets of co-ordinates specifying the opposite corners.

```
Line (10, 50)-(80, 60), , B
```

Note that the missing parameter, indicated by the pair of commas, is an optional one specifying the RGB colour to draw the line.

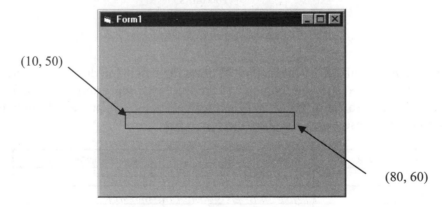

Figure 14.8: Drawing a box

5. Now simply add an **F** immediately after the 'B' in the previous Line example. This states that the box should be filled with the same colour used to draw it. In this case you'll get a rectangle coloured black.

Drawing bar charts

One useful application of the Line method is for drawing bar charts. Program 14.3 takes you through a detailed example, but first you need to understand the theory behind this technique. Assuming the ScaleHeight and ScaleWidth values of the form are 100, the first thing to do is work out the X and Y scales to use. If you had 8 values to represent by vertical bars you might decide to make the width of each bar 10 units. You'd need 80 units for the bars leaving 10 units either side. For the Y axis scale you must find the highest value to be represented by a bar and use this to work out the vertical scale. For example if the highest value is 400 you could decide on a scale of 1 unit for a value of 5. The longest bar would then be 400/5 = 80 units. These calculations are shown in figure 14.8. Note that 10 units in the vertical is smaller in length than 10 units in the horizontal because the form is rectangular. Only if the form was square would they be the same length. The numbering of lines 1 to 3 is taken up shortly.

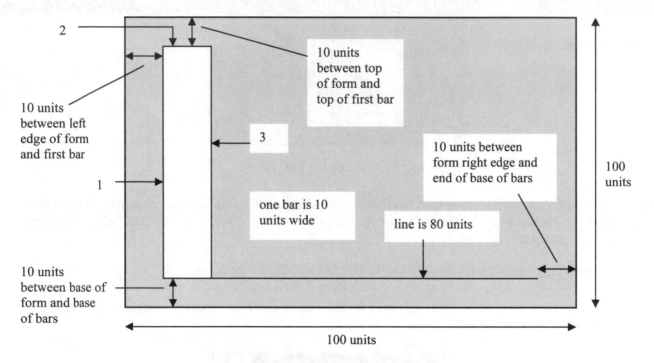

Figure 14.9: Calculating dimensions for a bar chart

There are several ways of using the Line method to draw the bars. One decision is whether to draw each line separately or use the 'box' method. Program 14.3 draws each separately. It is useful to draw up some rules about what you have to do to the X and Y co-ordinates as you proceed to drawing the next line. Figure 14.10 summarises these.

Line goes....	X co-ordinate	Y co-ordinate
Up		decreases
Down		increases
Left	decreases	
Right	increases	

Figure 14.10: Summary of using the X and Y co-ordinates when drawing lines

Assuming the base line for the bars is already drawn, to draw the bar in figure 14.9 requires the three lines numbered 1 to 3. Figure 14.10 shows that for line 1, X should not change but Y should decrease. If we set CurrentX and CurrentY to the starting point of line 1, i.e. (10, 90), then the finishing point would be (CurrentX, CurrentY – Height of Bar). If the height of the bar has been calculated and stored in BarHeight then the code is:

```
Line (CurrentX, CurrentY) - (CurrentX, CurrentY - BarHeight)
```

To draw line 2 the value for X must increase but Y remain unchanged. The increase is simply the width of the bar. For line 3 X must not change but Y must increase by the value of the height of the bar.

PROGRAM 14.3   *Drawing a bar chart*

Specification   Draw a bar chart to represent a given set of values.

Suppose a large firm records how many employees were absent from work on each weekday. How might we represent these values by vertical bars? Assume the numbers are as follows:

Monday	50	Thursday	10
Tuesday	25	Friday	30
Wednesday	75		

In real programs where bar charts (and other graphs) are appropriate, it is likely that the data is stored on file. Therefore program 14.3 uses the file **Numbers.txt**, which stores the five numbers above. You can download it from the web site, or if this is not possible create the file yourself in Notepad with one number on each line. The first part of the program reads these numbers from the file into an array. If you haven't done text files in Chapter 10 you won't understand the early code but you can still type it in.

The finished program is shown in figure 14.11. The form is divided into 100 x 100 units. Each bar is 10 units wide and the vertical scale is 1 unit for each person absent. Thus the first bar is 50 units in height (which can also be confirmed by the difference between its two Y co-ordinates, 90 and 40).

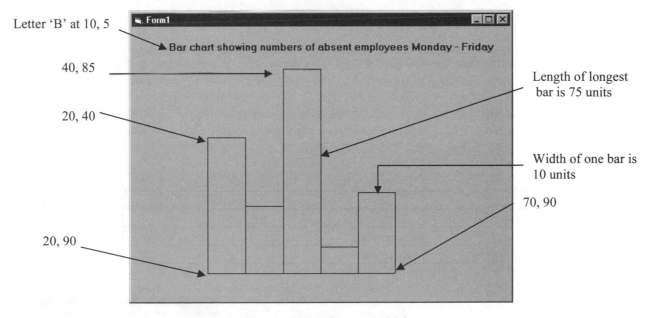

Figure 14.11: Program 14.3

1. Open a new project. Change the Font property of the form to **12 point Bold** so that the title can be clearly seen. Set its ScaleHeight and ScaleWidth properties to **100**.

2. Declare a global array to hold the five numbers from the file:

```
Dim Numbers(1 To 5) As Integer
```

3. In the form's Load event open the file and copy its contents to the array:

```
Private Sub Form_Load()
   Dim Filename As String
   Dim Index As Integer
   Filename = App.Path & "\Numbers.txt"   'set full path to the text file
   Open Filename For Input As #1           'open file for reading
   For Index = 1 To 5
      Input #1, Numbers(Index) 'read value from file and store in array
   Next Index
   Close #1                                'close file
End Sub
```

4. The code to display the title and the bar chart can go into the form's Click event. The bar width can be a constant but its height must be stored in a variable. The following code also handles the title:

```
Private Sub Form_Click()
   Const BarWidth = 10
   Dim BarHeight As Integer
   Dim Bar As Integer
   CurrentX = 10
   CurrentY = 5
   Print "Bar chart showing numbers of absent employees Monday - Friday"
```

5. The baseline is along Y co-ordinate 90 from X co-ordinate 20 to 70. Type this in on the next line:

```
Line (20, 90)-(70, 90)
```

6. Each bar is drawn by one repetition of a For...Next loop. The first thing inside the loop is to get the bar's height. Each of the Line statements draws one of lines 1 to 3 in figure 14.9.

```
   CurrentX = 20                    'set the starting point of the first bar
   CurrentY = 90
   For Bar = 1 To 5
      BarHeight = Numbers(Bar)
      Line (CurrentX, CurrentY)-(CurrentX, CurrentY - BarHeight) 'line 1
      Line (CurrentX, CurrentY)-(CurrentX + BarWidth, CurrentY)  'line 2
      Line (CurrentX, CurrentY)-(CurrentX, CurrentY + BarHeight) 'line 3
   Next Bar
End Sub
```

7. Run the program and click the form to produce the bar chart

end of Program 14.3

Summary of key concepts

- The X and Y co-ordinates of a form are numbered from 0 in the top left corner, X increases from left to right and Y increases from top to bottom.

- The default unit of measurement of a form is the **twip**. Use the **ScaleHeight** and **ScaleWidth** properties of the form to define your own unit of measurement.

- Use the **Move** method to move any control on a form.

- Use the form's **Circle** method to draw a circle and the **Line** method to draw a line.

- A form's **CurrentX** and **CurrentY** properties hold the X and Y co-ordinates for the next printing or drawing method.

Take it from here...

1. Investigate the form's **AutoRedraw** method which has a default value of False. Run any program from this chapter and then make the form smaller so that part of the graphic is lost. Enlarge it again and note what you get. Set AutoDraw to True and do the same again.

2. We used the **ScaleHeight** and **ScaleWidth** properties of the form to define our own units of measurement in programs 14.1 and 14.3. Find out about two related properties, **ScaleLeft** and **ScaleTop**.

3. Investigate the **Image** and **PictureBox** controls from the toolbox. For example find out which of them can stretch the image they contain when the control itself changes shape. Which of them allows graphics drawn at run time to draw over whatever they are currently displaying?

4. The two graphical methods not covered in this chapter are **Pset** and **Point**, which process individual points or pixels on the screen. Find out more about them.

5. Find out about how to use the form's **FillColor** and **FillStyle** properties to change the appearance of graphics drawn on the form.

6. The Circle method can do a lot more than just draw circles. Find out what else it can do, and in particular find out how to use it to draw simple pie charts.

Questions on the Programs

Program 14.1

*1. The amount of movement is fixed by the constant *Amount*. Replace this by letting the user determine the amount of movement using a horizontal scroll bar with a range of values from 1 to 20. Display the currently selected value next to the scroll bar. (You used this technique in program 2.4).

**2. Display the X and Y co-ordinates of the centre of the circle at all times, including when the program first runs.

Program 14.2

**1. Extend the program so that when the moving circle reaches the edge of the form it bounces off. Figure 14.12 shows an example trail after two bounces. Note that the initial direction of the circle is different from that in program 14.2. You would need to reset XCent and YCent to different values to achieve this, i.e. use two values instead of Amount. To achieve the bouncing effect you have to work out when the circle just touches the edge of the form. When you have done this, reset the two variables (in place of Amount) to negative values by multiplying them by –1 to effect the bounce.

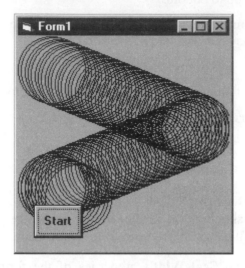

Figure 14.12: Exercise 1

Program 14.3

**1.   Add a label for the X axis. Under each bar write the initial letter of the day it refers to (M, T, W, T, F). You will need to use CurrentX and CurrentY to set the co-ordinates before printing. To get the letters printed in a straight line refer back to the use of the semi-colon (;) with the Print method in figures 3.7 and 3.11.

**2.   Add a label for the Y axis with the values 0, 20, 60 and 80. Add small horizontal lines at the 20, 60 and 80 values to indicate exactly where they come (like those in figure 14.16).

End of chapter exercises

*1.   Use the Line method to produce the shape shown in figure 14.13.

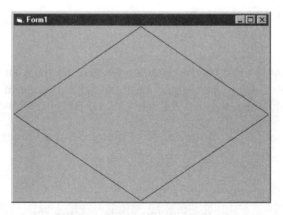

Figure 14.13: Exercise 1

**2. Use the Line method to draw three squares as shown in figure 14.14. The side of the second and third squares is twice the length of the one above. On the right of the form use the Print method to display the length of the square's side, the square's area and (for the second and third squares) how many times larger its area is than the previous square (not shown in the figure).

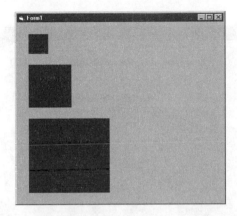

Figure 14.14: Exercise 2

3. Write a program to simulate the Kentucky Derby horse racing stall you often find in amusement arcades. Figure 14.15 shows the situation at the start of the race (left) and at the finish (right). The four 'horses' are different colours. Clicking Reset after a race positions them at the start again. The amount of movement of the horses should be calculated using random numbers. Look in Help at the **randomize statement and the **Rnd** function. The lines and circles are drawn using controls from the toolbox.

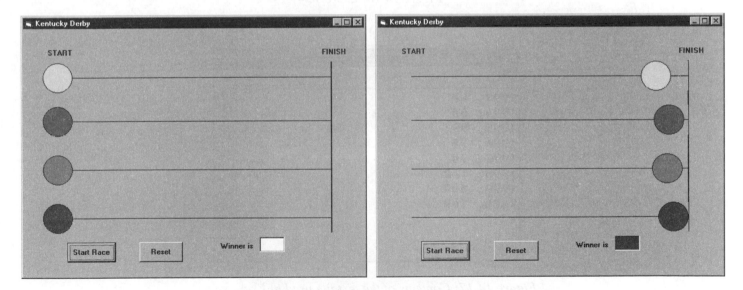

Figure 14.15: Exercise 3

4. Write a program to produce the line graph shown in figure 14.16. It uses data stored in the text file **SoftwareSales.txt which you can download from the web site. If you can't get this file create it quickly in Notepad. Figure 14.17 shows the contents. It contains the value of sales, in millions of pounds, for each year from 1993 to 2000 for a large software company. Work on getting the graph itself drawn, and only if you have time work on the labels for the two axes.

Since there are two items of data to read from the file with each read operation, use the Input statement to read them into two variables separated by a comma. (Step 3 in program 14.3 read in one item of data.)

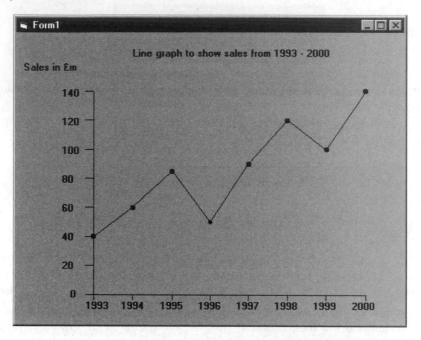

Figure 14.16: Exercise 4

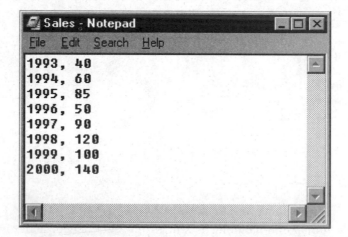

Figure 14.17: Contents of the text file used in Exercise 4

Chapter 15 – Relational Databases

Flat files and relational databases

Databases store data in tables. Tables are made up of fields (columns) and records (rows). Figure 9.1 in Chapter 9 is an example of a table – it stores details of how much customers currently owe an organisation such as a credit card company. Imagine a second table which stores details of daily payments made to the company, as shown in figure 15.1.

Account Number	Amount	Date of Payment
1208	£20.00	12/03/01
3593	£60.00	12/03/01
5552	£100.00	12/03/01

Figure 15.1: Table of payments

In a **flat file** system these two tables would be stored as separate files, most probably as random access files that you covered in Chapter 10. In a **relational database** they would be linked on their common field *Account Number*. When account numbers are entered into the payments file/table you would almost certainly wish to check that the account number exists in the customers file/table. With a flat file system you would have to program this yourself, but with a relational database the database software will handle it. Linking tables provides a host of things you can easily do which are difficult or impossible to do using flat files.

A database may have only one table, although it can't then use its relational power. Programs 15.1 and 15.2 use a single-table database. Program 15.3 uses a database with two linked tables.

The most popular database is Microsoft Access. This chapter shows you how to build a Visual Basic front end to an Access database, in particular how to display the data it contains, edit the data, query it and perform batch updates on it.

Random access files or a database?

In Chapter 10 you learned that random access files store records. They are therefore very similar to a database table, so which should you use? Some Visual Basic textbooks dismiss random access files altogether and say that interacting with a database is the modern way of doing things. If you're studying 'A' level Computing traditional file-handling is still firmly entrenched, and you are expected to know about it. The level of coding needed to process files and databases is about the same, though for performing queries databases are superior.

The Data control

Version 5 of Visual Basic has a tool in the standard toolbox called a **Data** control which allows you to use an Access database in your program. Version 6 introduced the **ADO** data control (ActiveX Data Objects) which allows programs to use other databases as well. Apart from the way you connect the database control to the database you wish to use, there's not much difference between the two controls. Since version 6 also provides the version 5 Data Control (see figure 1.7) we'll use this control throughout the chapter.

The Data control can only be connected to one table or one query in a specified database at any time. Programs 15.1 and 15.2 use an Access database called **HolidayHomes.mdb** which you can download from the web site. Have a look at it in Access before you do program 15.1. Holiday Homes is a small business which rents properties in the west of England. The single table in the database, Properties, holds details of 25 properties for rent.

PROGRAM 15.1 *Displaying data from a database*

Specification Display data from a database using two methods – a database grid and labels.

Figure 15.2 shows the program running. Record number 4 is selected in the grid (shown by the small triangle) and details of this property are also displayed in the six labels below it. The Data control allows you to scroll through the records by clicking the small buttons with triangles.

Database grid control

Data control

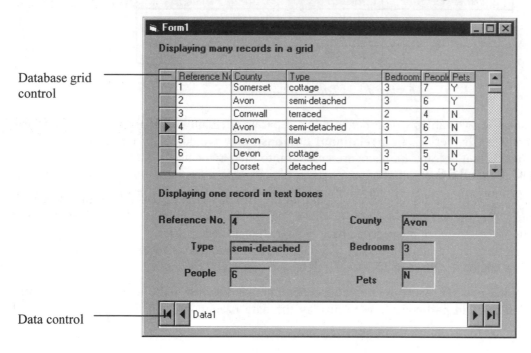

Figure 15.2: Program 15.1

1. Open a new project. Place a Data control from the toolbox as shown in figure 15.2.

2. To add a database grid control (DBGrid) to the toolbox select **Project/Components** and check the entry which lists a **Microsoft Data Bound Grid Control 5.0**. Click **OK** and the control will be added to the toolbox. If for some reason the control is not listed in the Components dialog box, you can still do the part of this program that displays a single record in the labels (and omit steps 3, 7 and 10 below). (Note that you can't use the version 6 DataGrid control with a Data control but only with an ADO Data control.)

3. Place a database grid on the form as shown in figure 15.2. In design view it looks a bit different from the one in figure 15.2.

4. Place all the labels on the form and set to blank the Caption property of those that display the data.

5. Find the DatabaseName property of the Data control, click the small button with the three dots, and specify the path to **HolidayHomes** in the resulting dialog box.

6. Click the small button in the RecordSource property of the Data control and select the name of the table from the drop-down list – **Properties**. The other items are queries stored in the database which we'll use in program 15.2.

7. Select the database grid control and set its DataSource property to the name of the main database control **Data1**. This is telling Visual Basic to connect the two controls so that the grid will display data from the table specified in step 6.

8. In the same way set the DataSource property of each of the 6 labels which will display data for one record to **Data1**.

9. Select the label that will display the reference numbers and set its DataField property to **Reference No**. Set the DataField property of the other 5 display labels to the appropriate fields.

10. To be able to change the contents of the Properties table make sure the data grid's **AllowAddNew**, **AllowDelete** and **AllowUpdate** fields are set to **True**.

11. Now run the program. You should be able to scroll through the records by clicking the buttons in the Data control. Check that you can change the data or add a new record. If you used labels rather than the database grid you can't edit the table – you would need to have used text boxes instead.

end of Program 15.1

Querying a database

Querying a database involves extracting part of its data. In the Holiday Homes example of program 15.1, sensible queries might be *find all properties in Cornwall* or *list detached houses which allow at least 6 people*. There are two ways you can query a database from a Visual Basic program:

- run a query which you have saved as part of the Access database
- run SQL code

SQL stands for **S**tructured **Q**uery **L**anguage and is the world's premier language for creating and querying databases. All good databases support it. It isn't the purpose of this chapter to teach you SQL but a little explanation is needed if you are to understand program 15.2. A typical SQL query has the form

    SELECT field names
    FROM   table(s)
    WHERE specify search condition

For example

    SELECT * FROM Employees WHERE [Days Absence] >= 10

extracts data in all fields (indicated by the '*') from the Employees table where the value in the Days Absence field is 10 or more. If a field name has spaces you must use square brackets. In Visual Basic code the SQL statement can be written on one line or over several and double quotation marks must be put around it. Upper case letters for SELECT etc. are not compulsory but it is common practice to use them.

Possibly the best way to learn SQL is to devise a range of queries in Access and then look at the SQL code which Access builds. When you save a query Access actually saves the SQL code.

PROGRAM 15.2   *Querying a database*

> **Specification**   Illustrate how to query a database, both by running stored queries and through SQL code.

The program is shown in figure 15.3 where the user has chosen to view the properties in Cornwall. Note that the selection from the other list box, the number of bedrooms, works independently of the county selected. If the user selects 2 from here all two-bedroom properties are displayed, not just those in Cornwall.

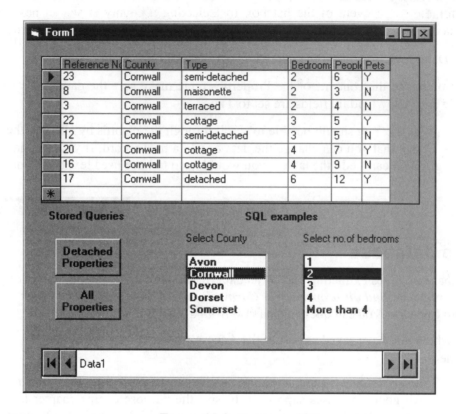

Figure 15.3: Program 15.2

1. Open a new project and repeat steps 1 –3 and 5 –7 from program 15.1. As before, if the database grid control is not available you'll have to use labels to display the table's data.

2. Place the two command buttons and name them **cmdDetached** and **cmdAll**.

3. The Holiday Homes database comes with two queries. One of these, qryDetachedProperties, selects those records with *detached* in the Type field. In the command button's Click event, assign this query name to the RecordSource property of the main database control and get the new data by calling its Refresh method:

```
Private Sub cmdDetached_Click()
   Data1.RecordSource = "qryDetachedProperties"
   Data1.Refresh
End Sub
```

4. For the other command button just set the RecordSource property to the name of the table:

```
Private Sub cmdAll_Click()
   Data1.RecordSource = "Properties"
   Data1.Refresh
End Sub
```

5. Run the program and try out the two buttons. Clicking the upper one should display the 5 detached properties.

6. Place the two list boxes on the form and set their List property to the items shown in figure 15.3.

7. The code for the Click event of the list box for selecting a county is shown next. The SELECT statement has an underscore but in this case it would produce a compiler error. Write it on one line instead.

```
Private Sub lstCounties_Click()
   Dim County As String
   County = lstCounties.Text
   Data1.RecordSource = "SELECT * From Properties WHERE [County] = _
            " & "'" & County & "'" & ""
   Data1.Refresh
End Sub
```

The SQL code above for setting the RecordSource of the database control looks messy with double quotation marks enclosing single ones, but this is how you must write it. If you had selected *Avon* the SQL boils down to:

```
"SELECT * From Properties WHERE [County] = 'Avon'"
```

8. The code for the Click event of the list box for selecting the number of bedrooms is:

```
Private Sub lstBedrooms_Click()
   Dim Bedrooms As Integer
   If lstBedrooms.Text = "More than 4" Then
      Data1.RecordSource = "SELECT * From Properties WHERE [Bedrooms] > 4 "
   Else
      Bedrooms = lstBedrooms.Text
      Data1.RecordSource = "SELECT * From Properties WHERE [Bedrooms] = _
            " & Bedrooms & ""
   End If
   Data1.Refresh
End Sub
```

As in step 7 write the SQL statement on one line and leave the underscore out. The last part of the SQL syntax is easier than for the county example because the variable Bedrooms is an Integer and doesn't need quotation marks.

9. Now try the whole program out. You should have quite a useful range of queries.

end of Program 15.2

Recordsets

A recordset is simply a set of records. It could be all the records in a table or perhaps some of the records extracted from one or more tables through a query. When you need to manipulate a database by going through its records, maybe searching for a particular record or updating the data in all or some of them, you can do this by using a recordset. A recordset is another object in Visual Basic and therefore has a number of properties and methods. The most useful are:

Properties

    RecordCount How many records are in the recordset.

Methods

Close	Closes the recordset.
Delete	Deletes the current record in a recordset.
Edit	Copies the current record in a recordset to a copy buffer ready for editing.
MoveFirst, MoveLast, MoveNext, MovePrevious	Moves to the first, last, next or previous record.
Requery	Updates the data in a recordset by re-executing the query on which it is based (if relevant).
Update	Copies the contents of the copy buffer (see Edit above) back to the recordset.

PROGRAM 15.3   *Using a Recordset*

Specification   Illustrate how to interact with a database by using a recordset.

Figure 15.4 shows the program. The database grid displays details of 5 students from an Access table, *Students*. Clicking Calculate Passes goes through a linked table, *Exam Results*, which stores details of the 'A' level results of these students (see figure 15.5). It calculates how many passes each student has achieved (grades A to E being a pass) and updates the Number Passed field in the *Students* table. This data is displayed when Show Passes is clicked. Clicking Reset Passes makes the Number Passed field empty once more, which can be seen by clicking Show Passes again.

1. Make sure you have the downloaded the Access database **Alevels.mdb** from the web site and have a look at it. It contains one form with two buttons which perform the same actions *from within Access* as the Calculate Passes and Reset Passes buttons in figure 15.4. The left button fires off Access Basic code (which is just about the same as the code you'll be writing in this program), and the right button fires off a macro which runs an update query to reset the Number Passed field to blanks. In this program you'll write code to do this.

2. Open a new project and place two Data controls as shown in figure 15.4, one each for the database tables. Name the left one **datStudents** and the right one **datExamResults**.

3. Set the DataBaseName property of each Data control to the Access database **Alevels.mdb**. Set the RecordSource property of datStudents to the table holding the data about the students – **Students**, and for datExamResults set the property to the other table – **ExamResults**.

4. Place a DBGrid control on the form (see step 2 in program 15.1) and set its DataSource property to **datStudents**. If this control is not available use two labels to display the Surname and Number Passed fields from the Students table (or labels for all the fields if you prefer). Set their DataSource property to **datStudents** and their DataField property to the appropriate field.

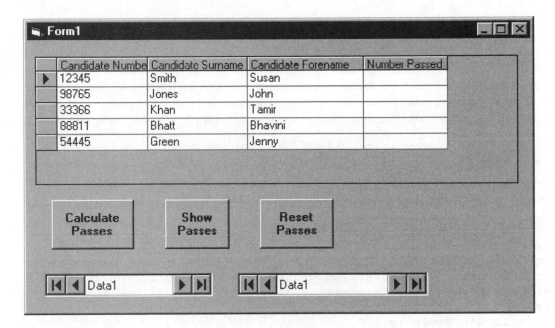

Figure 15.4: Program 15.3

Candidate Number	Exam	Result
12345	Maths	B
12345	Physics	C
12345	Chemistry	A
33366	Maths	D
33366	Biology	U
33366	English	C
54445	Geography	N
54445	History	N
54445	English	B
88811	History	C
88811	French	A
88811	German	C
98765	Chemistry	E
98765	Biology	N
98765	Computing	D

Figure 15.5: The contents of the Exam Results *table*

5. Run the program to check that the grid (or labels) displays the data from the Students table.

6. Place the command buttons on the form. Set their captions as shown in figure 15.4 and name them **cmdCalculatePasses**, **cmdShowPasses** and **cmdResetPasses**.

7. Declare global variables to store the two recordsets needed. Visual Basic supports a data type, *Recordset*, for this purpose.

```
Dim Students As Recordset
Dim ExamResults As Recordset
```

Before writing code to calculate how many passes each student has gained, you must be clear about the main steps involved. First we need to look at the initial record in the Students recordset and then go through all the records in the other recordset trying to find a match on the candidate number. If a match is found then look at the exam grade and increase a count of some sort if it's an E or better. Then go to the next record in the Students recordset and repeat the process of looking through all the records in the other recordset. The overall structure is an outer loop (one repetition processing one record in the Students recordset) driving an inner loop (one repetition processing one record in the ExamResults recordset).

8. The code for the Click event of the Calculate Passes button is shown below. First you must create the two recordsets with the word **Set**. The **MoveFirst**, **MoveNext**, **Edit** and **Update** methods are used. These were briefly described earlier. Note the use of the exclamation character (!) between the name of a recordset and a field, e.g. Students![Candidate Number].

```
Private Sub cmdCalculatePasses_Click()
   Dim CandidateID As String
   Dim Count As Integer                       'No. passes for one student
   Set Students = datStudents.Recordset        'Create the 2 recordsets
   Set ExamResults = datExamResults.Recordset
   Students.MoveFirst    'move to first record in the Students recordset
   Do While Not Students.EOF 'go through all records in Students recordset
     Count = 0
     CandidateID = Students![Candidate Number] 'find current candidate no.
                                    'square brackets contain field name
     ExamResults.MoveFirst 'go to first record in ExamResults recordset
     Do While Not ExamResults.EOF    'go through all records in ExamResults
                                     'recordset
       If CandidateID = ExamResults![Candidate Number] And _   'if the
                    ExamResults![Result] <= "E" Then 'candidate no.
          'if current record in ExamResults recordset matches that in
          'current record in Students recordset and the exam result is
          'E or better
         Count = Count + 1
       End If
       ExamResults.MoveNext 'move to next record in ExamResults recordset
     Loop
     Students.Edit 'get ready to edit current record in Students recordset
     Students![Number Passed] = Count'assign value to Number Passed field
     Students.Update                      'actually carry out the update
     Students.MoveNext    'move to next record in Students recordset
   Loop
End Sub
```

9. To display the new number of passes (by clicking the Show Passes button) use the Refresh method of the Data control:

```
Private Sub cmdShowPasses_Click()
   datStudents.Refresh
End Sub
```

10. To reset the entries in the Number Passed field, by clicking the Reset Passes button, loop through the Students recordset and set the field to **Null**:

```
Private Sub cmdResetPasses_Click()
  Set Students = datStudents.Recordset
  Students.MoveFirst
  Do While Not Students.EOF
    Students.Edit
    Students![Number Passed] = Null
    Students.Update
    Students.MoveNext
  Loop
End Sub
```

11. Finally, you should close recordsets when you've finished with them. When the program closes the form's Terminate event is fired off so do it there:

```
Private Sub Form_Terminate()
  Students.Close
  ExamResults.Close
End Sub
```

12. Run the program. You need to click the Show Passes button to display the results of clicking either of the other two buttons.

end of Program 15.3

Summary of key concepts

- A **relational database** is one that is capable of storing two or more tables linked together on a common field.

- A **Data** control is used to connect a Visual Basic program to an Access database.

- You can display data from a database using a **DBGrid** control which displays many records at once, or using labels (or text boxes) to display one record at once.

- You can query a database by setting the RecordSource property of a Data control either to the name of a stored query in an Access database or to an **SQL** statement.

- A **recordset** holds records from a database table or from the result of running a query on one or more tables. It is a Visual Basic object and so has properties and methods.

Take it from here...

1. If you have version 6 of Visual Basic experiment using the ADO Data control. Add it to the toolbox by selecting **Project/Components** and checking the appropriate entry in the list box of the Components dialog. To set its properties click the button in its Custom property. In the dialog box make sure the third option button is selected and click **Build**. Then select the entry which says **Microsoft Jet.....** Enter the database to connect to in the next dialog, click **OK** and then click the **RecordSource** tab. Select Command Type **1 - adCmdTable** in the next dialog and then select which table to connect to below this. If you're connecting to a query select **4 – adCmdStoredProc** instead. You can now use this control instead of the Data control for most of the things in this chapter. Note that in program 15.2, where you switch between using a table and a query for the RecordSource when the two command buttons are clicked, you must set the control's Command Type first, e.g.

```
Adodc1.CommandType = adCmdText    'to use an SQL statement
Adodc1.CommandType = adCmdTable   'to use a table
```

2. Visual Basic supplies an add-in feature called the **Visual Data Manager** which allows you to create Access databases without having to use Access. Have a look at it by selecting **Add-Ins** from the main menu, though if you know how to use Access to create databases, you'll no doubt stay with it.

3. Two database controls not used in this chapter are the **DBList** and **DBCombo** (**DataList** and **DataCombo** in version 6). Each of these can be populated with data from one field in a table. Try producing a list of candidate numbers from the database you used in program 15.3 (Alevels.mdb), as shown in figure 15.6. This has a Data control (Data1) which you have used throughout this chapter, rather than an ADO Data control, and so has a DBList control rather than a DataList control. You need to associate the DBList control to the Data control and then set its RowSource and ListField properties. There are several other interesting properties you might like to explore, especially DataSource, DataField, BoundColumn, Text and MatchEntry. To get the DBList control select **Project/Components** and then check the item containing Microsoft DBList or Microsoft DataList.

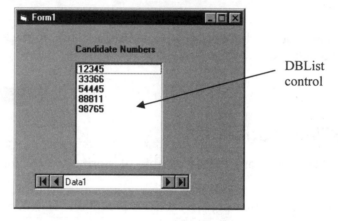

DBList
control

Figure 15.6: Using the DBList control

Questions on the Programs

Program 15.2

*1. In this program you used one of the two queries stored in the Holiday Homes database. In Access run the other query, qryPetsAllowed, to see what it does. Now add a command button to program 15.2 to run this query from Visual Basic.

*2. Add a third list box so that you can display properties of a selected type (detached, cottage etc.)

**3. The two list boxes, and the third one if you've done question 2 above, work independently of each other. Now try to get two of them working together so that a query might be *find all 4-bedroom properties in Cornwall*. You will need to write slightly more complex SQL code than in the examples in the program. Do the query in Access, look at the code produced and adapt it for your program.

Program 15.3

*1. Add controls to display the total number of 'A' level passes and the average number of passes per student. Use the RecordCount property of the recordset to help you.

**2.   Add a list box with the names of the 'A' level subjects. Then loop through the ExamResults recordset to display the number of students who have passed the course selected from this list box.

End of chapter exercises

To do these exercises you need to download three Access databases from the web site. Each has two linked tables. These are:

GNVQStudents   Don't confuse this with the text file of the same name that you might have used to do exercise 1 in Chapter 10. The Students table has details of GNVQ students. The Portfolio Grade field holds the overall grade for the coursework (D = distinction, M = merit, P = pass, X = not passed). Students have to pass a given number of unit tests. How many they have passed is stored in the Students table but how many they must pass in total is in the Courses table.

Repayments   The Customers table has a field storing how much each customer owes the company. The other table, Cheques Received, lists payments which have been made.

Wards.   The Patients table has details of which ward each patient is in. In the Wards table the field *No of Patients in Ward* is blank.

*1.   Design a form to display data from the Students table in the GNVQStudents database, as shown in figure 15.7. Use labels instead of the data grid if this component is not available.

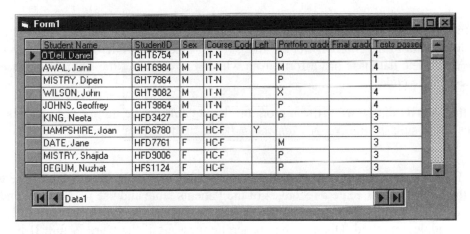

Figure 15.7: Program for exercise1

**2.   Build a program so that you can practise writing SQL, as shown in figure 15.8. The user writes SQL in the text box and clicks the OK button. Those records from the Students table in the GNVQStudents database matching the SQL query are displayed. In figure 15.8 the SQL query is searching for students with a distinction in their portfolio work.

**3.   Develop your form in question 1 above to allow the user to query the Students table. Display:

- Students on a given course (selected by the user).
- All students who have left.
- Students who have a given portfolio grade (selected by the user).

How you design the interface is up to you. If you use list boxes as in program 15.2 you will have to write SQL statements. Design the query in Access and then adapt the SQL code Access produces.

Instead you could build separate queries in Access for each possible selection made by the user, and then just use the query names in your code.

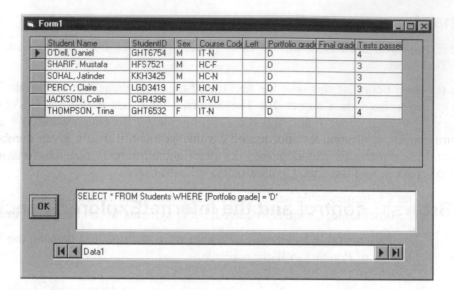

Figure 15.8: Exercise 2

4. Look at the **Repayments database. Write a program that updates the *Balance* field in the Customers table from the data in the *Amount* field of the *Cheques Received* table. Display the updated results if you have time. The database has a form from which you can reset the original balance values. This uses Access Basic code.

5. Look at the **Wards database. Write a program that calculates the number of patients in each ward and stores the results in the *No of Patients in Ward* field. Display the updated results if you have time.

***6. Design a form to enter new records into the Patients table of the Wards database. Use text boxes for entering the record data. Create a recordset of the Patients table and use its AddNew method to add a new record. When this is working extend the program to check that the ward isn't full after you have called the AddNew method. Display an appropriate message if the ward is full. If it is full then use the CancelUpdate method to cancel the new record.

***7. In the Students table of the GNVQStudents database the Final Grade field is blank. Write a program that updates this field with an appropriate grade (D, M, P or X). You need to know the following:

- if a student has not passed the required number of tests then the final grade is X, no matter what their portfolio grade
- if a student has passed the required number of tests their portfolio grade becomes their final grade

Note that students with no portfolio grade shown have either left the course, or they are on the first year of a two-year course and so have not completed their portfolio. No final grade should be filled in for these students.

The database has a single query which will reset the Final Grade field to blanks for your convenience.

Chapter 16 – Visual Basic and the Internet

Introduction

Visual Basic provides several controls and one object that you can use to explore the Internet. Two of these controls and the object are provided with the Learning Edition. In this chapter we'll look at one control, the **WebBrowser**, and the object, called **InternetExplorer**.

The WebBrowser control and the InternetExplorer object

The WebBrowser control lets you do many of the things you can do using Microsoft Internet Explorer. For example you can type in a web address or URL (Uniform Resource Locator) and go to it, or navigate forwards and backwards through documents that have been previously viewed.

Like all controls the WebBrowser has properties, methods and events. Program 16.1 uses a few of these in introducing you to the control.

Program 16.2 shows you how to use the InternetExplorer object, which lets you run Internet Explorer from a program. This has a similar set of properties, methods and events to the WebBrowser control. The important properties and methods of the WebBrowser control and the InternetObject are listed below.

Properties

Busy	If navigation to a new URL is going on, or a web page is being downloaded, this returns True, otherwise False.
LocationName	Title of the web page currently displayed.
LocationURL	The URL (address) of the web page currently displayed.

Methods

GoBack	Navigates back one item in the history list (i.e. to previous page/document).
GoForward	Navigates forwards one item in the history list.
GoHome	Navigates to the current home page.
GoSearch	Navigates to the search page.
Navigate	Navigates to a web address. Pass the address as a parameter.
Refresh	Reloads the page currently displayed.
Stop	Cancels any navigation or downloading currently going on.

PROGRAM 16.1   *A simple Web Browser*

Specification   Use the WebBrowser control to navigate the Internet. Use buttons to go forwards and backwards through previously viewed documents.

1. Open a new project. To use the WebBrowser tool select **Project/Components**. In the Components dialog box click the check box for **Microsoft Internet Controls** (see figure 16.1). Click **OK** and you'll have two more controls on the toolbox. One of these is the WebBrowser. (The other one is not covered in this chapter.)

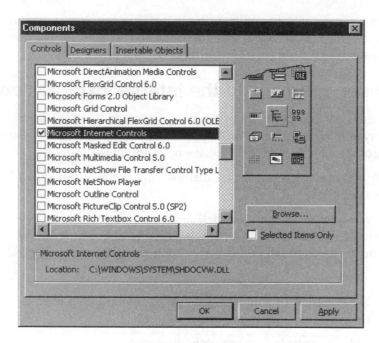

Figure 16.1: Selecting Internet controls for the toolbox

2. Design the form as shown in figure 16.2. Name the text box **txtAddress** and the command buttons **cmdWebAddress**, **cmdPrevious**, **cmdNext** and **cmdHome**. Place the WebBrowser control so that it occupies the lower two-thirds or so of the form. Don't change its default name of WebBrowser1.

3. Set the form's WindowState property to **2 – Maximized**. Most users of the web want a full-screen view immediately.

4. In the form's Load event procedure use the WebBrowser's GoHome method.

```
Private Sub Form_Load()
   WebBrowser1.GoHome              'navigate to current home page
End Sub
```

5. In the Click event procedures for the Previous and Next buttons use the WebBrowser's GoBack and GoForward methods:

```
Private Sub cmdPrevious_Click()
    WebBrowser1.GoBack            'navigate to previous page/document
End Sub


Private Sub cmdNext_Click()
    WebBrowser1.GoForward         'navigate to next page/document
End Sub
```

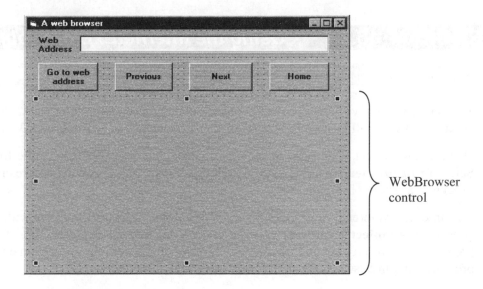

Figure 16.2: Design of program 16.1

6. In the Click event of the button to go to the web address enter code which uses the Navigate method of the WebBrowser control to go straight to a specified URL.

```
Private Sub cmdWebAddress_Click()
    Dim WebAddress As String
    WebAddress = txtWebAddress.Text
    If WebAddress <> "" Then      'has a web address been entered?
        WebBrowser1.Navigate (WebAddress)'pass it as a parameter to Navigate
    End If
End Sub
```

7. In design view the form occupies only part of the screen. When the program runs it will occupy the whole screen because in step 3 you set the WindowState property to Maximized. The text box for the web address, and the WebBrowser control which will display the documents from the web, must be made larger. In the form's Resize event use the ScaleWidth and ScaleHeight properties of the form to increase their size. You used these two properties extensively in Chapter 14. The value of 400 assumes the form's measurements are in twips (the ScaleMode property is set to 1- Twip).

```
Private Sub Form_Resize()
    txtWebAddress.Width = Form1.ScaleWidth - 400 'increase width of text
    WebBrowser1.Width = Form1.ScaleWidth - 400   'box and WebBrowser so
                                        'they are almost as wide as the screen
    WebBrowser1.Height = Form1.ScaleHeight - WebBrowser1.Top 'extend base
                                        'of WebBrowser to bottom of screen
End Sub
```

8. Run the program. The GoHome method in the form's Load event takes you to your home page and then you can type in a web address. Start the address with **http://www.** To get to the address you must click the left command button. Navigate through three or four pages from the opening page of your site and then try out the Previous and Next buttons.

end of Program 16.1

PROGRAM 16.2   *Using the InternetExplorer object*

Specification   Demonstrate how to use the InternetExplorer object.

In this program we'll have a small list of publishers who publish computing books. Selecting one of these and clicking a button will take you to that publisher's home web page. Figure 16.3 shows the program.

1. Open a new project. You need to tell Visual Basic that you wish to use the InternetExplorer class. Select **Project/References** and in the References dialog box check the **Microsoft Internet Controls** checkbox as shown in figure 16.4.

2. The InternetExplorer is not added to the toolbox, but if you're familiar with the Object Explorer (select **View/Object Explorer**) you can see that the InternetExplorer class has been added to the project. Classes are beyond this book, but are explained in the document on object-oriented programming in Visual Basic that you can download from the web site.

3. Design the form using figure 16.3. Name the list box **lstPublishers** and the command button **cmdWebSite**. Add the publishers to the list box either by using the List property or writing four AddItem methods in the form's Load event:

```
Private Sub Form_Load()
   lstPublishers.AddItem "payne-gallway"
   lstPublishers.AddItem "deitel"
   lstPublishers.AddItem "wrox"
   lstPublishers.AddItem "oup"
End Sub
```

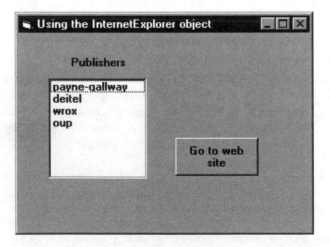

Figure 16.3: Program 16.2

4. In the General section declare an object variable of the InternetExplorer class. This type of declaration requires the keyword **New**. We're getting into object-oriented territory here!

```
Dim IE As New InternetExplorer
```

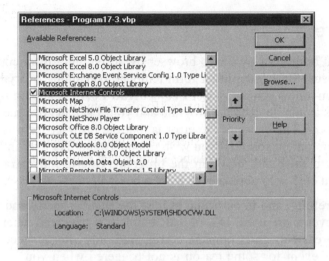

Figure 16.4: Referencing the InternetExplorer class

5. The web address of the first publisher is **http://www.payne-gallway.co.uk**. The other three have addresses ending in **com** rather than **co.uk**. So in the Click event for the command button type in:

```
Private Sub cmdWebSite_Click()
  IE.Visible = True
  If lstPublishers.ListIndex = 0 Then 'first publisher in the list selected?
    IE.Navigate ("http://www." & lstPublishers.Text & ".co.uk")
  Else
    IE.Navigate ("http://www." & lstPublishers.Text & ".com")
  End If
End Sub
```

You must use the **Visible** property of the InternetExplorer object to see anything of the web when the program runs. The **Navigate** method is used in the same way as you used it for the WebBrowser control in program 16.1.

6. Run the program. You must select a publisher before clicking the button or the Navigate method will try to take you to an address simply called *http://www* and fail.

end of Program 16.2

Summary of key concepts

- The **WebBrowser** control displays pages on the web. To navigate through the web you must provide your own navigation (command) buttons.

- The **InternetExplorer** object launches Microsoft Internet Explorer.

Take it from here...

1. In program 16.1 you built your own web browser by designing a form containing the WebBrowser control. Actually Visual Basic supplies a form template containing everything this program can do plus a bit more. Open a new project, select **Project/Add Form**, and then select **Web Browser** from the form icons if it is available. Run the program and you'll get an error message telling you *No MDI Form available to load*. The cause of the error is that the browser form is supplied as a child form but this project has no parent form. (If you wish to understand this look in Help.) Change the form's MDIChild property to **false** and now run the program. One useful extra thing this program does compared to program 16.1 is to populate the combo box with web addresses that you have used.

Look at the code carefully, and in particular at how the Busy property and DownLoadComplete and NavigateComplete events are used. DownLoadComplete is triggered when navigation has finished, halted or failed whereas NavigateComplete is triggered only after a successful navigation to a new location. If the latter event for some reason is not triggered when you run the program, and so the web address is not added to the combo box, copy the code from this event to DownLoadComplete and the combo box should get the address.

Questions on the Programs

Program 16.1

**1. Run the program and click the Previous or Forward buttons before a web address has been accessed. A run-time error results. There are at least two ways to get round this problem:

- write error-handling code (covered in Chapter 11)
- disable/enable the buttons as appropriate

Write code to carry out either or both of these solutions.

End of chapter exercises

*1. Create a program similar to 16.2 but in the list box put in the names of several of your favourite web sites.

Part Three – The Project

Chapter 17 – Introduction and Analysis

Requirements of an 'A' level project

The requirements of the 'A' level Computing project vary from board to board but for this part of the book we'll use the AQA syllabus. Module 6 of the syllabus requires candidates to "*demonstrate skills of practical application and problem solving, as well as the techniques of documentation and system testing. The system developed by the candidate should allow interaction with the user, storage and manipulation of data, and output of results.*" It is expected that the end-user should be a real person or group of people.

The AQA mark scheme for candidates who use a standalone programming language like Visual Basic to carry out their project (rather than a package with programming facilities such as Access), is shown in Appendix C. The project is divided into the following sections:

	Marks
Analysis	12
Design	12
Technical Solution	12
System Testing	6
System Maintenance	6
User Manual	6
Appraisal	3
Quality of Communication	3
Total	60

Analysis

This stage should report on what the user wants the computerised solution to do. The candidate should draw up a list of general and specific objectives of their solution, identify possible methods of meeting them, and justify the method they have chosen.

Design

Design covers several important topics. These include:

- what the interface will look like – use of various controls and so on;
- the files needed – their structure, organisation and processing;
- how the data will be validated;
- the procedures needed.

Quite clearly you cannot draw up a complete design unless you know Visual Basic reasonably well. Design is covered in Chapters 18 and 19.

Technical Solution

This is your Visual Basic program and is covered in Chapters 20 – 23.

System testing

Testing is evidence that the system you have implemented really does work. The evidence should normally be hard copy (printouts). You should first draw up a test plan and then carry out each test carefully. This is not covered in the sample project.

System Maintenance

This should include the following:

- A printout of your program code with suitable comments within the code itself or with handwritten annotations about how the code works. Using the commenting facility of Visual Basic is more sensible.

- A list showing all the variables and procedures you have used.

- Some sample algorithms using a recognised method of presentation.

The first of these is fully covered in the sample project. The second is partly covered in Chapter 19.

User Manual

This is a guide for the user, several pages in length, that explains how to use your system. It should include screen displays, refer to error messages which may crop up and how to recover from these errors. This is not covered in the sample project.

Appraisal

How well have the objectives listed in the Analysis been met? Feedback from the user would be very useful here. Are there any improvements you could make, either to the way you have coded your solution or in extensions to the program sometime in the future? This is covered in Chapter 24.

Quality of Communication

How well written and clearly set out is your report?

The mark scheme suggests that only 12 of the 60 marks come from coding, but the importance of coding is much greater than this. Many of the marks for system maintenance, testing and even the user manual can only be earned if your coding has been done reasonably well in the first place. You can't test what you haven't coded for example!

In Part Three of this book you will be shown how to design and code a full project of 'A' level standard. The Analysis stage will not be covered in great detail, but we do need to cover enough in order to know what to design and code.

Advanced VCE programming units

Two of the three Exam Boards have one programming unit which involves writing code; the other Board (Edexcel) has two units. Appendix D shows the Assessment Evidence for a typical programming unit. For a grade A you need to cover all the main sections listed earlier for the 'A' level project except Analysis.

Introducing the sample project – Smiley's Snooker Club

The project is based on a snooker club called Smiley's Snooker. It is a private club with 20 snooker tables and about 400 members. 300 of these are Seniors (over 18 years of age) and 100 are Juniors. The club is open from 10.00 am to 10.00 pm each day. There is no booking system at present. Members just turn up and ask to play. The part of the business that Smiley's has asked you to computerise is handling the allocation of tables and to keep a record of the membership of the club. These aspects will now be looked at in more detail in the Analysis stage which follows.

The Analysis stage

The Analysis stage covers your early discussions with Smiley's when you would make a careful study of how the present manual system works. You would try to find out in as much detail as possible just what Smiley's wants your computerised solution to do. The discussion below is deliberately too short for a good 'A' level project. For example it does not say much about how the club currently handles its games. However the purpose of the sample project is to concentrate on those aspects which are closely related to your Visual Basic work. It does not try to explain how to conduct a full analysis of an existing system. There is just enough detail in what follows to get on with the next stage, the design.

The initial findings

On your first visit to Smiley's you have gathered a range of details about how the club works and which part of it you need to computerise. The following is a summary of your findings.

It was mentioned above that Smiley's has 20 snooker tables and that there is no booking system at present. They do not wish to have a booking system and want your computerised solution to simply make the allocation of tables and calculating the cost of games much easier than it is at present.

A member may bring along one guest to play snooker. At present the charge to play is 4p a minute if a senior member is playing with a guest or another member (senior or junior) and 3p a minute if two juniors or a junior plus guest are playing. If two members play a game then one of them is responsible for the payment. If a member plays with a guest then this member is responsible for the payment. If a senior and junior member play then details of the senior member should be recorded as payment is based on this category of membership. When members come to play they should show their membership card. However, sometimes they forget so the system should be able to retrieve a particular membership number by the member's name.

Smiley's wants to be able to see on screen at any time which tables are free and which have games going on. For those tables with games going on, the times that the games started should be displayed. When a new game starts the system should display the membership number, the table number and the time the game started for the receptionist. When a game finishes the table number, membership number, category of membership, finish time, the length of playing time in hours and minutes and the cost should be displayed. A record of each completed game, containing the table number, details of how long the game took and the cost, should be kept. At the end of each day Smiley's wants a printed report showing the usage of each table. It should show the total length of time each table has been used that day, how many games have been played on it and the amount of income it has made. The overall income for the day is also required.

Smiley's wants to keep a record of all its members and so be able to add new members and delete others. The club requires, at any time, a printed list of their members. This should list the names alphabetically, the category of membership, the total number of senior and junior members and the overall total number of members.

Membership numbers have the format LLDDDD where L is an upper case letter and D a numeric digit from 0 to 9. The two upper case letters represent the member's first name and surname. No-one seems to know why there are four digits but Smiley's wishes to keep this format. Tables are numbered from 1 to 20.

Reflections

You have studied your initial findings at home and several questions spring to mind that you'd like to ask Smiley's about. These questions are:

1. *The costs per minute should be stored in a file, so when they inevitably go up will Smiley's know how to change them if they are stored in a text file?*

   The alternative to storing the costs per minute in a file is to code them into your program. But when the costs change Smiley's would require a programmer to change them. This would be good for you since they may need to pay you, but it would be more reasonable to allow Smiley's to change the prices themselves without getting involved in code. If the costs are stored in a text file Smiley's can change them in a simple text file editor, such as Notepad or WordPad that comes with Windows, or you can let this to be done through one of the forms in your program.

2. *Smiley's has said that it wants a printed report at the end of each day showing details of the usage of each table. Will Smiley's want to produce this report at other times of the day, sometimes at the end of the morning for example?*

   If Smiley's only wants to produce the report at the end of the day then you can delete the file that stores the data for this report immediately after the report is printed. The next day the file should start afresh again with no data in it. However if Smiley's wish to produce the report more than once in a day then you must not delete its contents.

3. *Smiley's closes at 10.00pm. Is this likely to be extended in the future so that games could finish after midnight?*

   You need to know this because even at this early stage you are thinking about how to calculate the cost of a game. It will be calculated by multiplying the number of minutes the game lasts by the rate per minute, and in turn the number of minutes will be calculated by doing some arithmetic on the start and finish times of the game. If games finish after midnight this will probably affect the way this arithmetic is done.

Second visit

The answers to the questions have been cleared up.

1. Smiley's does not want to change the contents of the file directly. You know their fears are exaggerated, but they are rather afraid of doing something wrong. They would prefer your program to handle this.

2. Yes, on reflection they would like to produce the daily usage report at any time during the day.

3. No, it is most unlikely that the closing time will be extended.

Final thoughts on the Analysis stage

The analysis stage is worth 12 marks and must be more thorough than the outline given here for Smiley's Snooker to earn these marks. For example it is very likely that the club would want more from the computerised solution to the membership part of the system than just adding and deleting members. The problem is that a few more requests from the user will generate a project that is just too big if implemented fully. In the analysis you should discuss all the needs of the user but make it clear, if these are too wide, where you are drawing the boundary for your computerised solution.

Chapter 18 – Design: Forms, Reports, Files and Data Validation

What is design?

Design is all about preparing the groundwork so that during the next stage, coding, the only major decisions that have to be made are about the coding itself. If an experienced Visual Basic programmer could take your design and get on with building the program without having to come back to you about non-coding issues, then you have probably done a good design. But since you are both designer and programmer it can be very tempting to start coding before a sound design is in place. But resist it if you can! It will pay off in the end.

Design covers quite a range of topics although some of these will be much more important than others in your project. For Smiley's Snooker we will concentrate on the big topics which have a bearing on how the program is coded. We'll cover the following in the order listed:

- form design
- design of printed reports
- file design – structure, organisation and processing
- data validation
- design of the overall modular structure

The hardest of these is designing the modular structure and is discussed in the next chapter.

Designing the forms

You should produce paper designs of all the forms in your project, drawn by hand or by using a software package. For Smiley's Snooker we will have four forms as outlined in figure 18.1.

General name	*Purpose*
Main form	Displays the 20 snooker tables and their state of play. Prints a report on daily usage of tables. Allows other 3 forms to be loaded
Game form	Input/output appropriate data when a game either starts or finishes. Calculates the cost of a finished game. Stores details of games on file.
Members form	Allows new members to be added and others to be deleted. Displays full list of members. Prints a membership report.
Utilities form	Creates lost or missing files. Backs up files. Changes price of snooker game.

Figure 18.1: The project's forms

Main form

Figure 18.2 shows a sketch of the design of the main form.

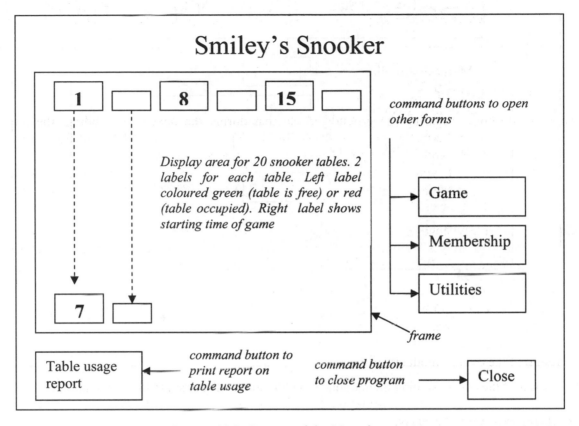

Figure 18.2: Design of the Main form

Game form

Figures 18.3 and 18.4 show sketches of this form. Depending on which option button is clicked, Start Game or Finish Game, a different set of controls is made visible. When the form first loads, by clicking the Game button on the Main form, the controls for starting a game will be visible.

Starting a game

The following will happen:

- The receptionist enters the person's membership number.

- The member's name and their category of membership will automatically appear. The receptionist confirms these details with the player.

- The combo box will display the numbers of all those tables which are available for play. When the receptionist selects a table number the current time is taken from the system clock and displayed in the Start Time control. The receptionist will confirm with the member the starting time of the game for payment calculations.

- Clicking the command button stores details of the game on a file and clears all the text boxes. It also changes the table's colour from green to red on the Main form and displays the starting time next to it.

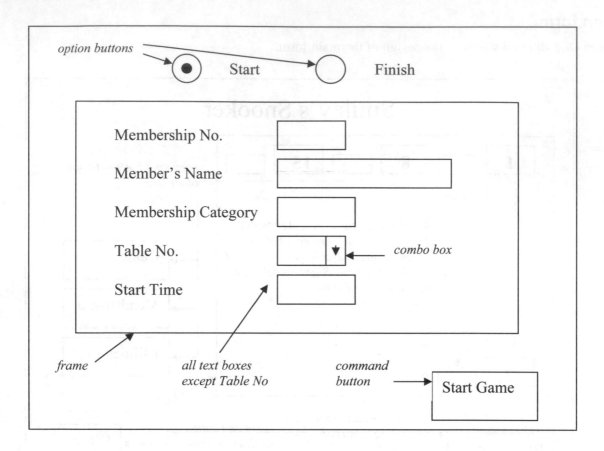

Figure 18.3: Design of the Game form – Starting a game

Finishing a game

The following will happen:

- The receptionist will ask the player which table they have been using and selects this from the tables currently in use that are displayed in the combo box.

- Selecting a table number triggers off the display of data in all the other controls.

- The finishing time of the game is taken from the system clock and the playing time and cost of the game calculated automatically.

- Clicking the command button stores details of the completed game on file and clears all the text boxes. It also changes the table's colour back to green and removes the start time next to it on the Main form.

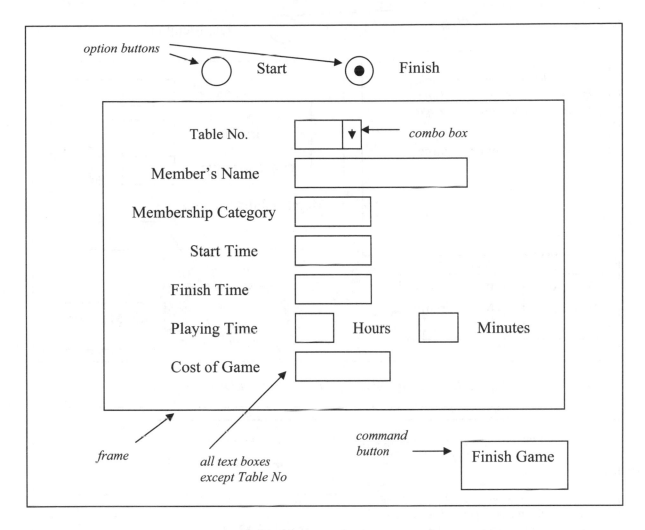

Figure 18.4: Design of the Game form – Finishing a game

Members form

Figures 18.5 and 18.6 show sketches of the form. Depending on which option button is clicked, Add Member or Delete Member, a different set of controls is made visible. When the form first loads the controls for adding a member will be available.

Adding a member

The receptionist enters a new membership number, the member's name and category of membership and then clicks the command button. The details are added to a file.

Deleting a member

The receptionist enters a membership number and clicks the command button. The member is deleted from a file.

The list box displays details of each member. These details can be printed out.

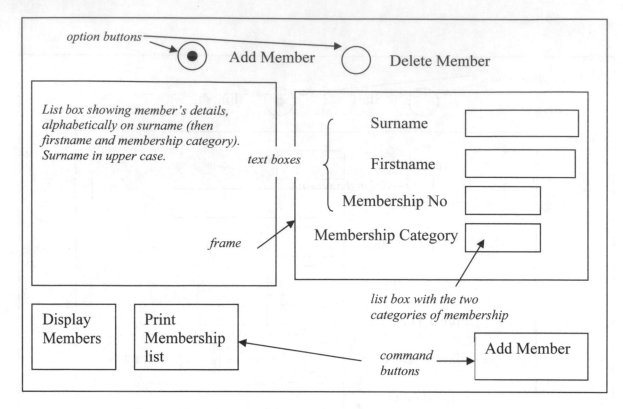

Figure 18.5: Design of the Members form – Adding a member

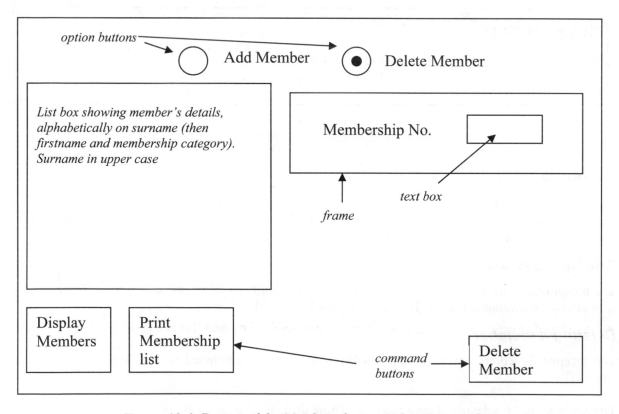

Figure 18.6: Design of the Members form – Deleting a member

Utilities form

Figure 18.7 shows a sketch of the form. The controls for entering new payment rates for a game are only made visible if the user clicks the appropriate option button.

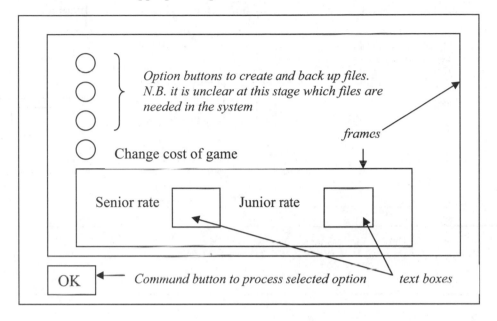

Figure 18.7: Design of the Utilities form

Printed reports

Our Analysis found that Smiley's wants two printed reports:

- At any time during the day, but most likely at the end of the day, a report showing the usage of each table. This includes the total length of time the table has been in use, how many games were played on the table and how much income the table made. The overall income for the day is also required.

- An alphabetical list of members showing their name and category of membership, the total number of senior and junior members and the overall total.

In your project you should draw sketches of all your reports. Figures 18.8 and 18.9 show sketches of the two reports for Smiley's.

Files

For each of the files your project uses you should state:

- its name
- its organisation (text file or random access file)
- its record structure (random access files) or "structure" of its data if it is a text file. If a random access file state the size of one record.
- the likely size of the file when in use
- how the file is processed – how data is added, deleted and changed
- what it is used for

Four files are needed for Smiley's Snooker. Three of these will store records and therefore be random access files (for which we'll use a '.dat' extension in the file name) and one is a text file ('.txt' extension).

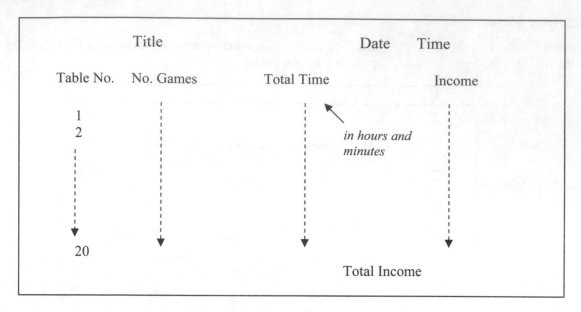

Figure 18.8: Report on table usage

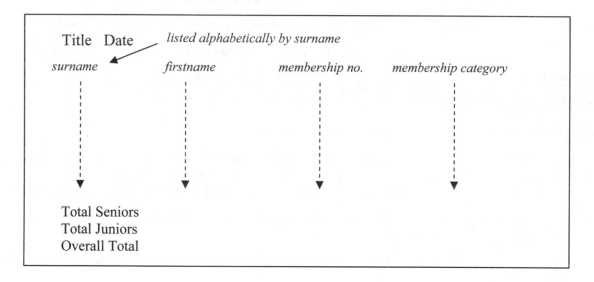

Figure 18.9: Report on membership

CurrentGames.dat   Stores details of the status of each table (in use or not) and the membership number of the player responsible for the game. Note that the data in this file *could* be stored only in RAM, but if the user accidentally closed the program, or even just the Main form, these details would be lost.

DailyGames.dat   Stores details of games that have finished. To be used for printing the report Smiley's wants on table usage. Smiley's does not require any details about which members used the tables in this report so these can be omitted. We do need to store details of the length of each game because the report needs to show the total amount of time each table has been used. A good rule in file design is not to store data that can be calculated from existing data. If there was a single cost rate at Smiley's, rather than senior and junior rates, we would not need to store how much each game cost because we would only have to multiply the rate by the number of minutes the game takes. Because there are different rates we must either store the cost of the game or the membership category of the member in charge of the game. Let's store the cost.

Costs.txt   Stores the senior and junior rates as pence per minute.

Members.dat   Stores details of each member – membership number, name and category of membership. As explained below it also has a flagged field to indicate if the member has been deleted.

CurrentGames.dat file

External file name	CurrentGames.dat		General name Current Games	
Description	Stores details of the current status of each table - if in use details of the game played on it			
Used for	Colouring the tables on the Main form green or red when the form loads Retrieving details of game when processing a finished game			
Organisation	Random access			
Processing	File is created with all records initialised to appropriate values. TableID values correspond to record numbers and are used for direct access			
Record structure				
Field name	**Field description**		**Data type (and length)**	**No. bytes**
TableD	Table number (1 to 20)		Integer	2
MemberID	Membership number		String	6
StartTime	If table has a game, time game started		Date	8
Occupied	Whether table has a game. Stores Y or N		String (1)	1
Record size	17 bytes			
Typical size of file	File always has 20 records (1 per table) – size is 340 bytes			

DailyGames.dat file

External file name	DailyGames.dat		General name Daily Games	
Description	Stores details of all completed games for the current day			
Used for	Producing the printed report on daily table usage			
Organisation	Random access			
Processing	New records appended. No deletions/changes to data required. Linear searching of file to produce printed report on daily table usage.			
Record structure				
Field name	**Field description**		**Data type (and length)**	**No. bytes**
TableID	Table number (1 to 20)		Integer	2
StartTime	Time game started		Date	8
FinishTime	Time game finished		Date	8
Cost	Cost of game		Currency	8
Record size	26 bytes			
Typical size of file	1 record for each completed game. Assuming all tables are used all day (12 hours) and that a game averages 1 hour, 12 x 20 records stored – maximum total size 6240 bytes			

Costs.txt file

External file name	Costs.txt	General name	Costs
Description	Stores the senior and junior rates per minute for a game		
Used for	Calculating cost of a finished game		
Organisation	Text file		
Structure of data	Only 1 line containing the two rates (e.g. 4, 3.5 etc)		
Typical size of file	A few bytes		

Members.dat file

Recall from the Analysis section that the only things Smiley's needs to store about a member is their membership number, name and category of membership. At this point, though, we have to consider how we will add and delete members from the file since this will affect how we design it. Take deleting a member first. Two algorithms you might consider are:

- Copy all the records except the one to delete to a new file, delete the old file and rename the new one with the same name as the old one. This **physically** deletes the record.

- Delete the record in the existing file **logically** by flagging one of its fields to indicate the record has been deleted. The record is still there physically.

If your own project has a file which will grow very large and contain many deletions, the first option might be the best since the file will not use a lot of wasted space storing deleted records. On the other hand how long would it take to carry out a deletion? If you need on-line processing and deletions are very frequent this method might be counterproductive. If you use batch processing you could flag the record for deletion and carry out all the deletions once every so often.

For Smiley's Snooker there's nothing to choose between the two algorithms. Let's use the second one, which means that we need a field to flag whether the record has been deleted. It will hold a single character Y or N.

To add a new record to the Members file we could simply append it (add it after the last record in the file). But let's keep the file as physically small as possible and overwrite the first record that has been flagged as deleted.

External file name	Members.dat		General name	Members	
Description	Stores details of all current members				
Used for	Displaying data on Game form when a new game starts or a game finishes Displaying list of members in Members form Producing printed list of members				
Organisation	Random access				
Processing	Records are logically deleted. Linear search made to find first logically deleted record when adding a new member – if none found record is appended.				
Record structure					
Field name	Field description		Data type (and length)		No. bytes
MemberID	Membership number		String (6)		6
Surname	Member's surname		String (14)		14
Firstname	Member's firstname		String (14)		14
Category	Category of membership – S (senior) or J (Junior)		String (1)		1
Deleted	Has this member been deleted? Stores Y or N		String(1)		1
Record size	36 bytes				
Typical size of file	1 record for each member. With 400 members = 14,400 bytes				

Data validation

Data input by the user may not be entered correctly. Any check to ensure that it is acceptable is called data validation. At the design stage of your project you are expected to list the validation checks you would like to build into your system. A word of warning here though. At design time you may think of plenty of checks but eventually find that the proportion of your code given over to validation is too high. In some projects to carry out very thorough validation could take up to half your code. By all means do it thoroughly at design time but be prepared not to implement all of it. You could refer to any uncoded validation in the Appraisal section of your project.

Figure 18.10 lists all the validation in Smiley's Snooker that will be coded in the chapters which follow. As we have no Visual Basic names for the controls yet, the identifiers below refer to the captions shown in the form design sketches earlier.

Control	*Form*	*Validation check*
Membership No, (Adding a member)	Members	• Length 6 characters • Not already used for another member. This means that the MemberID field in the Members.dat file is a primary key field (i.e. a field that cannot contain duplicate values)
Membership No. (Deleting a member)	Members	• Must not be blank
Surname	Members	• Must not be blank
Firstname	Members	• Must not be blank
Membership Category	Members (list box)	• Must be Senior or Junior
Senior (rate per game)	Utilities	• Must be a number
Junior (rate per game)	Utilities	• Must be a number
Membership No. (start a game)	Game	• Must not be blank • Membership number must exist (on Members file). This is a **file lookup check**, and since the membership number will be stored on the Daily Games file, it is also an example of **referential integrity**.
Table No. (start a game)	Game (combo box)	• Must be the number of a table available for play. • A value must be selected from the combo box
Table No. (finish a game)	Game (combo box)	• Must be the number of a table currently in use • A value must be selected from the combo box

Figure 18.10: Summary of validation checks

Entering the membership number of a new member lends itself to further validation. Since membership numbers consist of two characters followed by four digits you could check for this. This is briefly taken up in Chapter 24 which looks at how the project might be improved.

Visual Basic makes validating some data very easy by the use of list or combo boxes. In the three validation checks listed above that involve these controls, the user is forced to select a correct item of data. However you could still check that they have made a selection in the first place.

Chapter 19 – Design and System Maintenance: Modular Structure

Modular structure

The term 'modular structure' refers to the way in which the whole program is broken up into procedures and functions. Compared to a non-visual language, Visual Basic makes things a little easier by having event procedures. You have no choice but to structure your program using these event procedures. However you do have the choice about writing your own general procedures. A full-sized project ought to have general procedures for many reasons. The early part of Chapter 7 briefly described some of these.

Deciding on the general procedures you need at the design stage is not easy. You need to carefully work out what you want to happen when an event is triggered. If a particular task must happen that is not directly related to the event itself, then you should probably put it into a general procedure. If it needs particular items of data to do this task pass these as parameters. For example when the receptionist enters a player's membership number to start a new game and then tabs out of this control, the event procedure itself (the LostFocus event) can check if the user has actually entered a valid membership number. But checking that the valid membership number actually exists in the Members file can be done by a general procedure since this is a task one step removed from the event.

Event procedures

It's useful first to identify all the event procedures in your program, as shown in Figure 19.1. Notice the overwhelming dominance of the Click event. The asterisked tasks are those that will be assigned to general procedures.

Event	Control	Processing
Main form – command buttons		
Click	Close	Closes program
Click	Game	Displays/loads Game form
Click	Membership	Displays/loads Members form
Click	Utilities	Displays/loads Utilities form
Click	Table Usage Report	* Prints report on table usage * Deletes Daily Games file (if user requests this)
Main form – other		
Load	n/a	Colours tables red or green according to whether they are in use, and displays starting time of game next to red ones.
Game form – Starting a game		
Click	Start option button	Makes input controls for finishing a game invisible. Makes those for starting a game visible Changes caption of command button to 'Start Game' * Populates combo box (tables available for play)
LostFocus	Membership No. text box	* Displays member's name and category of membership

Click	Combo box	* Converts starting time of game to hours/minutes only Displays this starting time
Click	Start Game command button	* Stores record of game in Current Games file * Changes table's colour to red and displays starting time next to it * Populates combo box (available tables)
Game form – Finishing a game		
Click	Finish option button	Makes input controls for starting a game invisible. Makes those for finishing a game visible. Changes caption of command button to 'Finish Game' * Populates combo box (occupied tables)
Click	Combo box	* Retrieves record of game from Current Games file * Retrieves player's details from Members file * Calculates playing time in hours and minutes * Calculates cost of game * Converts starting and finishing times of game to hours/minutes Displays start and finish time and cost of completed game
Click	Finish Game command button	* Retrieves details of game from Current Games file * Updates record of finished table in Current Games file (sets Occupied field to 'N') * Changes colour of table to green and removes starting time * Stores record of finished game in Daily Games file * Populates combo box (occupied tables)
Members form – Adding a member		
Click	Add option button	Makes input control for deleting a member invisible. Makes controls for adding a member visible Changes caption of command button to 'Add Member'
Click	Add Member command button	* Checks that membership number has not been used before * Stores new member's details in Members file
Members form – Deleting a member		
Click	Delete option button	Makes input controls for adding a member invisible. Makes control for deleting a member visible Changes caption of command button to 'Delete Member'
Click	Delete Member command button	* Deletes member from Members file
Members form – other command buttons		
Click	Display Members	Displays details of all current members in list box
Click	Print Membership List	Prints report on current membership
Utilities form		
Click	Change Price of Game option button	Displays controls for entering new senior and junior rates
Click	OK command button	* Backs up Current Games and Daily Games files * Backs up Members file * Creates Current Games file * Stores new rates in Costs file

Figure 19.1: The tasks of the event procedures

General procedures

Ideally at design time you should be able to state the following for each general procedure that you intend to write:

- its name
- the type of general procedure – a sub Procedure or a function
- exactly what it does
- parameters – their data types and whether they are passed by value or by reference
- if a function, its return value
- where it is called from

This is a tall order for inexperienced programmers, and it is very likely that many of these items will be decided as you code. Some students doing the project will not have understood parameter passing and will therefore have to miss this part out. Your program can work perfectly without parameters, but the overhead is more global variables, the likelihood of more errors, and the perception by your assessor that the program is not quite as good as it could be.

One of the main stages of an 'A' level Computing project noted in Chapter 17 was Systems Maintenance. This covers three things – a code listing (with plenty of comments), samples of algorithms, and an overall system design including the modular design. Although the list of features about each procedure noted above should ideally be worked out at design time, realistically you won't draw these up completely until writing up the system maintenance. So the title of this chapter covers takes in two stages of the project. If you change any of the design time decisions when you code, these should be documented as part of the system maintenance.

Let's take some of the event procedures listed in figure 19.1, which call one or more general procedures, and see how to draw up a modular structure.

Clicking the Start/Finish option button on the Game form

If starting a game the appropriate combo box should list the free tables, and if finishing a game it should list the occupied tables. Both these tasks are similar and can be done by the same general procedure. No parameters are needed and nothing is returned so it can be a sub procedure. We will name it ListTablesAvailable.

A useful way of documenting a general procedure is shown in figure 19.2. You should do this for each of the general procedures in your own project. Figure 19.2 shows that ListTablesAvailable does not need any parameters, but you might be thinking that it needs to know whether a game has just started or finished. It does, and the caption of the command button on the form, which shows 'Start Game' or 'Finish Game', can be used for this (figures 18.3 and 18.4). You *could* pass this caption as a parameter but it really isn't necessary.

Name	ListTablesAvailable
Type	Sub Procedure
Parameters/ReturnValue	None
Called from	Click event of StartGame/Finish Game command button and the Start and Finish option buttons on the Game form
Purpose	If starting a game populates the 'start' combo box with table numbers that are free. If finishing a game populates the 'finish' combo box with table numbers that are occupied.

Figure 19.2: Documenting the general procedure ListTablesAvailable

LostFocus event of Membership No. text box (starting a game)

This event is triggered when the user tabs out of the text box. Figure 19.1 shows that the LostFocus event of the membership number text box (for starting a game) should display the name and category of membership of the player whose membership number has just been entered. As it is possible that the membership number does not exist we could consider breaking the task into two sub-tasks:

- check to see if the membership number exists
- retrieve the record from the Members file

The second sub-task will only be done if the first sub-task reports that the number does exist. Since the 'parent' LostFocus event calls these procedures, the question is how the first sub-task reports back that the membership number exists or not. A function is an appropriate type of procedure and a Boolean return value looks promising. But if the number does exist, the next sub-task needs to know which record number in the file to go to. It could search the file for the membership number, but this has already been done by the first sub-task. A good solution is to make the return value of the first sub-task the record number in the file if the membership number is there, and another integer value if the number does not exist. A value of 0 will do (since record numbers begin at 1).

Figure 19.3 uses a **module structure chart** to show the modular structure of this part of the program. An arrow going into a general procedure represents a value parameter and a return arrow represents a reference parameter (for a sub procedure) or a return value (for a function).

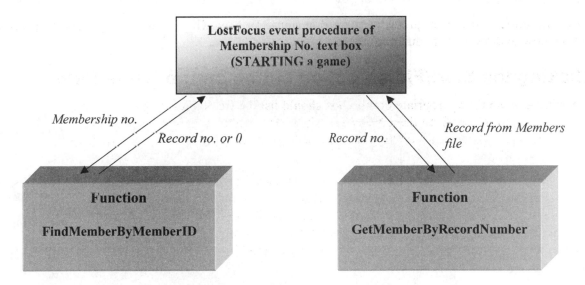

Figure 19.3: Modular structure chart for the LostFocus event of the membership no. text box (for starting a game)

Clicking the combo box (starting a game) to display start time

The start time of a game is taken from the system clock and this includes seconds as well as hours and minutes. The receptionist does not need the seconds part displayed so we will have a function, *ShortenTime*, that is sent a time and returns only the hours and minutes part. Figure 19.4 shows its documentation. Note that other events also call it, and that an identifier for the parameter, *FullTime*, has been used to make the description of the purpose easier to write.

Name	ShortenTime
Type	Function
Parameters/ReturnValue	String value parameter (FullTime) – a time Returns String
Called from	Combo box Click event (both for starting and finishing a game) Main form's Load event
Purpose	Strips off the seconds part of FullTime and returns the hours and minutes part

Figure 19.4: Documentation of function ShortenTime

Clicking the combo box for finishing a game

Each of the five asterisked tasks in figure 19.1 for this event procedure can be put into a general procedure. The last one, to convert the starting and finishing times to hours and minutes only, has already been designed – ShortenTime above.

Each of the general procedures can be written as a function since they all return one item of data. Figure 19.5 shows the details. The first function, to retrieve a particular table's details from the Current Games file, needs to be passed the table number. The second function, to retrieve a particular member's details from the Members file, needs to be passed the member's membership number. Function NumberOfMinutes needs to be passed the start and finish times of a game in order to calculate how many minutes the game took. Finally, to calculate the cost of a game requires the number of minutes it took (which has just been returned from NumberOfMinutes) and the category of membership. You'll see in Chapter 23 that the senior and junior rates, which function CalculateCost also needs, will be global variables, and are therefore not passed as parameters.

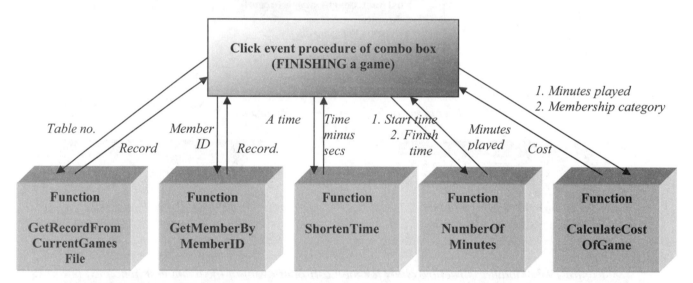

Figure 19.5: Modular structure chart for the Click event of combo box for finishing a game

Clicking the command button to process a new game

Figure 19.1 lists three tasks that must be done when processing a new game. These are:

- store details of the new game in the Current Games file
- change the table's colour to red and display the starting time
- repopulate the combo box so that the newly-used table is not listed

Figure 19.6 shows the modular structure chart for these tasks. No data needs to be returned to the calling event procedure and so sub procedures are used. We saw earlier that ListTablesAvailable does not even need to be passed any parameters (figure 19.2) and so the line connecting it to its parent event procedure in figure 19.6 does not have an arrow. Note that UpdateTableDisplay in turn needs to call ShortenTime. This is so it can display the start time of the new game on the Main form.

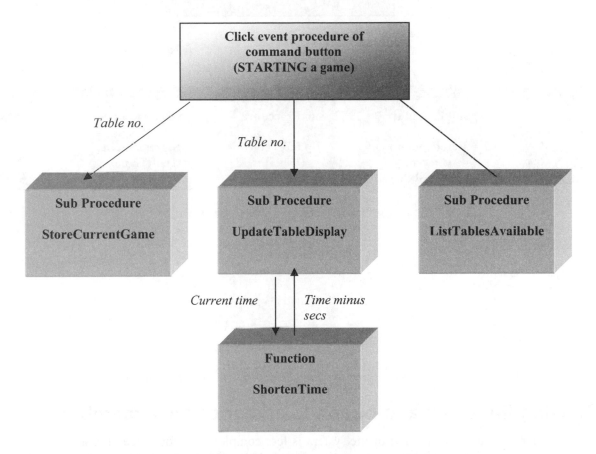

Figure 19.6: Modular structure chart for the Click event of command button for starting a game

Clicking the command button to process a finished game

Figure 19.1 lists five tasks that must be done when the user clicks the button to process a finished game:

- retrieve details of the game that has finished from the Current Games file
- update the record of this table in the Current Games file so that its Occupied field stores 'N'
- change the colour of the table to green and remove the starting time
- store details of the finished game in the Daily Games file
- repopulate the combo box with tables that are in use

Figure 19.7 shows the modular structure for these tasks. We have already designed procedures to handle the first and third tasks. Since ResetGameInCurrentGamesFile simply overwrites the occupied field with 'N', it only needs the table number. Procedure StoreGameInDailyGamesFile needs the table number and the start time. The start time will have been retrieved in the record returned from GetRecordFromCurrentGamesFile.

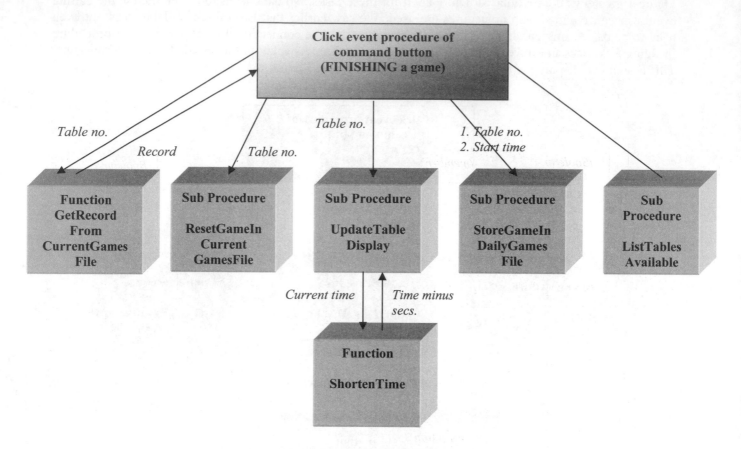

Figure 19.7: Modular structure chart for the Click event of command button for finishing a game

Clicking the command button to add or delete a member

The modular structure for this part of the system is less complex than for processing a game and we can put everything into one modular structure chart (figure 19.8). When adding a member we need to check that the new membership number does not already exist (unlikely but possible). This task is assigned to the function CheckDuplicateMemberID. It returns a Boolean value to indicate whether or not the membership number already exists.

Procedure AddMember actually writes the new record to the Members file, but recall from Chapter 18 that we decided to find the first logically deleted member (the Deleted field contains 'Y') and overwrite this record with the new one. The task of locating this deleted member is assigned to function FindDeletedMember. If there is a deleted one it returns the record number; if there isn't one it returns 0. It is the job of AddMember to handle the 0 if this is returned. Figure 19.8 shows the arrow connecting AddMember to its parent event procedure as a dashed line. Although the record passed into AddMember could theoretically be a value parameter, since it does not need to be changed and passed back again, ***Visual Basic will only allow user-defined types to be passed by reference***.

Only one general procedure, DeleteMember, is used to process a deleted member. It is passed a membership number and searches the Members file for this number. If it finds the number it logically deletes the member and returns True. If it doesn't find the number the return value is False, and no changes are made to the file. Note that we could have had a separate function to check if the membership number exists in the file and given DeleteMember the single task of deleting the appropriate record. Instead we have packed two closely related tasks into DeleteMember.

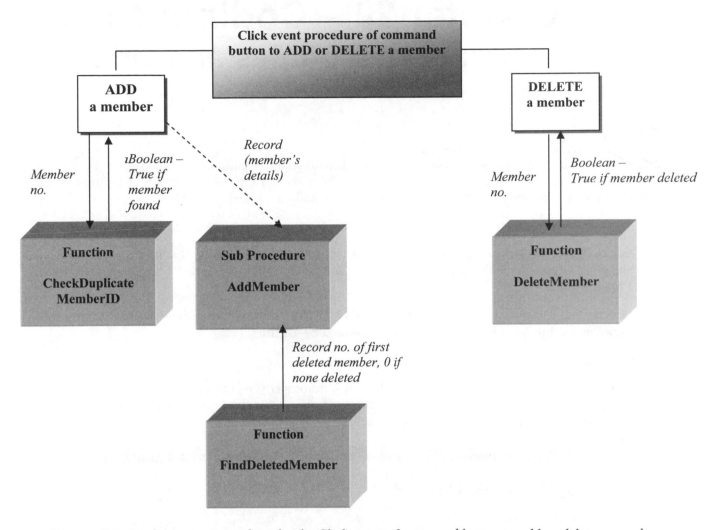

Figure 19.8: Modular structure chart for the Click event of command button to add or delete a member

Complete modular structure

There are several other tasks assigned to general procedures in figure 19.1 that we haven't covered above. These are called from the Click events of command buttons on the Main form to print the table usage report or on the Utilities form to carry out the task selected by the user. None of them needs parameters and none return any data, so they must all be sub procedures.

Final thoughts

It's worth repeating the point that all the details about the modular structure of your project *can* be done at the design stage. It's quite a skill getting everything worked out before you start to code and quite understandable that inexperienced programmers will shuffle between design and coding. Nevertheless it's worth spending some time trying to sort out the modular structure before coding as it will really help you with this later stage of the project.

Chapter 20 – Coding: Forms, Standard Modules and Utilities

The Forms

The design of the four forms in Chapter 18 can be used directly in building them in Visual Basic. The only thing we did not decide on at design time was the names of the controls that will be used in our coding. First let's tell Visual Basic that we want four forms in our project.

1. Open a new project and name the form **frmMain**. Delete its caption.

2. Select **Project/New Form**. Make sure the **New** tab is selected and that the **Form** icon is highlighted and click **Open**. Name the new form **frmGame** and set its caption to **Smiley's Snooker – Start and Finish a game**.

3. Get two more forms. Name them **frmMembers** and **frmUtilities** and set their captions to **Smiley's Snooker – Club Membership** and **Smiley's Snooker – Utilities**.

The Main form

Figure 20.1 shows the completed form. The BorderStyle property of the labels to display the starting times of games in play has been set to Fixed Single simply so that they can be seen in the figure. The default value, None, will be used in the project itself.

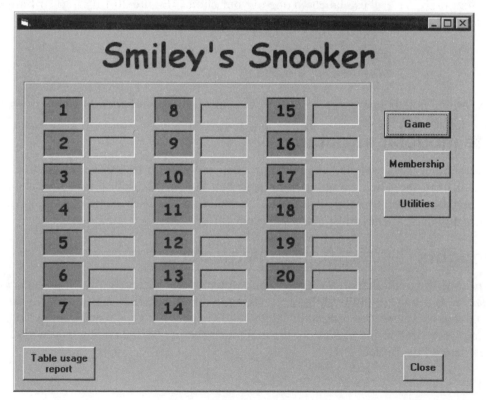

Figure 20.1: The main form

1. On frmMain place a label and enter the title **Smiley's Snooker**. The font in figure 20.1 is **30 pt bold Comic Sans MS**, but use whichever font you feel is appropriate.

2. Draw a frame to contain the tables. Delete its caption.

We've quickly reached the point where the most important decision in coding the whole project must be made. How are we to name the 40 labels to represent the 20 tables and their games' starting times? If you named them lblTable1, lblTable2, lblStartTime1, lblStartTime2 and so on you would find later that you have to write many dozens of lines of code where only a few would be needed if you use two control arrays, one for the tables and one for the starting times. Recall from Chapter 8 that a control array is a group of controls which are all of the same type, and that you set the Index property of each to a different value.

3. Place a label in the top left of the frame for table 1. Change its caption to **1** to indicate table number 1 and its name to **lblTables**. Set its Index property to **1**. It will now be known to Visual Basic as lblTables(1).

4. Now add 19 more labels (numbered 2 to 20 in figure 20.1). Name each of them **lblTables** and Index them from 2 to **20**. Set their the captions from **2** to **20** also. Note that you cannot copy and paste these labels because pasting won't attach them to the frame. You must drag and drop each one separately.

5. Press the **Shift** key and select all 20 labels. Change their BorderStyle property to **1 – Fixed Single** and set their BackColor property to a particular green colour. To set the colour click the small button in the BackColor property and click the **Palette** tab. Select the third green colour from the top in the column of greens. It's most important that this one is selected for some later code to work. You can check you have the right one by the BackColor property. It should contain &H0000FF00&, which corresponds to RGB(0, 255, 0) if you can remember doing program 2.4.

6. Set the Font property of these labels to one of your choice. Figure 20.1 uses **14 pt bold Comic Sans MS**. Set the Alignment property to **2 – Center**.

7. Now for the labels to display the starting times of games being played. Place a label to the right of the table 1 label. Name it **lblStartTimes** and set its Index to **1**. Delete its caption. You may wish to set its BorderStyle property to Fixed Single to be able to see exactly where it is on the form. You can change it back to Normal later. Accept the default Font but set it to **bold**.

8. Place 19 more labels next to the tables. Name these **lblStartTimes** and set their Index property to **2** to **20** as appropriate. Set the BorderStyle as in step 7.

9. Place the 5 command buttons shown in figure 20.1 on the form. Set their properties as shown in figure 20.2.

Name	Caption
cmdGame	Game
cmdMembership	Membership
cmdUtilities	Utilities
cmdPrintReport	Table usage report
cmdClose	Close

Figure 20.2: Properties of the command buttons on the Main form

10. If you have set the BorderStyle of the lblStartTimes control array to 1 - Fixed Single (step 8), change it back to **0 – Normal**.

11. As a final check make sure that all the members of each of the two control arrays have the same name and are indexed from 1 to 20. If there is just one mistake at this stage you will get run-time errors later that at first you may not be able to put right.

12. The code for the four command buttons on the right of the form is simple:

```
Private Sub cmdGame_Click()
   frmGame.Show
End Sub

Private Sub cmdMembership_Click()
   frmMembers.Show
End Sub

Private Sub cmdUtilities_Click()
   frmUtilities.Show
End Sub

Private Sub cmdClose_Click()
   End
End Sub
```

13. Test out the form by running the program and then save the form as **Main** and the project as **SmileysSnooker**.

The Game form

Figures 20.3 and 20.4 show the finished form based on the sketches in figures 18.3 and 18.4. Since several of the controls are duplicated on the two frames their names will end with Start or Finish as appropriate. Thus txtMemberIDStart refers to the membership number control in figure 20.3 and txtMemberIDFinish to the membership number control in figure 20.4.

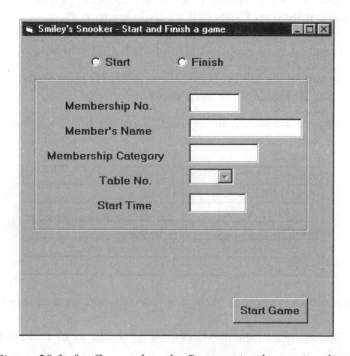

Figure 20.3: frmGame when the Start option button is selected

206

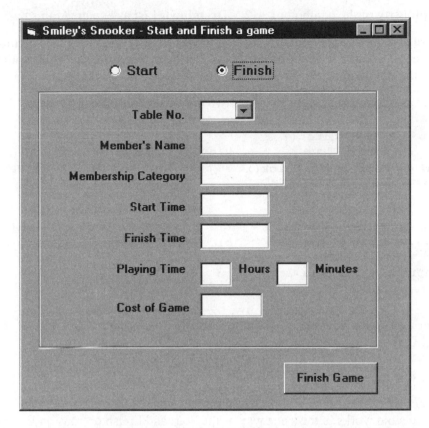

Figure 20.4: frmGame when the Finish option button is selected

1. Place the two option buttons, name them **optStart** and **optFinish** and set their captions to **Start** and **Finish**. Set the Value of optStart to **True** so that it is selected by default when the form loads.

2. Place a frame below the option buttons. Name it **fraStart** and delete its caption.

3. Put the 5 labels shown in figure 20.3 onto the frame and set their captions.

4. Position the 4 text boxes and the combo box. Set their Text property to blank and name them **txtMemberIDStart**, **txtMemberNameStart**, **txtCategoryStart**, **txtStartTimeStart** and **cboTableNumberStart**.

5. Set the Style property of the combo box to **2 – Dropdown List**. In a true combo box (with the default Style of 0 – Dropdown Combo) the user can either select an item or enter one that is not listed in the edit box at the top of the control. In our project the user must only select a table from those listed, which the Dropdown List type enforces.

6. The controls that display the member's name, category of membership and starting time of game should be read-only, so set their Enabled property to **False**.

7. Position another frame below fraStart. Name it **fraFinish** and delete its caption.

8. Put the 9 labels shown in figure 20.4 onto the frame and set their captions.

9. Place the combo box and the 7 text boxes. Set their Text properties to blank and name them **cboTableNumberFinish**, **txtMemberNameFinish**, **txtCategoryFinish**, **txtStartTimeFinish** **txtFinishTime**, **txtHours**, **txtMinutes** and **txtCost**.

10. Set the Style property of the combo box to **2 - Dropdown List** as explained in step 5.

11. Move fraFinish so that its upper edge is over the upper edge of fraStart. Place a command button as shown in figure 20.3. Name it **cmdOK** and set its caption to **Start Game**. This caption will change if the user clicks the option button to finish a game.

12. Make sure the code for the Click events of the two option buttons on frmGame is:

```
Private Sub optStart_Click()
   fraStart.Visible = True        'hide controls for starting a game
   fraFinish.Visible = False      'and show those for finishing one
   cmdOK.Caption = "Start Game"
End Sub

Private Sub optFinish_Click()
   fraFinish.Visible = True       'hide controls for finishing a game
   fraStart.Visible = False       'and show those for starting one
   cmdOK.Caption = "Finish Game"
End Sub
```

13. Save the form as **Game**. Run the program and test that the option buttons make a different set of controls visible.

The Members form

Figures 20.5 and 20.6 show the finished form based on the sketches in figures 18.5 and 18.6. Making the frame visible and invisible works in the same way as the Start and Finish options on frmGame.

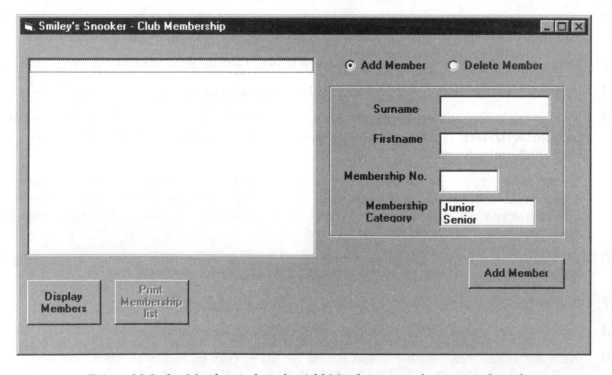

Figure 20.5: frmMembers when the Add Member option button is selected

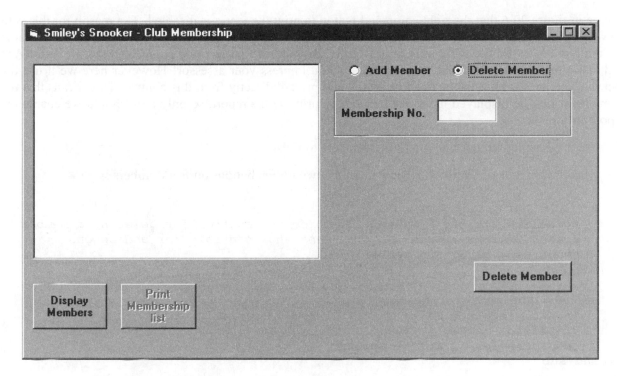

Figure 20.6: frmMembers when the Delete Member option button is selected

1. On frmMembers place the two option buttons near the top. Name them **optAdd** and **optDelete** and set their captions to **Add Member** and **Delete Member**. Set the Value property of optAdd to **True** since we want this option selected by default when the form loads.

2. Place a frame below the option buttons. Name it **fraAdd** and delete its caption.

3. Put the 4 labels shown in figure 20.5 onto the frame and set their captions.

4. Position the 3 text boxes and the list box. Set their Text property to blank and name them **txtSurname, txtFirstname, txtMemberIDAdd** and **lstCategory**.

5. Add the two items **Junior** and **Senior** to the List property of the list box.

6. Position another frame below fraAdd. Name it **fraDelete** and delete its caption.

7. Put the label and text box shown in figure 20.6 onto the frame. Name the text box **txtMemberIDDelete**.

8. Move fraDelete so that its upper edge is over the upper edge of fraAdd.

9. Place a command button below the bottom right of fraAdd. Name it **cmdOK** and set its caption to **Add Member**. This caption will change if the user selects the option button to delete a member.

10. Position the list box and name it **lstMembers**. Since it must display members alphabetically by surname, set its Sorted property to **True**.

11. Since we want the member details displayed in columns we need an even-spaced font. Change the Font property of the list box to **Courier.**

12. Place two command buttons below the list box. Figure 20.6 shows their captions. Name them **cmdDisplayMembers** and **cmdPrintMembers**.

Notice in figure 20.6 that the right command button to print the report is disabled. The reason for this is to do with the method we'll use later to print the membership list. The report must list members by surname but the records in the file will not be in this order. In your own project you *could* read the file into RAM and call a procedure to sort the records. This would impress your assessor! However here we'll use the fact that the items in the list box can be sorted and printed directly from this control. This means that the items must first be displayed in the list box before printing the report, so only then should we enable the report button.

13. Set the Enabled property of cmdPrintMembers to **False**.

14. Make sure the code for the Click events of the two option buttons on frmMembers is:

```
Private Sub optAddMember_Click()
    fraDelete.Visible = False      'hide the control for deleting a member
    fraAdd.Visible = True          'and show controls for adding one
    cmdOK.Caption = "Add Member"
End Sub

Private Sub optDeleteMember_Click()
    fraAdd.Visible = False          'hide controls for adding new member
    fraDelete.Visible = True        'and show control for deleting one
    cmdOK.Caption = "Delete Member"
End Sub
```

15. Save the form as **Members**. Run the program and test that the option buttons make a different set of controls visible.

The Utilities form

This is based on the sketch in figure 18.7 and is shown in figure 20.7. When the option to change the price of a game is selected the Senior and Junior controls and the short instruction are made visible.

1. On frmUtilities place the large frame. Leave its default name but delete its caption.

2. Put the 4 option buttons onto the frame and set their captions. Store them as a control array using the name **optUtilities** and set their Index properties from **1** to **4**.

3. Place the smaller frame within the larger one below the last option button. Name it **fraCosts** and delete its caption. Set its Visible property to **False**.

4. Place labels and text boxes on fraCosts as shown in figure 20.7. Name the text boxes **txtSeniorCost** and **txtJuniorCost**. Place the label to the right of the frame. Name it **lblHelp** and set its caption as the instruction to the user shown in figure 20.7. Set its Visible property to **False**.

5. Double-click on any of the options buttons to get the code template for the control array. Notice that Visual Basic supplies a parameter which the code uses to work out which button has been selected. This concept was covered in program 8.4. Its code is:

```
Private Sub optUtilities_Click(Index As Integer)
    If Index = 4 Then               'option to change costs of game selected?
        fraCosts.Visible = True
        lblHelp.Visible = True
    End If
End Sub
```

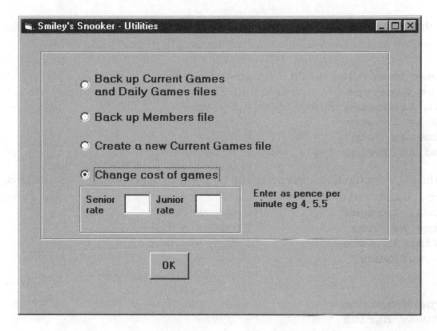

Figure 20.7: frmUtilities when the option to change the cost of a game is selected

6. Place the command button. Name it **cmdOK** and set its caption to **OK**.

7. Save the form as **Utilities**. Run the program and test that clicking the last option button on frmUtilities displays the cost controls.

Standard modules

Recall that a standard module cannot contain any controls, only code, and that when saved it has a **.bas** extension. For Smiley's Snooker we will use standard modules to do the following:

- Declare a constant to hold the number of tables (20). This will be used in several loops to process all the tables. If Smiley's ever adds more tables in the future only this constant needs to be changed.

- Declare user-defined data types for processing records in the Current Games, Daily Games and Members files. Each file is processed by code on more than one form and so the declarations must be made on a standard module. (This was explained in step 8 of program 9.1.)

- To calculate the cost of a game you need to multiply the number of minutes it lasted by the cost per minute. We decided on function NumberOfMinutes in Chapter 19 (see figure 19.5). It is passed two time values and returns the number of minutes difference between them.

- When displaying the start and finish times the receptionist would be put off by having the seconds shown. We decided on function ShortenTime in Chapter 19 (figures 19.4 to 19.6). It is passed a time value and returns the hours and minutes part.

The two functions referred to above are used only on the Game form and so *could* be written there. But in your own project it is a good idea to put functions like these, which might be used in other programs dealing with time, into a standard module. At least it shows your project assessor that you understand another important part of Visual Basic.

Declarations

1. Select **Project/Add Module**. Name it **basDeclarations** and save it as **ProjectDeclarations**.

2. Declare the three user-defined types for storing records. Recall from Chapter 10 that when writing a record to a random access file you must declare the length of any String fields.

```
Public Const MaxTables = 20      'Smiley's has 20 tables
Public Type GameType        'data type for a record to store one current game
   MemberID As String * 6        '6 bytes
   TableID As Integer            '2 bytes
   StartTime As Date             '8 bytes
   Occupied As String * 1        '1 byte
End Type                         'one record is 17 bytes

Public Type GameFinishedType     'data type for record for a finished game
   TableID As Integer            '2 bytes
   StartTime As Date             '8 bytes
   FinishTime As Date            '8 bytes
   Cost As Currency              '8 bytes
End Type                         'one record is 26 bytes

Public Type MemberType           'data type for a record to store one member
   MemberID As String * 6        '6 bytes
   Surname As String * 14        '14 bytes
   Firstname As String * 20      '20 bytes
   Category As String * 1        '1 byte
   Deleted As String * 1         '1 byte
End Type                         'one record is 42 bytes
```

Library of time functions

3. Add a second module to the project. Name it **basTimeFunctions** and save it as **TimeFunctions**.

4. Write code for the function to calculate the number of minutes between two time values. It uses the two built-in time functions Hour and Minute. Chapter 6 has a similar example to this.

```
Public Function NumberOfMinutes(ByVal Time1 As String, ByVal Time2 As _
                                            String) As Integer
'Returns the number of minutes difference between Time1 and Time2
'Time1 and Time2 must be strings in the form of "19:42:54" or "19.42.54"
'Time1 must be a later time than Time2
   Dim HoursDiff As Integer
   Dim MinutesDiff As Integer
   HoursDiff = Hour(Time1) - Hour(Time2)
   MinutesDiff = Minute(Time1) - Minute(Time2)
   NumberOfMinutes = (HoursDiff * 60) + MinutesDiff
End Function
```

5. The code for the function to display a time minus the seconds uses the Left string-handling function which was covered in Chapter 6.

```
Public Function ShortenTime(ByVal FullTime As String) As String
'Removes the seconds from a time value and returns the hours and minutes
'FullTime is a string in the format "19:42:54".
   ShortenTime = Left(FullTime, 5)
End Function
```

Utilities

Figures 18.7 and 20.7 show the four utilities we need to code. The user selects one of the option buttons and then clicks OK. Figure 19.1 suggested that each of these utilities would be coded in a separate procedure. Each of them is called from the Click event of the single command button.

1. In the Click event for cmdOK find out which option button has been selected by using a **For...Next** loop to examine each of them. Then use a **Select Case** to call the relevant procedure.

```
Private Sub cmdOK_Click()
'Finds out which option has been selected and calls relevant procedure
   Dim Index As Integer
   Dim OptionChoice As Integer        'option button selected (1 to 4)
   For Index = 1 To 4                 'find which option has been selected
      If optUtilities(Index).Value = True Then   'true if option selected
         OptionChoice = Index
      End If
   Next Index
   Select Case OptionChoice
      Case 1
         Call BackupGamesFiles
      Case 2
         Call BackupMembersFile
      Case 3
         Call CreateCurrentGamesFile
      Case 4
         Call ChangeCostOfGame
   End Select
End Sub
```

2. Select **Tools/Add Procedure** and get the code template for **BackupGamesFiles**. The code uses the FileCopy statement to copy the two games files to the root directory of a floppy disk:

```
Public Sub BackupGamesFiles()
   Dim Source1 As String
   Dim Source2 As String
   Dim Destination1 As String
   Dim Destination2 As String
   Source1 = App.Path & "\CurrentGames.dat"
   Destination1 = "a:\CurrentGames.dat"
   FileCopy Source1, Destination1
   Source2 = App.Path & "\DailyGames.dat"
   Destination2 = "a:\DailyGames.dat"
   FileCopy Source2, Destination2
End Sub
```

3. The procedure to make a backup of the Members file is the same as the previous one:

```
Public Sub BackupMembersFile()
   Dim Source As String
   Dim Destination As String
   Source = App.Path & "\Members.dat"
   Destination = "a:\Members.dat"
   FileCopy Source, Destination
End Sub
```

4. To create the Current Games file requires a **For...Next** loop. Each repetition writes one record to the file with details of one table:

```
Public Sub CreateCurrentGamesFile()
'Creates Current Games file with one record for each table
   Dim OneGame As GameType
   Dim TableNumber As Integer
   Open App.Path & "\CurrentGames.dat" For Random As #1 Len = Len(OneGame)
   For TableNumber = 1 To MaxTables       'loop 20 times, once for each table
      OneGame.MemberID = ""               'set to blank
      OneGame.TableID = TableNumber       'assign a number from 1 to 20
      OneGame.Occupied = "N"              'set to not occupied
      Put #1, TableNumber, OneGame        'write record to file
   Next TableNumber
   Close #1
End Sub
```

5. To change the cost of a game simply requires writing the two new values to the Costs file. Recall that this is a text file consisting of one line only - senior and junior rates in pence per minute.

```
Public Sub ChangeCostOfGame()
'Stores new senior and junior rates in Costs file
   Dim FileName As String
   Dim SeniorCost As String
   Dim JuniorCost As String
   SeniorCost = txtSeniorCost.Text                 'get the two new rates
   JuniorCost = txtJuniorCost.Text
   If (Not IsNumeric(SeniorCost)) Or (Not IsNumeric(JuniorCost)) Then
      MsgBox ("One or both of the rates are not numbers. Please re-enter")
   Else
      FileName = App.Path & "\Costs.txt"
      Open FileName For Output As #1
      Print #1, SeniorCost, JuniorCost             'and write them to the file
      Close #1
   End If
End Sub
```

One of the data validation checks we decided on at Design time was that valid numbers are entered for the new costs (see figure 18.10). In the code above the **IsNumeric** function returns True if its argument forms a valid number. The expression Not IsNumeric therefore means *does not form a valid number*.

6. The Utilities are now ready for trying out. To test the two backup options you need any three files with the names (and extensions) used in the code above in your current directory and a floppy disk. To check that the Current Games file has been created go to Windows and look for CurrentGames.dat. It should be 340 bytes in size. To check that the costs of a game have been stored look for **Costs.txt** in Windows and open it in Notepad or WordPad. When you run the code for changing the costs Visual Basic will create the file if it doesn't exist. Changing the cost of a game only takes effect the next time you run the program (see *Getting the payment rates* on page 231).

Chapter 21 – Coding: Membership

Declaration and Loading the form

The Members file will be used by several procedures on the Members form, so we can declare it as a global variable and use the form's Load event to assign it a value.

1. On frmMembers declare the file variable as follows:

```
Dim FileName As String
```

2. Assign it the file name in the form's Load event:

```
Private Sub Form_Load()
   FileName = App.Path & "\Members.dat"
End Sub
```

Adding a new member

The sequence of events when the user clicks the command button on the Members form to add a new member is:

- A validation check is made that the membership number has 6 characters.
- A check is made that the membership number is not already being used by calling function CheckDuplicateMember.
- A check is made that the user has entered data in the surname and firstname controls.
- If the above three checks are satisfied the procedure AddMember is called.
- Procedure AddMember calls the function FindDeletedMember to get the record number of the first logically deleted record in the Members file.
- AddMember stores the record in the first logically deleted record space if there is one, otherwise it appends the record to the file.

First let's write the code for the general procedures. Look back at figure 19.8 to remind yourself of the modular structure for adding a member. We decided on three general procedures.

Function CheckDuplicateMemberID

1. This function needs to be passed one parameter – the membership number to search for in the file. As this is not changed inside the function it can be passed by value.

```
Private Function CheckDuplicateMemberID(ByVal MemberID As String) As _
                                        Boolean
'Returns True if MemberID has already been used as a membership number,
'otherwise returns False
   Dim Found As Boolean
   Dim OneMember As MemberType
   Found = False
   Open FileName For Random As #1 Len = Len(OneMember)
   Do While (Not EOF(1)) And (Found = False) 'keep looping until a
            'a duplicate ID has been found or the end of file reached
```

215

```
      Get #1, , OneMember        'second parameter not needed, so 2 commas
      If (MemberID = OneMember.MemberID) AND (OneMember.Deleted = "N")Then
         Found = True          'member ID used?
      End If
   Loop
   CheckDuplicateMemberID = Found        'return True or False from function
   Close #1
End Function
```

Function FindDeletedMember

2. This function does not need any parameters. Recall that Visual Basic numbers the records in a random access file from 1. The function returns this number for the first record with a 'Y' in its Deleted field., or returns 0 if it can't find a deleted record. Type in the following code:

```
Private Function FindDeletedMember() As Integer
'Finds the first record in Members file that is logically deleted
'A logically deleted record has the Deleted field set to Y
'Returns the record number of the first deleted record, or returns 0 if
'there are none
   Dim Found As Boolean
   Dim RecordNumber As Integer
   Dim OneMember As MemberType
   Found = False
   RecordNumber = 0
   Open FileName For Random As #1 Len = Len(OneMember)
   Do While (Not EOF(1)) And (Found = False)
      RecordNumber = RecordNumber + 1        'to get to the next record
      Get #1, RecordNumber, OneMember        'read record from file
      If OneMember.Deleted = "Y" Then        'is record logically deleted?
         Found = True
      End If
   Loop
   If Found Then                             'there IS a deleted record so
      FindDeletedMember = RecordNumber       'return its number
   Else
      FindDeletedMember = 0       'return 0 if no deleted record in file
   End If
   Close #1
End Function
```

Note the difference in the **Get** statements used in the two functions above. In CheckDuplicateMemberID commas are used for the missing second parameter. In FindDeletedMember a variable, RecordNumber, is used instead because this is needed as the return value if a deleted record has been found.

Sub Procedure AddMember

3. This procedure is passed a record to add to the Members file. It first calls FindDeletedMember to see if there is an existing record it can use. If there is it uses the record number returned from FindDeletedMember to write the new record to this space. If there is no deleted record, because FindDeletedMember returned a 0, it appends the new record. Note that the parameter is passed by reference even though it is not changed and does not need to be passed out again. Visual Basic does not allow user-defined types, MemberType for example, to be passed by value. A dashed line in figure 19.8 was used to represent this. The code is:

```
Private Sub AddMember(ByRef OneMember As MemberType)
'Stores record in Members file. Calls FindDeletedMember function to get
'first logically deleted record in the file and uses this space for the
'new record.If no such record it appends new record
  Dim NumberOfRecords As Integer
  Dim DeletedRecordNumber As Integer
  DeletedRecordNumber = FindDeletedMember
  Open FileName For Random As #1 Len = Len(OneMember)
  If DeletedRecordNumber <> 0 Then        'there is a deleted record that
                                          'can be used
    Put #1, DeletedRecordNumber, OneMember   'store record in this space
  Else                                       'no deleted records so
    NumberOfRecords = LOF(1) / Len(OneMember)'calc no. of records in file
    Put #1, NumberOfRecords + 1, OneMember      'append new record
  End If
  Close #1
  Call cmdDisplayMember_Click   'so that new member appears in list box
End Sub
```

The LOF (**L**ength **O**f **F**ile) function was covered in step 4 of program 10.2. The last line of code is the only example in Smiley's Snooker of calling an *event* procedure from code. You haven't written the Click event for cmdDisplayMember yet but its task will be to display all the members' details in the list box. Calling it here will have the effect of adding the new member to the list box.

Deleting a member

This is more straightforward than adding a member. Only one procedure is needed, DeleteMember.

Function DeleteMember

1. This function must be passed a membership number. It searches the file for the record with this membership number, and if it finds it checks whether this member has already been logically deleted. (This is unlikely but possible - the receptionist would have accidentally just entered the membership number of a member who has left the club, but their record space in the file had not yet been used for a new member.)

```
Private Function DeleteMember(ByVal MemberID As String) As Boolean
'logically deletes record with membership no. MemberID from Members
'file by setting its Deleted field to Y. Returns True if deletion
'is successful, otherwise returns False
  Dim OneMember As MemberType
  Dim RecordNumber As Integer
  Dim Found As Boolean
  RecordNumber = 0
  Found = False
  Open FileName For Random As #1 Len = Len(OneMember)
  Do While (Not EOF(1)) And (Not Found)
    RecordNumber = RecordNumber + 1
    Get #1, RecordNumber, OneMember               'read one record from file
    If OneMember.MemberID = MemberID Then 'is this the required record?
      If OneMember.Deleted = "Y" Then       'member previously deleted
        MsgBox "This member does not exist"
      Else
        OneMember.Deleted = "Y"
        Found = True
```

```
      End If
    End If
  Loop
  If Not Found Then                    'no record in file to delete
    DeleteMember = False
  Else                                 'a record has been deleted
    DeleteMember = True
  End If
  Put #1, RecordNumber, OneMember      'write record to file
  Close #1
  Call cmdDisplayMember_Click  'so that member disappears from list box
End Function
```

Calling the adding and deleting procedures

Now that the general procedures are in place we need to write code for the Click event of cmdOK, the button that actually fires everything off. First, though, we need to decide which option button the user has selected, Add or Delete. One way of doing this is to look at the current caption of cmdOK. When we built the Members form in the last chapter, in step 14 we set the caption to *Add Member* or *Delete Member* according to which option was selected.

1. The code for the Click event of cmdOK is quite long so take it slowly and read the comments carefully. The **If** statement is nested to four levels, largely to validate and check that a membership number entered for a new member is not in current use. When you type in the code below don't split the MsgBox parts over two lines as you are liable to make errors. (They are split here to fit on the page.) The only new things in the code below are to do with the MsgBox function. The example which asks the user to confirm a deletion includes the parameter **vbYesNo**. The *Take it from here...* section in Chapter 4 invited you to investigate the parameters you can pass MsgBox. The parameter vbYesNo means that Yes and No buttons will be placed in the message box. The function returns the value 6 if the user clicks Yes (and 7 for No).

```
Private Sub cmdOK_Click()
'processes either adding or deleting a member
  Dim MemberID As String
  Dim MemberDeleted As Boolean         'return value from DeleteMember
  Dim Duplicate As Boolean  'True if membership number already in use
  Dim Response As Integer 'reply when asked to confirm impending deletion
  Dim OneMember As MemberType
  If cmdOK.Caption = "Add Member" Then                 'add a member
    If Len(txtMemberIDAdd.Text) = 6 Then     'a 6-character ID entered
      MemberID = txtMemberIDAdd.Text
      Duplicate = CheckDuplicateMemberID(MemberID)    'is membership
                                         'number already in use?
      If Not Duplicate Then      'membership number does not already exist
          'member's details have been entered on form so use them
        If (txtSurname.Text <> "") And (txtFirstname.Text <> "") And _
                            (lstCategory.Text <> "") Then
          OneMember.MemberID = txtMemberIDAdd.Text      'collect details
                                           'into one record
          OneMember.Surname = txtSurname.Text
          OneMember.Firstname = txtFirstname.Text
          If lstCategory.Text = "Senior" Then
            OneMember.Category = "S"
          Else
            OneMember.Category = "J"
```

```
              End If
              OneMember.Deleted = "N"
              Call AddMember(OneMember)        'add new record to file
              txtMemberIDAdd.Text = ""         'clear member details
              txtSurname.Text = ""
              txtFirstname.Text = ""
            Else
              MsgBox ("You have not filled in all details of the member")
            End If
          Else                   'user has entered a duplicate membership number
            MsgBox "Membership No. " & MemberID & " has been used. Enter", _
                                                  "a different one"
            txtMemberIDAdd.SetFocus
          End If
        Else                     'not enough characters typed in for membership no.
          MsgBox ("You must enter a membership number with 6 characters")
          txtMemberIDAdd.SetFocus
        End If
      Else 'Else part of (If cmdOK.Caption = "Add Member") ie delete a member
        MemberID = txtMemberIDDelete.Text
        If MemberID = "" Then    'user has not entered a membership number
          MsgBox ("You haven't entered a membership number")
        Else
          Response = MsgBox("Confirm you want to delete this member?", _
                                                  vbYesNo)
          If Response = 6 Then                  'user does wish to delete
            MemberDeleted = DeleteMember(MemberID)    'True if deletion
                                              'successful
            txtMemberIDDelete.Text = ""
            If Not MemberDeleted Then           'deletion not successful
              MsgBox "Member not deleted. Membership number " _
                                      & MemberID & "does not exist"
            End If
          End If
        End If          'end of (If MemberID = "")
      End If            'end of (If cmdOK.Caption = "Add Member")
End Sub
```

2. Run the program and try adding and deleting members. You will need to comment out the last line in AddMember and DeleteMember which calls the Click event of cmdDisplayMembers because you haven't written this procedure yet. You can only check that members have been added by noting that Members.dat has been created, and that for every record you add it should grow in size by 42 bytes. Since deleting a member does not physically delete a record the file size won't change. You'll have to wait for the next section to prove to yourself that this part works.

Displaying members in the list box

Clicking the Display Members command button loops through all the records in the Members file. If the record is not logically deleted, because the Deleted field stores 'N', the surname and first name are concatenated. The surname is changed into upper case by using the UCase function. The two name fields total 28 characters, and in order to fit all the data about the members across the width of the list box, this is reduced to 24 using the Left function. Whether you *have* to do this depends on the size of your form and thus the list box itself, but do it anyway.

1. Copy the code below for the Click event of cmdDisplayMembers.

```
Private Sub cmdDisplayMembers_Click()
'displays full name, membership no, and category of membership
'of all members in list box
  Dim FullName As String
  Dim Category As String
  Dim MemberID As String
  Dim OneMember As MemberType
  lstMembers.Clear
  Open FileName For Random As #1 Len = Len(OneMember)
  Do While Not EOF(1)
    Get #1, , OneMember              'read one record from Members file
    If OneMember.Deleted = "N" Then  'record has not been deleted
      FullName = Left(UCase(OneMember.Surname) & " " & _
                                    OneMember.Firstname, 24)
      MemberID = OneMember.MemberID
      If OneMember.Category = "S" Then   'S or J stored on file - change
                                         'to Senior or Junior
        Category = "Senior"
      Else
        Category = "Junior"
      End If
      lstMembers.AddItem FullName & MemberID & "    " & Category
    End If
  Loop
  Close #1
  cmdPrintMembers.Enabled = True      'can print report only after list
    'box displays members' details since report takes details from
    'list box rather than the file
End Sub
```

2. Remove the commenting out of the calls to cmdDisplayMembers_Click you added in step 2 above and run the program. Check that the list box displays only those members who have not been deleted. Because the Sorted property is True you can't visually see that a new member physically occupies the space of the first deleted one in the file. Experiment by changing the property to False, delete the first member and then add a member. It should be the first one displayed in the list box.

Printing the membership report

Clicking the Print Members button prints the report on the current members. We designed this in figure 18.9. Since Smiley's wants the members listed alphabetically by surname we can simply use the contents of the list box, although there is a slight drawback with this method here. The width used for one member's details on the report is determined by the spacing used in the list box. Recall that we restricted the surname and first name to 24 characters in the list box.

If you took the details from the Members file instead you would have more control over the spacing of the output. However the members would not be sorted. (In your own project always take every opportunity to demonstrate the use of advanced techniques, and here is a good one. You *could* copy the Members file into an array of records and write code to sort it on the surname field. Then print from this sorted array.)

1. Copy the code below for the Click event of cmdPrintMembers. The only new things here that were not covered in programs 12.1 and 12.2 are the use of the **NewPage** method, to force output to a new page, and the **Page** property to print page numbers. In the code below the method used to print in vertical columns is to use an even-spaced font. In Chapter 12 we used tabs for this, which we'll use again in printing the report on table usage in Chapter 23.

```
Private Sub cmdPrintMembers_Click()
'Prints a list of all current members. Prints membership no., name and
'category of membership. Gives totals of senior, junior and all members
'Data is taken from the list box showing members' details
    Dim NumberSeniors As Integer
    Dim NumberJuniors As Integer
    Dim Category As String
    Dim OneMemberDetails As String
    Dim NumberLines As Integer
    Dim Index As Integer
    NumberSeniors = 0
    NumberJuniors = 0
    NumberLines = 0
    Printer.Print                          'prints a blank line
    Printer.Print
    Printer.Font.Name = "Courier"  'to format output in vertical columns
    Printer.FontSize = 15
    Printer.Print "Page " & Printer.Page          'print page number
    Printer.Print
    Printer.Print "Smiley's Snooker. List of current members on " & Date
    Printer.Print
    Printer.Print
    For Index = 0 To lstMembers.ListCount - 1'process each item in list box
        OneMemberDetails = lstMembers.List(Index)   'current item in list box
        Printer.Print OneMemberDetails
        If InStr(OneMemberDetails, "Senior") <> 0 Then  'Instr returns 0 if
                                                'search string not present
            NumberSeniors = NumberSeniors + 1
        Else
            NumberJuniors = NumberJuniors + 1
        End If
        NumberLines = NumberLines + 1
        If NumberLines = 50 Then              'new page after each 50 members
            Printer.NewPage                   'print on a new page
            NumberLines = 0
            Printer.Print
            Printer.Print
            Printer.Print "Page " & Printer.Page
            Printer.Print
            Printer.Print
        End If
    Next Index
    Printer.Print
    Printer.Print "Total Seniors   " & NumberSeniors
    Printer.Print "Total Juniors   " & NumberJuniors
    Printer.Print
    Printer.Print "Overall Total   " & NumberSeniors + NumberJuniors
    Printer.EndDoc
End Sub
```

2. Run the program and try out your report. To test the page numbering you will probably need to change how many members are printed on each page (50 in the code above).

Chapter 22 – Coding: Starting a Game

Displaying a member's details automatically

The first thing the receptionist does onscreen when handling a new game is to get to the Game form. If the option button to start a game is not selected she should click it to display the appropriate controls. You have already coded this in Chapter 20. Then she enters the player's membership number and tabs out of this control (or clicks in another one) so that this member's name and category of membership are displayed. The LostFocus event of the control in which the membership number is entered will handle this.

As in the last chapter let's start with the general procedures and work back to the event procedure that calls them. For automatically displaying a member's details our design identified two of these – FindMemberByMemberID and GetMemberByRecordNumber (see figure 19.3).

Function FindMemberByMemberID

This is passed a membership number and uses it to search the Members file for a match. If a match is found it passes back the record number in the file; if not it passes back 0.

1. The function has one formal parameter, MemberID, which it uses to search the Members file.

```
Private Function FindMemberByMemberID(ByVal MemberID As String) _
                                                    As Integer
'searches Members file for membership number MemberID. Returns
'the file record number if this ID exists, otherwise returns 0
   Dim RecordNumber As Integer
   Dim OneMember As MemberType
   Dim FileName As String
   Dim Found As Boolean
   RecordNumber = 0
   Found = False
   FileName = App.Path & "\Members.dat"
   Open FileName For Random As #1 Len = Len(OneMember)
   Do While (Not EOF(1)) And (Found = False)
      RecordNumber = RecordNumber + 1        'to go to next record in file
      Get #1, RecordNumber, OneMember        'and read it
      If OneMember.MemberID = MemberID Then   'is its member ID the one
                                              'we are looking for?
         Found = True
      End If
   Loop
   If Found Then
      FindMemberByMemberID = RecordNumber     'return record no.
   Else
      FindMemberByMemberID = 0                'or return 0
   End If
   Close #1
End Function
```

Function GetMemberByRecordNumber

The record number that is passed back by FindMemberByMemberID can in turn be passed into GetMemberByRecordNumber to retrieve the record.

2. The parameter RecordNumber is not changed in any way and so can be by value. Type in the code below.

```
Private Function GetMemberByRecordNumber(ByVal RecordNumber As Integer) _
                                          As MemberType
'returns record from Members.dat file at RecordNumber position
  Dim OneMember As MemberType
  Dim FileName As String
  FileName = App.Path & "\Members.dat"
  Open FileName For Random As #1 Len = Len(OneMember)
  Get #1, RecordNumber, OneMember
  Close #1
  GetMemberByRecordNumber = OneMember
End Function
```

Note the data type of the returned value. MemberType was declared in basDeclarations and can store a record for one member.

The LostFocus event procedure for txtMemberIDStart

Now that the two general procedures are in place we can look at the event that calls them.

3. The code for the LostFocus event is shown below. The only validation done on the membership number is that it is not empty. We don't really need any more ambitious validation since the call to FindMemberByMemberID will report whether the membership number exists. Recall that it returns 0 if the membership number does not exist, or the record number in the file if it does exist. If the membership number is found this record is retrieved from the file as the return value of the function GetMemberByRecordNumber (see figure 19.3). This is then used to display the member's name and category of membership.

```
Private Sub txtMemberIDStart_LostFocus()
'Calls FindMemberByMemberID to check that membership number entered when
'starting a game exists. If it does exist then calls
'GetMemberByRecordNumber to retrieve record and displays member's name
'and category of membership
  Dim MemberID As String
  Dim RecordNumber As Integer
  Dim OneMember As MemberType
  MemberID = txtMemberIDStart.Text
  If MemberID <> "" Then  'something entered into member ID control?
    RecordNumber = FindMemberByMemberID(MemberID)
    If RecordNumber = 0 Then           'membership number does not exist
      MsgBox "Membership Number " & MemberID & " does not exist"
      txtMemberIDStart.SetFocus
    Else                               'membership number does exist
      OneMember = GetMemberByRecordNumber(RecordNumber) 'retrieve record
      txtMemberNameStart.Text = Rtrim(OneMember.Firstname) _
                                & " " & UCase(OneMember.Surname)
      cboTableNumberStart.Enabled = True   'allow user to select a table
      If OneMember.Category = "S" Then
        txtCategoryStart.Text = "Senior"
```

```
        Else
            txtCategoryStart.Text = "Junior"
        End If
    End If                          'end of (RecordNumber = 0)
  Else                             'a membership ID has not been entered
    MsgBox("You must enter the member's ID")
    txtMemberIDStart.SetFocus
  End If                           'end of (If MemberID <> "")
End Sub
```

4. Run the program and try out what you've coded. Enter one membership number you know exists and one that does not.

Populating the combo box with available tables

In our design we decided to have one sub procedure, ListTablesAvailable, for populating the combo boxes with the appropriate table numbers when starting or finishing a game (see figure 19.2). This procedure is called when the user indicates they want to start or finish a game by clicking the appropriate option button.

1. The procedure uses the caption of the command button on the form to determine whether the user wishes to start or finish a game, in the same way as we used the command button's caption to decide on whether adding or deleting a member had been chosen on frmMembers. Enter the code below.

```
Private Sub ListTablesAvailable()
'Populates combo boxes of table numbers with appropriate table numbers
'If starting a game then only green tables listed. If finishing then
'only red tables listed
  Dim Index As Integer
  If cmdOK.Caption = "Start Game" Then                    'a new game
    cboTableNumberStart.Clear
    For Index = 1 To MaxTables
      If frmMain.lblTables(Index).BackColor = vbGreen Then    'check each
                                          'table on Main form - is it green?
          cboTableNumberStart.AddItem Index 'if it is, display its number
      End If
    Next Index
  Else                                           'a finished game
    'to be coded later
  End If
End Sub
```

Note the following:

- You declared MaxTables in basDeclarations to be available for use anywhere in your program.

- When you built frmMain in Chapter 20 it was stressed that you had to set the BackColor property of the labels that represent the snooker tables to a particular shade of green (see step 5). This shade is identified by the colour constant vbGreen in the code above. If you have not set the colour correctly the code above will not work. Note that you could have written

```
If frmMain.lblTables(Index).BackColor = RGB(0, 255, 0) Then
```

2. To call ListTablesAvailable add the following line to the end of the code you already have in optStart_Click.

```
Call ListTablesAvailable
```

Displaying the start time of a new game

After the receptionist has entered a player's membership number and their name and category of membership have been displayed, she must select an available table from the combo box. When a table has been selected the starting time of the game will be displayed as hours and minutes (since seconds would probably be annoying to the user). The receptionist can inform the player when the cost of the game will be calculated from. For this we need the Click event of the combo box that displays the tables available for use.

1. This event procedure calls the function ShortenTime you wrote in the standard module basCalculations (step 5 under Standard Modules in Chapter 20). You pass a time in the form hh:mm:ss and it returns the hours and minutes part only.

```
Private Sub cboTableNumberStart_Click()
'Display starting time of a new game
  Dim StartTime As String
  StartTime = basTimeFunctions.ShortenTime(Time())
  If Hour(Time()) > 11 Then
    txtStartTimeStart.Text = StartTime & " " & "PM"
  Else
    txtStartTimeStart.Text = StartTime & " " & "AM"
  End If
End Sub
```

Look at the **If** statement carefully. If your system displays time as AM/PM then this is lost when ShortenTime removes the seconds part of the time sent to it. The Hour function is used to see if the current time is after midday, and PM or AM added appropriately to the returned time from ShortenTime. If your system displays time according to the 24-hour clock you don't need AM/AM added to it, so you could omit the **If** statement.

Processing a new game

When the receptionist clicks the command button, details of the new game should be stored in the Current Games file, and the table on the Main form changed to red with the game's starting time displayed next to it. Our design settled on two new sub procedures to handle this processing, StoreCurrentGame and UpdateTableDisplay, and two we've already coded, ListTablesAvailable and ShortenTime (figure 19.6).

Sub procedure StoreCurrentGame

1. This procedure is passed a table number (which the user will have selected from the combo box). It's quite a simple one – wrap the details up in one record and send it off to the file. The Put statement is used with the content of the parameter TableNumber, first to position the file pointer at the required record, and then to write the record to the file.

```
Private Sub StoreCurrentGame(ByVal TableNumber As Integer)
'stores details of one game in CurrentGames.dat file
  Dim OneGame As GameType
  Dim Filename As String
```

```
                'get details of game from form's controls and store in a record
    OneGame.MemberID = txtMemberIDStart.Text
    OneGame.TableID = TableNumber
    OneGame.StartTime = Time()
    OneGame.Occupied = "Y"

                                        'write record to file
    Filename = App.Path & "\CurrentGames.dat"
    Open Filename For Random As #1 Len = Len(OneGame)
    Put #1, TableNumber, OneGame          'go straight to required record
    Close #1
End Sub
```

There's one minor thing to point out in the code above. Note that the starting time is taken from the system clock, not from the text box displaying the start time. Recall that the text box did not display the seconds. In practice there could be a slight discrepancy between the two, but only if the receptionist for some reason took some time over clicking the command button after entering details of the game. This might be something to talk over with Smiley's.

Sub procedure UpdateTableDisplay

2. This procedure is used to change the colour of the table on which a new game has just started to red, and of a table that has just had a finished game to green. The code for the finished game will be dealt with later. Notice in the code that the control array of lables, lblTables, must be prefixed by the name of the form it is on. A call is made to the ShortenTime function in the standard module basTimeFunctions to display the starting time (minus the seconds). Note the use of the nested **If** to handle the display of AM/PM. This was discussed earlier.

```
Private Sub UpdateTableDisplay(ByVal TableNumber As Integer)
'If a new game then changes table TableNumber from green to red and
'displays start time of game. If a finished game then changes table from
'red to green and removes starting time
   If cmdOK.Caption = "Start Game" Then        'a new game
      frmMain.lblTables(TableNumber).BackColor = vbRed
      If Hour(Time()) > 11 Then
         frmMain.lblStartTimes(TableNumber).Caption = _
                        basTimeFunctions.ShortenTime(Time()) & " " & "PM"
      Else
         frmMain.lblStartTimes(TableNumber).Caption = _
                        basTimeFunctions.ShortenTime(Time()) & " " & "AM"
      End If
      txtMemberIDStart.Text = ""              'clear text boxes for next game
      txtMemberNameStart.Text = ""
      txtCategoryStart.Text = ""
      txtStartTimeStart.Text = ""
   Else                                        'a finished game
      'to be coded later……….
   End If
End Sub
```

Consider how you would have to write the code to set the colour of the table to red if you had not used a control array to store the tables. In the code above one line is needed. If you had stored the tables as lblTable1 to lblTable20 instead of lblTables with indexes of 1 to 20, you would need 42 lines of code:

```
Select Case TableNumber
   Case 1
      frmMain.lblTable1.BackColor = vbRed
   Case 2
      frmMain.lblTable2.BackColor = vbRed
   'and 18 more Cases up to…..
   Case 20
      frmMain.lblTable20.BackColor = vbRed
End Select
```

Click event procedure of command button

The receptionist will click the single command button, cmdOK, to complete the processing of either a new game or one that has finished. The modular structure (figure 19.6) showed that three sub procedures are called, to store a record in the Current Games file, to update the table display by colouring the table red and to repopulate the combo box of tables.

1. Before calling the first two of these three sub procedures we have to check that the user is starting a game, rather than finishing one, by using the button's caption. We must further check that a table has been selected from the combo box.

```
Private Sub cmdOK_Click()
'completes the processing of either a new game or a finished game
   Dim Table As Integer
   If cmdOK.Caption = "Start Game" Then                'a new game
      If cboTableNumberStart.Text <> "" Then    'table selected?
         Table = cboTableNumberStart.Text         'select table to play on
         Call StoreCurrentGame(Table)    'to store details of game on file
         Call UpdateTableDisplay(Table)           'to colour table red
      Else
         MsgBox "You have not selected a table number"
      End If
   Else
      MsgBox "You have not entered a member ID"
   End If
   Else                                            'a finished game
      'to be coded later….
   End If
   Call ListTablesAvailable       'to populate combo box with table numbers
End Sub
```

ListTablesAvailable to repopulate the combo box is called whether a new game or a finished game is being processed, and so is outside the main If statement. This procedure is shown in both figures 19.6 and 19.7, but of course is the same procedure call.

2. Everything is now in place for starting a new game. Try it out and check that the tables used are coloured red and the start time is displayed next to them. You can't check that details of a game have been written to the Current Games file by looking at the file size because this never changes from 340 bytes. You can open it up in Notepad or WordPad and see data in the string fields. Figure 22.1 shows the file in Notepad when table 2 has been used by member number FF6767. You may wish to recreate CurrentGames.dat again from the Utilities form as you try the code out.

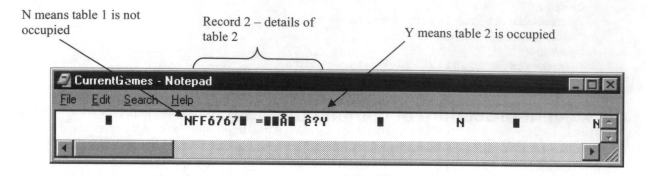

Figure 22.1: CurrentGames file in Notepad after table 2 has been used for a new game

Displaying table information when the program loads

UpdateTableDisplay colours a table red and displays the starting time of its game. But if the receptionist accidentally closed the whole program, or even just the Main form, this information would not be displayed when the Main form is reloaded. We can write code in its Load event to display the colours of the tables and the starting times of the red tables.

1. In the Load event for the Main form enter the following code:

```
Private Sub Form_Load()
'reads from Current Games file to set table display
   Dim Table As Integer
   Dim Filename As String
   Dim OneGame As GameType
   Filename = App.Path & "\CurrentGames.dat"
   Open Filename For Random As #1 Len = Len(OneGame)
   For Table = 1 To MaxTables
      Get #1, , OneGame        'could use Table as missing parameter, but
                               'not necessary
      If OneGame.Occupied = "Y" Then       'table in use?
         lblTables(Table).BackColor = vbRed
         lblStartTimes(Table).Caption = _
                     basTimeFunctions.ShortenTime(OneGame.StartTime)
      End If
   Next Table
   Close #1
End Sub
```

You might possibly have noticed that this does not display the AM/PM format you allowed for earlier. The possible improvements to the project listed in Chapter 24 do not cover this point. It's a minor thing, but one which you may feel should be implemented.

Chapter 23 – Coding: Finishing a Game

When a game has finished the receptionist must get to the Game form and, if the controls for a new game are currently displayed, click the option button for a finished game. She asks the player which table they used and selects this from the occupied tables displayed in the combo box. All the other details (see figures 18.4 and 20.4) are automatically filled in and she just has to click the command button. This will write a record of the finished game to the Daily Games file, update the appropriate record in the Current Games file (so that the table is now unoccupied), change the colour of the table to green and remove the displayed start time on the Main form.

Before the receptionist can select the table from the combo box, however, we have to write code to populate it with the appropriate tables.

Populating the combo box with occupied tables

1. In Chapter 22 we wrote part of the code for populating the combo box with tables available for a new game. In that part of sub procedure ListTablesAvailable with the comment *to be coded later* (the Else part of the If statement) insert the following:

```
cboTableNumberFinish.Clear
For Index = 1 To MaxTables
    If frmMain.lblTables(Index).BackColor = vbRed Then      'check each
                                    'table on Main form - is it red?
        cboTableNumberFinish.AddItem Index 'if it is, display its number
    End If
Next Index
```

2. In Chapter 22 we called this procedure, ListTablesAvailable, from the Click event of the option button for starting a game (optStart). To do the same thing for the other option button to finish a game, optFinish, add the line below to the three lines you have previously coded:

```
Call ListTablesAvailable
```

3. Try out the combo box by entering data for one or more games and then inspecting the list of tables in the combo box for finishing a game. Only the occupied tables should be there.

Selecting a table from the combo box

In our modular structure design (figure 19.5) we identified three main processing stages that occur as soon as a table has been selected from the combo box. The functions ShortenTime and NumberOfMinutes in figure 19.5 play a supporting role.

- Retrieve the record from the Current Games file for the table that has just had the finished game.
- Retrieve the record from the Members file for the member who has just finished playing.
- Calculate the cost of a game.

Retrieving a record from the Current Games file

1. The function GetRecordFromCurrentGamesFile handles this (figure 19.5). It needs to be passed the table number to go to in the file.

```
Private Function GetRecordFromCurrentGamesFile(ByVal TableNumber As _
                                          Integer) As GameType
'returns record of the current game for table TableNumber
  Dim Filename As String
  Dim OneGame As GameType
  Filename = App.Path & "\CurrentGames.dat"
  Open Filename For Random As #1 Len = Len(OneGame)
  Get #1, TableNumber, OneGame 'go straight to record, retrieve it and
  GetRecordFromCurrentGamesFile = OneGame        'return it from function
  Close #1
End Function
```

Retrieving a record from the Members file

The previous function returns a record from the Current Games file. This record includes the membership number of the player who has finished the game. This can be used to find the member's details from the Members file in order to display them onscreen for the receptionist.

2. The function GetMemberByMemberID (figure 19.5) is passed a membership number. It searches the Members file for the record with this membership number and returns the record.

```
Private Function GetMemberByMemberID(ByVal MemberID As String) _
                                        As MemberType
'returns record from Members.dat file with membership number MemberID
  Dim Found As Boolean
  Dim OneMember As MemberType
  Dim Filename As String
  Dim RecordNumber As Integer
  Found = False
  Filename = App.Path & "\Members.dat"
  RecordNumber = 0
  Open Filename For Random As #1 Len = Len(OneMember)
  Do While Not Found                     'loop until record found in file
    Get #1, , OneMember
    If OneMember.MemberID = MemberID Then   'membership no. of record
                                        'same as search membership no?

      Found = True
    End If
  Loop
  GetMemberByMemberID = OneMember            'return record from function
  Close #1
End Function
```

Just in case you thought the loop above might never stop, think about what switches Found to True. If the membership number passed into the procedure is present in the file, Found is set to True. Actually it *must* be present because it was taken from the record retrieved by GetRecordFromCurrentGamesFile above, and this record in turn was stored in Current Games only after getting the player's membership number from the Members file in the first place.

Calculating the cost of a game

To calculate the cost of a game you need to know how long the game lasted and the cost per minute. The cost per minute depends on whether the player is a senior or junior member. Function CalculateCostOfGame (figure 19.5) returns the cost of a game.

3. Two parameters are passed to the function – the number of minutes the game took and the category of membership. The code below uses two variables, SeniorRate and JuniorRate, which our program knows nothing about yet. We'll come to these next.

```
Private Function CalculateCostOfGame(ByVal MinutesPlayed As Integer, _
                            ByVal Category As String) As Currency
'calculates the cost of one game
  If Category = "Senior" Then
     CalculateCostOfGame = (SeniorRate * MinutesPlayed) / 100
  Else
     CalculateCostOfGame = (JuniorRate * MinutesPlayed) / 100
  End If
End Function
```

Getting the payment rates

The senior and junior rates per minutes are stored in the text file Costs.txt. We could have included code in the previous function to open the file and read in the rates. Instead we'll use another technique in order to add to your understanding of building a Visual Basic project.

When the program loads we want the rates read from the file and stored in variables that can be accessed from the Game form. If we coded this in the Load event for the Main form it would work until the user for some reason closed this form but still needed to process a game. Instead we can use a standard module with a procedure called Main. When your program loads you can direct Visual Basic to load any form of your choice or a sub procedure called Main. (See steps 4 and 5 of program 8.2 and Exercise 1 at the end of Chapter 8.) We'll declare two variables and write the Main procedure on one of the standard modules we have already created, basDeclarations.

4. In basDeclarations add the two declarations below. These variables can be accessed anywhere in the program. The syntax for opening and reading the file is different from the syntax we've used on the Members and Game forms because this is a text file. Note the line that calls the Show method of frmMain; we must open the Main form otherwise our program stops here!

```
   Public SeniorRate As Single
   Public JuniorRate As Single

Public Sub Main()
   Dim Filename As String
   Filename = App.Path & "\Costs.txt"
   Open Filename For Input Access Read As #1
   Input #1, SeniorRate, JuniorRate
   Close #1
   frmMain.Show
End Sub
```

5. Select **Project/Project1 Properties**, select **Sub Main** as the Startup Object and click **OK**.

Click event procedure of the combo box

Now we need to return to what happens when the receptionist selects a table from the combo box. Apart from calling the three functions you've just coded it has to display several items of data, and calculate and display how many minutes the game took and how much the game costs.

6. The code is shown below. Two calls are made to DisplayTime in basTimeFunctions to display the start and finish times minus the seconds. The start time has just been retrieved from the Current Games file where it is stored as a Date data type. A call is made to the other function in basTimeFunctions, NumberOfMinutes to calculate the number of minutes the game took. Finally it expresses this in hours and minutes and calculates the cost of the game.

```
Private Sub cboTableNumberFinish_Click()
'Calls functions to retrieve player's details and table's start time from
'file. Displays these and calls function NumberOfMinutes to calculate
'length of time game took in minutes. Then calcs and displays game time
'in hrs and mins and calls a function to calculate cost of game
  Dim Table As Integer
  Dim MinutesPlayed As Integer
  Dim Hours As Integer
  Dim Minutes As Integer
  Dim OneGame As GameType
  Dim OneMember As MemberType
  Dim MembershipNo As String
  Dim Category As String
  Table = cboTableNumberFinish.Text
  OneGame = GetRecordFromCurrentGamesFile(Table) 'retrieve details of
                              'game just finished from Current Games file
  MembershipNo = OneGame.MemberID
  OneMember = GetMemberByMemberID(MembershipNo)  'retrieve player's
                                    'details from Members file

  If OneMember.Category = "S" Then
    txtCategoryFinish.Text = "Senior"
  Else
    txtCategoryFinish.Text = "Junior"
  End If
  FinishTime = Time()
  txtMemberNameFinish.Text = RTrim(OneMember.Firstname) & "   " & _
                          UCase(OneMember.Surname)
  txtStartTimeFinish.Text = basTimeFunctions.ShortenTime(OneGame.StartTime)
  txtFinishTime.Text = basTimeFunctions.ShortenTime (FinishTime)
  MinutesPlayed = basTimeFunctions.NumberOfMinutes(FinishTime, _
                                    OneGame.StartTime)

  If MinutesPlayed >= 60 Then            'calculate number of hours played
    Hours = MinutesPlayed \ 60      'the '\' calculates an integer result
  Else
    Hours = 0
  End If
  Minutes = MinutesPlayed Mod 60     'calculate number of minutes played
  txtHours.Text = Hours
  txtMinutes.Text = Minutes
  Category = txtCategoryFinish.Text
  CostOfGame = CalculateCostOfGame(MinutesPlayed, Category)  'calculate
  txtCost.Text = Format(CostOfGame, "Currency")    'cost and display it
End Sub
```

Note the use of the two arithmetic operators '\' and Mod to change the length of the game in minutes into hours and minutes. If you don't understand them look back at figure 3.7 to see them in action.

There's one small, but crucial, point to make about the code above. The variables FinishTime and CostOfGame are not declared in the procedure. Let's deal with them separately.

- FinishTime stores the finishing time of the game by using the function Time to get the system time. At this point the receptionist has not yet clicked the command button (with the caption Finish Game) to finally complete the processing. As you'll see later, this stores the finishing time on file by calling procedure StoreGamesInDailyGamesFile. There may well be a time delay between clicking the combo box and this command button, which would mean that the finish time on file (assuming Time would be used again to get it) would be different from the one used to calculate the cost. This in turn would produce a mismatch between actual income and calculated income on the report Smiley's require on daily table usage. If we could send FinishTime from the event procedure above directly to StoreGameInDailyGamesFile there would be no problem. Although this is possible it would create other difficulties in our situation. The solution is to declare FinishTime as a global variable so both procedures can use it.

- CostOfGame stores the cost of a game, and this will also be needed later when details of a finished game are stored in the Daily Games file. As with FinishTime we will declare it as a global variable.

7. Declare FinishTime and CostOfGame as global variables:

```
Option Explicit
Dim FinishTime As String
Dim CostOfGame As Currency
```

8. You can now try out the code to see what happens when a table is selected from the combo box.

Click event of the command button (cmdOK)

When the receptionist clicks the button with the caption Finish Game, the following should happen:

- details of the finished game should be retrieved from the Current Games file
- the table's colour should change to green and the start time next to it removed
- the table's record in the Current Games file should be updated to indicate the table is not occupied
- details of the finished game should be stored in the Daily Games file
- the combo box should be repopulated with tables which are available

Our modular structure design allocated each of these to a general procedure (see figure 19.7). You have already written the first and last ones, GetRecordFromCurrentGamesFile and ListTablesAvailable. The former is called when the receptionist selects a table from the combo box. We *could* have stored the record returned from this function as a global variable in step 6 so that the Click event of the command button would not need to call the function again. However it is good practice to reduce global variables to a minimum, so we will call it again in the Click event of cmdOK.

Sub procedure ResetGameInCurrentGamesFile

1. This procedure needs to be passed the table number of the finished game. To indicate that the table is free again it changes the Occupied field of this table's record in the Current Games file from Y to N.

```
Private Sub ResetGameInCurrentGamesFile(ByVal TableNumber As Integer)
'Updates record in Current Games file for table TableNumber by setting
'occupied field to N
  Dim Filename As String
  Dim OneGame As GameType
  Filename = App.Path & "\CurrentGames.dat"
  Open Filename For Random As #1 Len = Len(OneGame)
  Get #1, TableNumber, OneGame
  OneGame.Occupied = "N"
  Put #1, TableNumber, OneGame
  Close #1
End Sub
```

Complete procedure UpdateTableDisplay

In Chapter 22 you wrote code for procedure UpdateTableDisplay to handle a new game. The table's colour was changed to red and the start time displayed next to it. Now you need to complete the code to handle a finished game.

2. In the commented section *to be coded later* of UpdateTableDisplay add the code below. The first two lines change the table's colour and remove the start time. The rest just clears out the controls on the Game form ready for the next finished game.

```
    frmMain.lblTables(TableNumber).BackColor = vbGreen   'change to green
    frmMain.lblStartTimes(TableNumber).Caption = ""
                                        'clear text boxes
    txtMemberNameFinish.Text = ""
    txtCategoryFinish.Text = ""
    txtStartTimeFinish.Text = ""
    txtFinishTime.Text = ""
    txtHours.Text = ""
    txtMinutes.Text = ""
    txtCost.Text = ""
```

Sub procedure StoreGameInDailyGamesFile

We haven't used the Daily Games file yet in this project. You declared a data type, FinishedGameType, in basDeclarations in Chapter 20 (step 2 under Standard Modules) for processing its records.

3. The procedure StoreGameInDailyGamesFile needs to be passed the table number and the time the finished game started. Recall in step 7 above that the finishing time and cost of the game were assigned to global variables so that they could be accessed by this procedure.

```
    Private Sub StoreGameInDailyGamesFile(ByVal TableNumber As Integer, _
                                      ByVal StartTime As Date)
'Stores record of finished game in Daily Games file
  Dim NumberOfRecords As Integer
  Dim Filename As String
  Dim OneFinishedGame As GameFinishedType
  Filename = App.Path & "\DailyGames.dat"
  OneFinishedGame.TableID = TableNumber
  OneFinishedGame.StartTime = StartTime
  OneFinishedGame.FinishTime = FinishTime     'uses two global variables
  OneFinishedGame.Cost = CostOfGame           'assigned values by
                                              'cboTableNumberFinish_Click
```

```
    Open Filename For Random As #1 Len = Len(OneFinishedGame)
    NumberOfRecords = LOF(1) / Len(OneFinishedGame)
    Put #1, NumberOfRecords + 1, OneFinishedGame
    Close #1
  End Sub
```

The LOF (**L**ength **O**f **F**ile) function was covered in step 4 of program 10.2. To append the finished game record to the file we need to position the file pointer just beyond the last record. Dividing the total length of the file in bytes by the length of one record in bytes gives the number of records in the file. The Put statement adds 1 to this value to get beyond the last record.

Completing the code for cmdOK_Click

The procedures above to update the finished game's table details in the Current Games file and store details of the finished game in the Daily Games file are called from cmdOK. You've already coded that part dealing with a new game in Chapter 22. Now to complete the coding for cmdOK's Click event.

4.   Two more local variables are needed:

```
    Dim OneGame As GameType
    Dim StartTime As Date
```

5.   Add the code below in place of the comment *'to be coded later*. This consists of another **If** statement to ensure something has been selected from the combo box.

```
    If cboTableNumberFinish.Text <> "" Then
       Table = cboTableNumberFinish.Text
       OneGame = GetRecordFromCurrentGamesFile(Table)
       StartTime = OneGame.StartTime
       Call ResetGameInCurrentGamesFile(Table)
       Call UpdateTableDisplay(Table)
       Call StoreGameInDailyGamesFile(Table, StartTime)
    Else
       MsgBox "You must select a table number"
    End If
```

6.   Now try out the code for steps 1 to 5 above to process a finished game when the command button is clicked. When StoreGamesInDailyGamesFile is run for the first time the file will be created for you by the Open statement. It was different for the Current Games file, where you needed to create the file with 20 records before using it for the first time. You can check that records have been stored in the Daily Games file by looking at its size in Windows; each finished game requires 26 bytes.

Printing the report on table usage

Remind yourself how we designed this by looking back at figure 18.8. Clicking cmdPrintReport on the Main form will produce the report. This is a long piece of code so let's look at it in three steps.

1.   In the Click event of cmdPrintPreport on the Main form declare the local variables and write code to print the report heading and column headings:

```
Private Sub cmdPrintReport_Click()
'prints a report on table usage. For each table displays number of games,
'total playing time and income. Gives overall total income also
```

```
Dim Index As Integer
Dim OneFinishedGame As GameFinishedType
Dim NumberOfRecords As Integer
Dim RecordNumber As Integer
Dim Table As Integer
Dim GamesForOneTable As Integer        'no. games played on a given table
Dim TimeForOneTable       'total time in minutes a table has been in use
Dim IncomeForOneTable As Currency      'total income for given table
Dim TotalIncome As Currency            'total income from all tables
Dim MinutesPlayed As Integer           'no. minutes a given game lasted
Dim Hours As Integer
Dim Minutes As Integer
Dim Filename As String
TotalIncome = 0
Printer.Print
Printer.Print
Printer.FontSize = 15                        'or whatever font size you want
Printer.FontBold = True
Printer.Print "Smiley's Snooker.  Table use for " & Date 'report header
Printer.Print
Printer.Print
Printer.FontSize = 12
Printer.FontBold = False
Printer.Print "Table No."; Tab(15); _                 'column headings
            "No.Games"; Tab(30); "Total Time"; Tab(50); "Income"
Printer.Print
```

- The Now function is used rather than Date because this gives both the date and time. Recall that Smiley's will usually print this report at the end of the day, but sometimes during the day as well, so knowing the time it refers to would be useful.

- In the members report in Chapter 21 we used an even spaced font (Courier) to produce straight columns of data. In this report the Tab function is used (covered in detail in Chapter 12.)

2. Add the following to the code above to print the details of each table:

```
Filename = App.Path & "\DailyGames.dat"
For Table = 1 To MaxTables                              'loop for each table
  Open Filename For Random As #1 Len = Len(OneFinishedGame)
  NumberOfRecords = FileLen(Filename) / Len(OneFinishedGame)
  GamesForOneTable = 0
  TimeForOneTable = 0
  IncomeForOneTable = 0
  For Index = 1 To NumberOfRecords          'search whole file for records
                                            'of the current table
    Get #1, , OneFinishedGame                         'read one record
    If OneFinishedGame.TableID = Table Then           'current table found
      GamesForOneTable = GamesForOneTable + 1     'one game more
      MinutesPlayed = basTimeFunctions.NumberOfMinutes _
              (OneFinishedGame.FinishTime, OneFinishedGame.StartTime)
      TimeForOneTable = TimeForOneTable + MinutesPlayed
      IncomeForOneTable = IncomeForOneTable + OneFinishedGame.Cost
    End If
  Next Index
  TotalIncome = TotalIncome + IncomeForOneTable  'add table's income
                                                 'to running income total
```

```
      If TimeForOneTable >= 60 Then          'calculate hours played on
         Hours = TimeForOneTable \ 60        'current table
      Else
         Hours = 0
      End If
      Minutes = TimeForOneTable Mod 60       'calculate minutes played
      Printer.Print Tab(5); Table; Tab(15); GamesForOneTable; Tab(30); _
                       Hours & " hrs " & Minutes & " mins"; Tab(50); _
                       Format(IncomeForOneTable, "Currency")
      Close #1
   Next Table
```

- The outer loop will be executed 20 times, once for each table. It is essential that the file is opened and closed each time round the loop because you must start at the first record again when the next table is processed. If you opened the file once before the loop and closed it after the loop only table 1's details would be calculated.

- The inner loop is repeated once per record. The start and finish times are sent to the NumberOfMinutes function, and then calculated as hours and minutes.

3. To print the total income at the end of the report is straightforward:

```
   Printer.Print
   Printer.Print Tab(30); "Total Income"; Tab(50); Format(TotalIncome, _
                                          "Currency")
   Printer.EndDoc
End Sub
```

Creating a new Daily Games file each day

In our Analysis we learned that Smiley's does not wish to keep permanent records of past games. If the report is printed at the end of the day the Daily Games file should be emptied, but if printed before this time the records should be kept until the report is printed at the end of the day. One way of doing this is to ask the user, when the report is being printed, whether they would like to purge the file.

1. Write a sub procedure DeleteDailyGames to delete the file. The next finished game that is processed will create the file again (by the Open statement in StoreGameInDailyGamesFile).

```
Private Sub DeleteDailyGamesFile()
'deletes Daily Games file. NB file does not go to Recycle Bin
   Dim Response As Integer
   Dim Filename As String
   Filename = App.Path & "\DailyGames.dat"
   Response = MsgBox("Delete today's games from the file?", vbYesNo)
   If Response = 6 Then         'user replied Yes
      Kill Filename             'delete it
   End If
End Sub
```

2. Finally, call this procedure by inserting the following line after Printer.EndDoc (step 3 above).

```
      Call DeleteDailyGamesFile
```

237

Chapter 24 – Appraisal

Chapter 17 listed Appraisal as the last stage of a project. It is worth 3 marks. Appendix C shows that you should cover three things (probably 1 mark for each):

- discuss how far your project meets the system objectives listed in the Analysis
- discuss any improvements you could make and indicate how you might make them
- get some feedback from your user on what they think of the solution

Meeting the system objectives

All the objectives referred to in the Analysis have been implemented. In your own project you should briefly go through each one indicating whether or not it has been met. It may be that some of the objectives have only been partly implemented. Point out which parts have and which have not, with a brief explanation for those things not covered.

Improvements

List a few ways you might improve the interface, the efficiency of your coding, the design of your files or whatever, and briefly say how you would do these. The following are some improvements we might make to the sample project.

1. Since the first two characters of membership numbers are supposed to be the initial letters of the member's firstname and surname, these two characters could be automatically displayed in the membership number text box when the user has typed in the new member's name. To do this write code in the GotFocus event procedure of txtMemberIDAdd. It may be that the code here should simply display these letters and that a function be written to return them to this event procedure code.

2. When the user backs up the files from the Utilities form the code copies them to a floppy disk. It would provide more flexibility if the user could choose the drive and directory. A text box could be made visible in which the path is entered by the user, although this assumes the user will enter a valid path. You might remember that Smiley's is not very good at using a computer. (Recall that they wanted to be able to change the payment rates from inside the program rather than change the contents of the text file directly.) The toolbox has two standard controls which together allow a user to indicate a drive and directory. These are the DriveListBox and DirListBox controls.

3. The Main form has command buttons to open the other three forms but the only way of moving between these three forms, or back to the Main form, is either by closing one or more of them by clicking the Windows Close button or by clicking somewhere on the form you wish to return to. If the form you wish to leave is maximised then the second method is not an option. To move around the forms more freely a simple four-item menu on each form, except possibly on the Main form since this has command buttons for the job, could be added. A drop-down menu on each form with two main menu items, Forms and Exit, and three submenu items under Forms, to open each of the other three forms, would be useful. The menu would need to be built separately on each form using the Menu Editor, and one line of code attached to each submenu item to call the Show method of the form to open. This is the same code as used for the three command buttons on the Main form to open the other forms (see step 12 for the Main Form in Chapter 20).

4. When the user chooses any of the utilities a message to say the action has been successful might be useful. A message box could be used for this.

5. When the user clicks cmdOK to process a new game the various controls are cleared ready for the next game. If the player has forgotten which table he has been given, and the receptionist also can't remember, the only way to find out is by looking for the most recent start time displayed on the Main form. This isn't very time consuming, but it would be a little easier if the table could be spotted at once. Perhaps the most recent start time could be displayed in a colour, or the most recent table number displayed in a separate label.

6. If for some reason the Members or Daily Games files are not present in the same directory as the project, the Open statement creates them again when the file needs to be used. It would be better, though, if the user was aware that the file is missing. You can check if a file exists by using the Dir function.

7. A record in the Daily Games file stores the start and finishing times of a game. When the report on table usage is printed these times are passed to the function NumberOfMinutes to calculate how many minutes the game lasted. Strictly this is an example of inefficiency. Why not store the number of minutes in the record instead, since this will have just been calculated before the record of a finished game is written to the file? Of course the amount of time taken to do the calculations again before the report is printed is undetectable (any noticeable time taken is in doing the printing itself) so the inefficiency is really only a theoretical one.

8. Another possible example of inefficiency is storing the membership categories as 'S' and 'J' in the Members file. In several places these codes need to be changed and displayed as full words. The conversion code wouldn't be necessary if the full words were stored on file in the first place (and recall that the user wouldn't be typing them in since they are selected from a list box). An alternative might be to avoid repeating the code and put it into a sub procedure.

Another area you might wish to refer to, if you haven't used it already in your project, is the use of error-handling code. If your testing has thrown up a number of run-time errors you could briefly point out how in principle to handle these. Chapter 11 covered this topic.

Feedback from user

Get your user to confirm in writing what they think of your solution. Take care here – assessors are used to candidates writing their own letters, which usually say how wonderful the project is! No-one is expecting your user necessarily to really use your project, though it is very gratifying if they want to. An honest opinion about what they think of your efforts is what is needed.

Appendices

Appendix A – Summary of topics covered in Parts One and Two which are used in the sample project in Part Three

Chapter	*Topic covered*	*Relevance to the sample project*
1	The programming environment	All relevant
2	Controls	Project uses labels, text boxes, command buttons, frames, combo boxes, list boxes, option buttons
3	Data types Variables Displaying output	All relevant. Note: Mod operator used in project.
4	If…Then…Else Select Case	Both selection statements used
5	For…Next Do While...Loop Do…Loop Until	Used extensively Used extensively Not used
6	Strings Dates Time	InStr, Left, UCase, RTrim functions used. Concatenation used. No date functions used Hour function used
7	General procedures Standard modules Parameters	Sub procedures and functions used extensively. Used Extensive use of value and reference parameters
8	Arrays Control arrays	Not used Used
9	Records	Used extensively
10	Files CommonDialog control	Project uses one text file and three random access files Not used
11	Error-handling	Not used
12	Printed output	Two reports printed as part of project
13	Menus	Not used
14	Graphics	Not used
15	Relational databases	Not used
16	Internet	Not used

Appendix B – Summary of the practical programs

Program No.	Program name	Main new topic(s) covered
1.1	Display your name	Print text on form
1.2	Change a message	Click command buttons
2.1	A list box of countries	List box
2.2	Option buttons, check boxes and frames	Option button, check box, frame
2.3	Displaying the time	Timer
2.4	Changing a form's colour using scroll bars	Scroll bar, RGB function
3.1	Add two numbers	Variables, Addition, input box
3.2	Illustrating global and local scope	Scope of variables
3.3	Using a static variable	Static variables
3.4	Calculating the average exam mark	Initialising variables, Enabling/disabling controls
4.1	Deciding exam grades	If statement, Message box
4.2	Selecting cutlery	Selecting option buttons and check boxes
4.3	Rent a property	Logical operators AND and OR
4.4	Wards and Patients	Select Case statement
5.1	Multiplication table	For…Next loop
5.2	Addition table	Nested For…Next loops
5.3	Driving test	Do While…Loop
5.4	Password entry	Do…Loop Until
6.1	Ensuring a person's name has one space	String functions Len and Mid
6.2	Extract the area telephone code	Building a string by repeated concatenation
6.3	College library issue desk	Processing dates
7.1	Avoid repeating code	Putting repeated code into a sub procedure
7.2	Value and reference parameters	Passing parameters by value and by reference
7.3	Calculating interest	User-defined function
7.4	A standard module function	Using a standard module
8.1	Array to hold numbers	One-dimensional array
8.2	Program 8.1 with a function to search array	Startup Object, Arrays as parameters
8.3	A control array of text boxes	Control array
8.4	A control array with a shared event procedure	Shared event procedure
9.1	Football team players	Record, Array of records, 2 forms in project
10.1	Text file to hold names and ages	App.Path, Reading to/writing from a text file
10.2	Random access file of garden centre products	CommonDialog control, Random access file
11.1	Stepping through code and setting watches	Stepping through code, Setting watches
11.2	Breakpoints and the Immediate window	Breakpoints, Using the Immediate window
11.3	Simple error handling	Use of OnError GoTo
11.4	Advanced error handling using the Err object	Using the Err object
12.1	Printing reports on sales staff	Printing from a text file
13.1	A drop-down menu	Drop-down menu
13.2	A pop-up menu	Pop-up menu
14.1	Moving a shape control by button clicks	Move method
14.2	Animate a circle moving across a screen	Simple animation
14.3	Drawing a bar chart	Line method
15.1	Displaying data from a database	Database controls
15.2	Querying a database	Using SQL to query a database
15.3	Using a recordset	Using a recordset
16.1	A simple Web Browser	WebBrowser control
16.2	Using the InternetExplorer object	InternetExplorer object

Appendix C – Assessment criteria for the stages of Analysis, Design, Technical Solution, System Maintenance and Appraisal of an 'A' level Computing project (AQA Examining Board)

Analysis			
Marks: 0 – 2	Marks: 3 – 6	Marks: 7 – 9	Marks: 10 – 12
Little or no evidence of any analysis Little or no evidence of investigation of a problem or an appropriate problem selected, that does not produce a useable computer-based solution No measurable system objectives No consideration of user needs	Some analysis but limited in scope and perception Some evidence of investigation of a problem with limited scope resulting in a standard exercise with no external constraints System objectives unclear or implicit Little evidence of consideration of user needs	Evidence of a well-structured analysis Evidence of a structured investigation into a problem demonstrating consideration of the realistic needs of a real user Statement of measurable system objectives but lacking in scope	Evidence of an extensive well-structured analysis Extensive investigation of a demanding open-ended problem showing realistic appreciation of system needs and demonstrating a high level of perception of a real user's needs Clear and comprehensive set of measurable system objectives

Design			
Marks: 0 – 2	Marks: 3 – 6	Marks: 7 – 9	Marks: 10 – 12
Little or no evidence of design with detail and/or content insufficient to produce a useable system	Evidence of design but lacking the necessary detail to produce a useable system without further development	Evidence of a feasible design. Majority of aspects are documented so that a useable system could be developed	Design well-fitted to the situation and incorporating all the required aspects to support the development of a fully-working system

Technical Solution			
Marks: 0 – 2	Marks: 3 – 6	Marks: 7 – 9	Marks: 10 – 12
Unstructured program that is trivial and/or incomplete with little evidence that it is working	A working program that produces some correct results but for a standard exercise and/or programmed in an unstructured way	Program showing reasonable structure, use of parameters and user-defined data structures	Well-structured program demonstrating methodologies appropriate to the programming language used

System Maintenance			
Marks: 0	Marks: 1 or 2	Marks: 3 or 4	Marks: 5 or 6
No samples of algorithm design. Program listing not self-documenting or with little annotation	Overall system design including information about modules / procedures. Some examples of algorithm design. Program listing clearly set out with some annotation	Overall system design including information about modules/ procedures. Representative samples of algorithm design. Program listing clearly set out - self-documented or clearly annotated	Same requirements as for 3 or 4 marks except that representative samples of algorithm design should use an appropriate standard method

Appraisal			
Marks: 0	Marks: 1	Marks: 2	Marks: 3
None provided or a few inappropriate comments	Little attempt made to relate achievement to the original objectives and / or shortcomings not identified	Achievement related to objectives. Analysis of and improvements needed and indication of how these could be achieved	As for 2 marks, plus… Analysis of feedback from user

Appendix D — Assessment evidence for Programming unit of Advanced VCE (Edexcel Examining Board)

You need to produce
- a working program to meet stated user needs. The program(s) must include most of the data types, objects and events listed under 'program design'.
- user and technical documentation including a test report for the most comprehensive program.

To achieve a grade E for your work you must show:	*To achieve a grade C for your work you must show:*	*To achieve a grade A for your work you must show:*
• a clear and accurate specification that meets user needs and defines the input, processing and output needs • a modular program design • suitable data entry facilities in your program(s) • appropriate use of sequence, selection and repetition in your program(s) • appropriate use of objects and events in your program(s) • suitable data processing methods in your program(s) including calculation and text manipulation • use of your program(s) to generate screen or printed reports that the user needs correctly • clear user documentation that enables a non-specialist to use the program(s) effectively and technical documentation that includes detailed program listings containing suitable comments	• accurate technical documentation that defines fully all calculation and manipulation, provides clearly commented program listings of all modules and details all user screens and dialog boxes • good quality user documentation which makes appropriate use of graphic images and screen prints and includes examples of data input screens, output screens, printed output and error messages • that you can work independently to produce your work to agreed deadlines	• a good understanding of programming through an effective modular design and in your imaginative use of events, objects and controls • creation of data entry facilities that are clear, well laid out and suitably labelled, correct validation of input data and provision of appropriate user guidance • design and implementation of imaginative and customised screen or printed output to provide content and layout that are well matched to user needs • provide records of thorough module and program testing that checks all major paths, acceptable and unacceptable input and all possible events, and show clearly how any identified problems were resolved to produce a good operational program(s)

Index